JOHN E. NIXON, Ed.D., University of Southern California, is Associate Professor and Director of the Professional Physical Education Program at Stanford University. He previously taught at The Pennsylvania State University and Los Angeles State College and was formerly Chief of Athletic Service at the Veterans Administration, Washington, D. C.

ANN E. JEWETT, Ed.D., Stanford University, is Director of Physical Education for Women at Springfield College. Dr. Jewett previously taught at the University of Illinois, where she was also Supervisor of Student Teachers in Women's Physical Education.

PHYSICAL EDUCATION CURRICULUM

JOHN E. NIXON
STANFORD UNIVERSITY

and

ANN E. JEWETT
SPRINGFIELD COLLEGE

THE RONALD PRESS COMPANY • NEW YORK

Copyright © 1964 by
THE RONALD PRESS COMPANY

All Rights Reserved

No part of this book may be reproduced
in any form without permission in writing
from the publisher.

7MP

Library of Congress Catalog Card Number: 64–17166
PRINTED IN THE UNITED STATES OF AMERICA

Preface

The authors view physical education as a continuous school program, basically instructional in nature, from grades one to twelve. Programs in both the elementary and secondary school are studied.

Today's physical education must find ways to individualize instruction so that each student may best develop his own personality, abilities, and interests. This book is addressed to students of physical education, both at the undergraduate and graduate levels, and to those supervisors and administrators who seek more effective ways of planning and conducting physical education in their schools.

The first half of the book focuses on modern principles of curriculum development. Several major curriculum patterns typically found in American public educational systems are discussed along with their implications for physical education programs. Examples are cited for various grade levels. An extensive analysis of influences that affect physical education teachers and administrators interested in curriculum change is included. It also provides many "down-to-earth" procedures for the analysis of curriculum deficiencies and describes methods for initiating and carrying through the improvement of local school programs. The second half of the book analyzes different patterns for organizing physical education curriculum content and cites examples of actual curricula in operation at various grade levels. It offers suggestions for teaching values through physical education, delineates procedures for grouping pupils and for organizing and conducting the program to better individualize instruction. It highlights fundamental principles for optimum staff assignment and utilization. New theories and practices are applied in flexible scheduling to the individualization of instruction and staff utilization.

This material will provide further insight and stimulation to those who seek improved ways to achieve qualitative excellence for every student.

The authors are indebted to many colleagues and friends at the University of Illinois, Springfield College, and Stanford University for personal inspiration, professional stimulation, and constructive help in the preparation of this manuscript, as well as for provision of specific materials that appear throughout the text. Particular gratitude is expressed to those University of Illinois cooperating teachers who demonstrate daily the practical possibilities for improving public school physical education. Their consistent professional dedication and teaching effectiveness have contributed significantly to the faith in the future of physical education that underlies this work.

The contents of Chapter 7 have developed to an important degree from a cooperative action research project in the River Forest, Illinois, Public Schools. Sincere appreciation is extended to Mr. W. E. Sugden, Superintendent; Mr. Edward Steadman, Assistant Superintendent; and to the members of the Physical Education Staff: Mr. Frank C. Brown, Mr. Gilbert Magida, Miss Helen Moody, Mr. Robert Skinner, Jr., and Mr. Donald P. Slutz. Professional associations with these colleagues have contributed far more than the specific references in this volume can indicate.

A special word of thanks is expressed to Miss Roberta S. Bennett for extensive editorial and typing assistance. Personal appreciation is also extended to Dr. Camille Brown, Dr. Rosalind Cassidy, and Dr. Seth Arsenian. The authors are happy to acknowledge the less direct, but nonetheless genuine, contributions of many former students.

JOHN E. NIXON
ANN E. JEWETT

Stanford, California
Springfield, Massachusetts
  April, 1964

Contents

Part I
FOUNDATIONS FOR CURRICULUM DEVELOPMENT

1   Functions of the American Public School   3
   The School's Role in Cultural Transmission, 3 · The School's Role in Cultural Change, 9 · The School's Role Based on Learning Principles, 17

2   Principles of Curriculum Development   22
   Determining Objectives, 23 · Selection of Subject Matter, 25 · Sequence of Materials, 27 · Selection of Methods, 29 · Broad Participation in Curriculum Development, 31

3   Curriculum Patterns and Physical Education . . .   34
   The Separate-Subjects Curriculum, 34 · The Broad-Fields Curriculum, 40 · The Core Curriculum, 43 · Other Curriculum Patterns, 49

4   Influences Toward Change in the Physical Education Curriculum   53
   National Influences, 53 · State Organizations, 60 · College and University Consultants, 68 · County School Office and District Consultants, 70 · Colleges and Universities, 73 · Colleagues, 75

5   Role of the Physical Educator in Curriculum Change . .   78
   Curriculum Change as Problem-solving, 78 · Defining Problems, 79 · Collecting Data, 86 · Selecting and Testing Solutions, 91 · Evaluating Results, 92 · The Teacher and Curriculum Development, 93 · Challenges for Physical Education Curriculum Change, 101

Part II

CURRICULUM CHANGE AND EDUCATIONAL PROBLEMS

6 Content Selection and Organization 105

Standards for Organizing Physical Education Curricula, 105 · Basic Core of Physical Education, 108 · Patterns for Organizing Elementary School Physical Education Curriculum Content, 111 · Patterns for Organizing Secondary School Physical Education Content, 116 · Co-Educational Programs in Physical Education, 131 · Intramural, Extramural, Interscholastic, and School Recreation Programs, 133 · Continuity in Physical Education Programs, 134

7 Teaching Values 136

Significance of the Problem, 136 · Unique Responsibilities of Physical Education, 141 · Learning Values by Imitation, 142 · Studying Values as Subject Content, 143 · Teaching Values Through Individual Counseling, 147 · Teaching Values Through Environmental Modification, 150 · Use of Reward and Punishment in Teaching Values, 152 · How Shall We Teach Values? 155

8 Individualizing Instruction 157

Significance of the Problem, 157 · Individualization Through Rate of Progress, 161 · Individualization Through Methodology, 163 · Individualization Through Grouping, 168 · Individual Differences Among Teachers, 172 · Practices in Individualizing Instruction, 173

9 Staff Utilization 180

Basic Assumptions, 181 · The Evolving Roles of Teachers, 181 · Traditional Teacher Utilization, 182 · Improving Teacher Utilization, 184 · Professional and Non-Professional Duties of Teachers, 184 · Differentiation of Staff Personnel, 188 · Team Teaching, 192 · Staff Utilization in Elementary School Physical Education, 195 · Staff Utilization in High School Physical Education, 196 · Physical Education Staff Utilization in the Future, 198

10 Flexible Scheduling 202

Basic Assumptions Concerning Flexible Scheduling, 204 · Schedule Modifications, 206 · Physical Education Flexible Scheduling in Elementary Schools, 213 · Physical Education Flexible Scheduling in Secondary Schools, 213 · Physical Education Flexible Scheduling in the Future, 217

11 Facilities and Instructional Technology 227

Definition, 227 · Buildings, Structures, and Areas for Physical Education, 228 · Educational Specifications, 230 · Physical Education Facilities for the Future, 232 · Instructional Technology, 233 · Physical Education and Instructional Technology, 251

Appendix

TABLES OF FLEXIBLE SCHEDULING POSSIBILITIES

Explanatory Notes for the Physical Education Structure, 263 · Schedule for Physical Education Student, 265 · Schedule for Physical Education Teacher, 267 · Suggested Curriculum for Group V, Girls, Gifted, 267 · Suggestions for Small and Large Group Activities, 270

Selected References 271

Index 287

Part I

FOUNDATIONS FOR CURRICULUM DEVELOPMENT

Functions of the American Public School

Faith in the importance of public education has been one of the more stable characteristics of American culture. Development of sound curricula for the public schools is a major concern of American democracy. Yet sound curriculum development is a highly complex task. A curriculum that is designed to achieve carefully selected goals does not result from a haphazard accumulation of desirable knowledges. On the contrary, it requires careful study of the sources of curriculum materials; a depth of understanding of principles of curriculum development; and the active participation of teachers, administrators, and lay citizens in action research and curriculum experimentation.

Curriculum materials find their sources in the culture of the society that chose to establish schools and in the nature of the human individual who lives in that society and who will learn through his curriculum experiences. A study of these foundations is beyond the scope of this volume. The following paragraphs are intended simply to review and summarize the highlights of such study. It is hoped that the reader whose background in these areas is limited will consult a number of the references in the bibliography.

THE SCHOOL'S ROLE IN CULTURAL TRANSMISSION

Schools are established by any society to insure the continued existence of the society. All children and youth must learn certain essentials of their culture in order to perpetuate their society as adults. Not all societies require schools to achieve this purpose, however. In primitive societies children, for generations, learned to be competent adults without any schools at all. In primitive Samoan society, when a boy was relieved of baby-tending responsibilities at the age of eight or nine, he learned to fish by making himself useful to the older boys who were already competent fishermen. His older sister was taught weaving by some older woman in the household. Generations of Zuñi children memorized the word-perfect rituals required in their complex ceremonial life through association with the adults of the pueblo. In all simpler cultures, the young have learned to obtain and prepare food, to make tools, to build homes, and to respect given attitudes and traditions by observing and imitating their elders, and through the pressures of public approval or disapproval.

But as a culture becomes more complex, as specialization increases, as cultural elements become more numerous, as essential learnings multiply, it becomes increasingly difficult for the family to educate its children adequately. As the members of a community begin to specialize in different kinds of work for mutual benefit, it is logical that someone should specialize in educating the children so that others will have more time for the different specialized functions they perform for the community. As education of the young grows more complex, it is more efficient to organize children into groups under the supervision of one adult who possesses special skills for performing this vital function. Thus, the school becomes an important social agency in any but the simplest cultures.

The public school in the United States of America, as in every nation, is charged with the responsibility of transmitting to the next generation the knowledges, skills, and attitudes needed in order to maintain the national culture. Throughout our history, important cultural changes have been reflected in changing educational aims, curricula, and methods.

The seventeenth-century schools were dominated by the religious aims of the churches that controlled them; reading and religion were the common subjects of elementary education in all the colonies. A strong Humanistic tradition kept vocational training out of the schools and led to an emphasis in the early secondary schools on the teaching of Latin grammar. The rising commercial interests of the eighteenth century produced new types of schools taught in English and offering instruction in English grammar, practical mathematics, history, commercial subjects, and modern languages. The patriotic sentiments of the Revolutionary period led to more secular text materials and to increased state and federal interest in strengthening the common schools. American education in the nineteenth century responded to the forces of democracy, industrialism, humanitarianism, and secularism with the development of a universal, free, co-educational, and compulsory school system, with the establishment of the public high school designed to provide both terminal and college preparatory education, and with tremendous expansion in higher education, both in private colleges and in the new state universities.

Twentieth-century American schools reflect the conflicts in modern American culture in controversies over increased emphasis upon scientific and technical education; racial integration; and government financial aid for educational facilities, scholarships, and salaries. The efforts of United States schools in mid-twentieth century to provide professional and vocational competence together with a sense of social responsibility have brought both curriculum expansion and election to stimulate individual development and core curriculum requirements and designs to ensure a minimum of general education. Research and experimentation have resulted in new patterns of educational organization and staff utilization and new teaching methods, techniques, and devices. New developments include programs of vocational education, citizenship education, guidance and counseling, and education of exceptional children.

Individual Survival and Self-Protection

Since any society consists of individual human beings, the individual's ability to survive and protect himself is essential to societal survival. If the American public school is to transmit to the next generation the learnings essential to the maintenance of our culture, certainly the curriculum must prepare the individual to protect himself under modern living conditions.

Today's American adult needs muscular strength and physical endurance sufficient to put screens on his home's windows, to shovel snow from his driveway, to carry a young child, to load luggage into his automobile, and to combat fatigue from ironing or waiting tables or retail selling. He also needs a reserve of physical endurance to survive such emergencies as the capsizing of a fishing boat or the forced landing of an airplane in inhospitable terrain.

He needs to understand the value of various immunization procedures, to recognize the early symptoms of cancer, and to seek competent professional assistance in solving his personal health problems. He needs to learn how to avoid safety hazards in his home and on our crowded highways. He needs to be prepared to protect himself and others through simple first-aid procedures and the administration of artificial respiration when necessary. He needs knowledge of the safest procedures to follow in the event of possible exposure to atomic radiation. These and many other aspects of promoting individual health must be considered in building a curriculum that will successfully maintain contemporary American culture.

Health in the modern world includes the promotion of sound mental hygiene. Some authorities have concluded that prisoners-of-war and human beings in circumstances of similar hardship more often die because of a lack of will to live than from physical weakness. It is estimated that one out of every ten babies born in the United States today will be hospitalized for mental illness at some time during his life.[1] While a portion of these individuals will return to useful citizenship, from the standpoint of cultural survival they must be considered partial casualties.

The American public school curriculum certainly cannot overlook the importance of promoting mental health. It must help each individual to understand himself and to value himself as a person of worth, to recognize and use his strengths, and to identify and try to improve his weaknesses. It must help each individual to achieve the security that comes from knowing he can earn his own living. It must help him to develop avocational interests and skills to provide satisfactions that his job cannot offer. It must help him to establish the kind of personal relationships that lend meaning to life in a world of people. It must help him to build and clarify a personal philosophy that will give purpose to his life, a pattern of beliefs that will provide direction amid the confusions so characteristic of life in our culture today.

Literacy has traditionally been an important objective of the public school curriculum. Communication skills are essential to survival in any culture in which the individual is to any degree dependent upon other human beings. Everyday living in the United States requires that the individual be able to state what he wishes to purchase in a department store. He must be able to read the labels on shelves, packages, and cans if he shops in a supermarket. He must be able to read warning signs on the highway. Most of the mechanical devices that are so prevalent in our culture must be operated in accordance with brief written instructions and simple cues indicating speed, direction, and application of power. Each person must be able to describe his wants to others whom he must ask for assistance in meeting his needs.

It has been suggested that reading and writing skills are less in demand in the era of radio and television and the long distance telephone. But certainly no thinking person would argue that an illiterate can participate fully in our culture. If the school is to fulfill its role in ensuring cultural survival, it must help each child to master the essential communication skills basic to maintenance of individual physical and mental well-being and to the capacity for protection against increasingly numerous, complex, and hazardous threats to individual survival.

---

[1] According to estimates of the National Association for Mental Health, New York City.

Occupational Self-Sufficiency

Human survival entails productive work on the part of individual members of every society in order to secure the food, clothing, and shelter necessary to sustain life. In America today, this work is highly specialized. The individual must be able to perform some function of value to his society in order that he can earn money to purchase the essentials he no longer produces independently. To provide for his own needs and the well-being of his dependents, he must be able to meet the demands of some occupation needed in his culture.

What does this mean for the public school curriculum? It does not mean that the school should attempt the impossible task of training boys and girls in all the skills and knowledges required by the myriad of jobs in the current American scene. Nor does it mean that the school should try to educate each boy and girl for competence to enter a specific job immediately after leaving school. It *does* mean that the schools should teach the knowledges, skills, and attitudes common to many vocations; and that the schools should offer basic vocational education for certain families of occupations.

The basic language skills are required of effective workers in almost all vocations. A worker must be able to read and/or listen to instructions with a satisfactory level of comprehension if he is to perform his job adequately. Most jobs entail the abilities to ask questions, call attention to irregularities, and make routine reports. Many jobs require computational skills—accurate counting of inventories, making change, simple arithmetic in estimating needed quantities of work supplies, and keeping accurate records of all kinds. Job success often depends upon the ability to submit a written application in acceptable form or to perform creditably in an interview situation. Such personal qualities as good grooming, promptness, honesty, dependability, and appropriate response to authority may be critical in almost any occupation.

In addition to educating children and youth in the essential knowledges, skills, and attitudes that are required as a foundation for achieving success in any occupation, the school should offer basic vocational education for various families of occupations. Boys and girls who plan to find work in the business world immediately after graduation from high school should have the opportunity to develop beginning skills in typing, bookkeeping, and the use of office machines. Those who are interested in trades or industrial occupations can profit from instruction and practice in the use of hand tools and the simpler standard power tools. To those who intend to devote full time to homemaking immediately after high school, the curriculum should offer instruction in nutrition, food preparation, child care, home beautification, and family budgeting.

Boys and girls who prepare for occupations requiring college or university education also need "basic vocational education." Some may object to the use of this phrase in reference to college preparatory curricula. But, in the broad sense, this is vocational education too. Curriculum decisions based upon college admission requirements or upon prerequisites to specific university curricula are tentative vocational decisions.

The school should offer alternative possibilities for basic vocational education. The number and variety and specific alternatives available will depend upon the needs of youth in the local community. Curriculum electives for groups of students sharing similar vocational objectives must receive the attention of educational planners. More specific vocational interests that are of direct concern to only a few students can be encouraged and guided by the personal leadership of interested teachers and through such activities as a mathematics club, the school newspaper, a Junior Achievement Club, a photography group, a physical education leaders' organization, and the school orchestra. Whether vocational education occurs through course offerings or more informal curriculum activities, it should be stressed that the school's objective is not preparation for specific job opportunities but only occupational orientation and elementary skills.

The fact that certain curriculum materials may be selected to serve a primarily vocational purpose does not by any means justify a predominant emphasis upon vocational education in the secondary schools. Education to provide a foundation for developing occupational proficiency is but one of many legitimate goals of the curriculum. No American public school is fulfilling its role adequately if it allows this goal to preempt other important functions.

Adaptation to Group Living

Group living is a condition of contemporary American culture for which every functioning citizen must possess basic skills. The young child being reared in an American family learns to respond to parental authority; as he matures, he needs to learn how to participate in family decision-making and how to assume responsibility in carrying out decisions requiring of him specific actions or behavior. As a member of the family group, he must develop his own individuality while adjusting to conflicting patterns and demands of others. He must learn to take responsible care of himself and his personal possessions, to share his playthings, parental attention, enjoyment of family possessions, and the use of his home, with other family members. He should cultivate habits of satisfying participation in family recreation and homemaking activities. The school must reinforce effective group living patterns taught within the family; and, for those children and youth whose homes have not provided the desired experiences, the public school must offer supplementary guidance in achieving minimum skills for democratic living.

During the school years, increasing emphasis is placed upon secondary group relationships. The individual must learn to live harmoniously in numerous and varied groups. He shares classroom experiences with twenty to thirty children of the same age; as he reaches the secondary school, these groups may differ in composition and size from hour to hour. He may participate in youth service organizations, church-affiliated groups, athletic teams, and school clubs. In all probability, during his out-of-school hours, he will be associated with one or more social groups whose specific nature reflects his age, social status, and current interests.

The young adult in our society needs skills for group living in order to fulfill his own individual potential as a human being and to contribute to the maintenance of American democratic culture. The school can provide innumerable learning experiences in groups; these experiences can be so organized that youth learn, in addition to traditional subject content, to relate themselves to changing social groups, to maintain personal ethical codes when challenged by conflicting peer values, to select friends and establish satisfying personal relationships, to appreciate differences in persons, to encourage the optimum personal development and the maximum social contribution of other individuals, to participate in setting and achieving group goals, to take leadership as appropriate, and to fulfill a wide variety of adult group roles.

THE SCHOOL'S ROLE IN CULTURAL CHANGE

The maintenance of democratic culture under present world conditions requires more than transmission of the status quo. Continuous improvement of contemporary American culture is essential. The school's role in cultural change is a vital one.

Educators have engaged in lengthy debates concerning the appropriate role of the school in social change. The authors hold the view (discussed in Chapter 5) that it is a function of the American public school to contribute to improvement of the culture through education of young people to critically evaluate current cultural patterns and to direct carefully selected social changes. A major goal of every local school system should be to equip graduates to deal effectively with contemporary social problems.

Optimum Individual Development

Democracy respects and values individual differences. Individual abilities must be stimulated, challenged, and developed to the highest possible level. The strength of our nation is the collective strength of many individuals. Our total capacity is directly dependent upon the degree to which the capacity of each individual is extended. We are not equal in our potential; yet the continuing growth and improvement of American society requires each of us to utilize our own unique talents and abilities to the top limits. The American public schools must provide the means for greater self-realization, for more complete development of individual capacities.

From each individual we need the highest intellectual power of which he is capable. The advances of science and technology in the past generation have been fantastic; future findings are beyond our present comprehension. Yet we are assured that education that builds upon present scientific knowledge and that leads to critical study and creative thought will inspire our young scientists to even more startling breakthroughs.

No one questions our country's need for the intellectual power required to push forward technological frontiers. Unfortunately, however, the importance of top-flight intelligence in solving the social problems inevitably associated with advances in the physical sciences is sometimes underestimated. The future course of world events may well be determined by our insight in identifying anachronistic social institutions, by our wisdom in exploring new directions for existing social agencies, and by our creative intelligence in devising new social arrangements to facilitate progress under new conditions.

Desirable cultural change demands tremendous and ever-increasing intellectual power in our physical and social scientists; in our experts in the humanities and sciences; and in our political, military, civic, spiritual, and educational leaders. It further requires extensive utilization of the potential intellectual power of individual citizens at all levels. Our awesome scientific capabilities cannot be supported without technical knowledges and skills never before needed on so widespread a basis. Our vast industrial complex constantly demands more technicians and skilled workers; the knowledges and skills possessed by the average worker are increasingly complicated. Our political responsibilities require unlimited persons with mastery of long-ignored foreign languages and realistic understandings of differing cultures and peoples. Effective participation in civic affairs continually grows more difficult; indifference to civic responsibility can be overcome only if we succeed in challenging more and more citizens to develop individual intellectual potential beyond current levels of aspiration.

To further these goals, the schools must help students to acquire basic skills for seeking information, reading skills adaptable to varying purposes, sound study habits, and competence in expressing ideas. Students must be guided in developing skills of reflective thinking and stimulated to extend their creative powers. Perhaps most important, the schools must encourage favorable attitudes toward learning as a lifelong activity and foster genuine enthusiasm for the pursuit and application of knowledge.

Not only do we need each individual's best intellectual power, but long-range cultural improvement also necessitates optimum development of his resources for "re-creation," for moral and spiritual well-being. We live in a tension-producing society in which the daily demands of our lives can best be met if we establish a rhythm or a balance between work and constructive hobbies, rewarding avocations, or satisfying recreation. The individual human being is a single entity. All phases of his growth and development are interrelated. A large proportion of potential human productivity will be lost to the improvement of our culture if we fail to stimulate avocational interests that lead to individual satisfaction and personality integration.

Many persons find better outlets for their creative energies in recreational activities than during hours of employment. Not infrequently talents that contribute significantly to the enrichment of our culture are discovered and developed in the pursuit of avocational interests. We cannot afford to lose these contributions of optimum individual development.

Elementary and secondary schools must foster recreational interests by encouraging hobbies children cultivate outside of school, by introducing students to many activities with recreation potential, by ensuring sufficient breadth in the curriculum to stimulate new interests for every student, by inspiring creative expression in many curriculum areas, by providing for group enjoyment of special interests in extensive extraclass programs, and by guidance of students into constructive hobbies and rewarding recreation. The schools have a further responsibility for the development of knowledges and skills that lead to safe and satisfying participation in leisure-time activities. They must strengthen recognition of the importance of balanced living and the desire for worthy use of leisure time. Beyond these tasks, schools must cultivate attitudes of responsibility for providing adequate facilities and leadership for public recreation, substantial support for the growth of the fine arts, and encouragement for the spontaneous development of local crafts and interest groups.

The complete utilization of an individual's capacities encompasses the establishment of a personal moral code, commitment to carefully chosen ethical standards, and acceptance of a scale of values consistent with democratic living. As each youth grows into adulthood, he must develop his individual philosophy of life. Wide latitude in religious preference is guaranteed by our Constitution; spiritual development of individual citizens is a must. Educators must learn more about the teaching of moral and spiritual values and find more effective means for making ethical learnings vital content of the public school curriculum.

Achievement of optimum health and fitness is basic to optimum self-realization. Every individual must achieve his highest possible level of fitness for maximum personal satisfaction and for realization of his potential social effectiveness. Total fitness includes physical, mental, social, emotional, and spiritual well-being. As modern medicine advances, the difficulties of separating physical causes of ill health from other causes become increasingly apparent. In regard to his health, as in other respects, we must deal with the individual as a whole.

Individual fitness is achieved through many channels, through the cooperation of many social agencies, through participation in a wide variety of activities at many different times and in many different places, but never without the individual's assumption of responsibility for personal fitness. It is understood that the school cannot accomplish this task alone, but it can play an important role. Every school should offer a scientifically sound, dynamic, and challenging health education curriculum. Every school should provide a healthful learning environment, essential health services, and up-to-date health instruction. Every schoolchild should participate in a physical education program geared to his physical developmental needs. Every school curriculum should include a required core of learnings to fit the individual for healthful participation in contemporary life, and opportunities to select learning experiences that will fit him for his unique role in his society. Above all, public education must inculcate in each individual an attitude of personal responsibility for the achievement of optimum fitness.

National Economic Well-Being

If our culture is not only to maintain itself but also to improve and prosper, American schools must provide a foundation for strengthening the national economy. A first step toward this goal is to improve individual work habits and attitudes. Machines have displaced many workers. Automation has multiplied industrial productivity. Yet the individual worker still plays an important role in the United States economy. For optimum production, he needs to be accurate, reliable, punctual, cooperative, and willing to receive suggestions. He must find value in his work, take pride in a job well done, seek to improve his performance, feel responsibility toward his job, be willing to recognize appropriate authority and to follow essential regulations, and ally himself with organizational goals. These are habits and attitudes that can be learned in school; they should be encouraged by constant striving to stimulate and maintain superior performance standards in classroom work, in daily preparation and study, and in extraclass activities.

Another means by which the school can contribute to national economic well-being is to place emphasis upon problem-solving skills. The individual who learns how to identify a problem correctly masters a skill as useful in the business world as in school. The student who acquires the habit of applying the scientific method to the solution of problems encountered in the laboratory or classroom becomes the worker who uses problem-solving techniques to deal with shop or office problems. Individual workers capable of recognizing and solving problems can contribute to more effective work methods and increased job efficiency.

The United States labor force is steadily growing and changing. The number and proportion of unskilled workers continually decreases, while our expanding economy demands proportionally more highly skilled specialists and technicians. The average young person in school today can assume that he must become a specialist if his job security is to be assured. At the same time, however, rapid advances in technology, industry, and automation periodically eliminate certain categories of jobs or drastically reduce the need for certain job specialties. Since the specific directions of economic progress cannot be accurately forecast, the individual worker must be able to adapt his education and training to productivity in other related jobs.

What does this mean for American education? It means that basic knowledges and skills useful in all occupations should receive emphasis. Vocational education for various job families, as discussed above, will continue to be appropriate. The individual student should have opportunities to develop skills needed in a specialized occupational field of his choice. But it is essential that he also have a broad general education, familiarity with basic knowledges required in many vocational fields, and competence in a sufficient variety of elementary skills to make him flexible in adapting to occupational changes. Vocational guidance must stress the importance of avoiding too much specialization too soon.

Another challenge to greater national economic well-being lies in the need for increasing individual ability to manage money successfully. A financially responsible adult must understand budgeting, simple bookkeeping, installment buying, credit plans, mortgages and loans, and savings and investments. The actions of individuals in handling their personal financial affairs necessarily affect the nation's economy. It is also important that the individual adult grasp the essentials of government financing; too many of today's citizens are unable to vote intelligently on bond issues, tax proposals, and other measures involving the raising or expenditure of public funds. This is a vital need for strengthening the economy and improving our way of life.

Consumer economics is important content in the public school curriculum. Every young person should understand the basic principles of our economic system. He should have opportunities to study its foundations and long-range operations as well as its current strengths, contemporary crises, and continuing problems. His learning experiences should include the acquisition of elementary knowledges and the development of fundamental skills required in establishing his own financial independence. He must learn to appreciate the importance of his responsibility to his local community and to his nation as an intelligent voter and a taxpayer in a democracy. Desirable cultural change must necessarily be supported by strength in the national economy.

Successful Group Participation

One of the constant challenges of democracy is to promote the general welfare by directing our efforts toward the best interests of the group while encouraging the optimum devolpment of each individual. At times, these two emphases appear to conflict; but in actuality, the individual and the group are mutually interdependent; the long-range good of the group is also the long-range good of the individual. Provision of experiences in successful group living is a major responsibility of the American public school.

One of the most difficult, yet most urgent, tasks of the school is to equip the individual to make the moral choices required in daily living. Democracy is built upon certain basic values that must be understood by every member of the group. More frequent adherence to the Hebraic-Christian ethic upon which our country was founded would minimize our problems. Yet many young people have not developed an adequate system of values and are unable to apply these values consistently in their daily lives. Ethical values should be taught by the home and by the church, but they must also be taught by the school. It is the school's responsibility to teach the values cherished in our democracy, to delineate the significance of these values in the development of our culture, and to guide the application of democratic values in the daily behavior of individual students.

In our society, the family is the basic unit, the primary group. In recent decades, the family unit has been weakened by many factors. Industrialization has made the family a less self-sufficient unit, no longer producing its own food or making much of its own clothing. Mechanization has drastically reduced the time required to maintain a home and all but eliminated the need for children to contribute to the work of operating the home. Urbanization has resulted in greater diversification of interests among family members and the pursuit of varied responsibilities and interests at increasing distances from the home. The constantly rising standard of living has led to employment of both parents. Increasing population mobility moves individual families away from relatives and the stabilizing influences of long-standing friendships and community traditions. Compulsory military service has separated family members for long periods under difficult circumstances. There have been many significant corresponding changes in popular mores and attitudes toward family living. Rising divorce rates, increasing incidence of venereal disease and illegitimacy, and growing juvenile delinquency attest to the breaking down of traditional patterns of family living.

Sociologists, psychologists, and educators all recognize the need for strengthening the American family unit. The schools must accept their responsibility for improving education for family living. Adolescents need both family and professional guidance in establishing satisfactory heterosexual relationships and in developing sound criteria for selection of a marriage partner. Knowledges relating to the common and unique responsibilities of the two partners to a succcessful marriage, current scientific information on child-rearing, and elementary knowledges in such less-glamorous fields as family budgeting and finance are appropriate secondary-school curriculum content for both boys and girls. School learning experiences should also include knowledges, skills, and attitudes for joint participation in the physical improvement and beautification of the home, and in wholesome family recreation.

Youth of both sexes should understand the value of broad general education as a foundation for establishing meaningful common interests and for sharing in each other's changing occupational lives. Boys as well as girls must recognize that woman's role in our culture has changed, that the typical American married woman will be gainfully employed for a total of twenty-five years of her adult life, although her career is likely to be interrupted during the child-rearing years. It is important for young people to understand that the American woman, like her husband, needs an education appropriate to her individual interests and abilities and the opportunity to prepare adequately for an occupation of her own choosing. The schools will render a valuable service to our nation if they can further the attitude that preparation for successful marriage is important, and help to counteract some of the pressures on youth for earlier marriage.

The schools can educate for successful living in other types of groups by offering group participation experiences in extraclass programs. A wide variety of activities should be available, including athletic teams and sports clubs, musical organizations, theatre groups, special interest clubs, and service and junior achievement organizations. Individual students should be guided in their selection and encouraged to develop judgment in the number, breadth, and specific nature of the groups in which they elect membership. Sponsors of student organizations and extraclass activities should be carefully chosen from among those faculty members most skillful in stimulating broad student participation, in challenging students to assume responsibility, and in encouraging and developing student leadership. Capably guided experiences in student activities should further the growth of adults who select wisely and participate effectively in civic and social groups.

American citizens must also learn to strengthen intergroup relations. Since the diversity of our peoples constitutes one of the sources of our nation's strength, we wish to maintain this diversity while increasing our national unity. We need the continued contributions and the unique talents of individuals of all groups, but we must learn to live together more successfully. We cannot afford the interracial strife that characterizes our society today. We cannot take the consequences of prolonging our ethnic group conflicts. We must resolve the tensions in our relationships among citizens of different religious faiths. We must find workable solutions to problems dividing one social class from another. If our nation is to survive in world competition, we need the unique abilities, the productive capacities, and the constructive contributions of all our citizens.

Our schools can strengthen intergroup relations if they become true laboratories in democratic living. Children develop prejudice only in environments that encourage it, through the adult behavior observed and imitated. A public school classroom that houses children representing a cross-section of the local population offers opportunities for boys and girls to know each other as individuals, to appreciate the abilities and personalities of other children without reference to subgroup membership. School policies that make no discrimination with regard to race, creed, social status, or ethnic background permit all children to identify with and give their individual talents to the larger group. Teachers who believe in the worth and dignity of every individual, who understand how to deal with intergroup tensions and how to build sound democratic human relationships must rise to the challenge to create a more perfect union of these United States.

Living in a democracy also demands from the individual citizen knowledgeable participation in his government. He has obligations toward local, state, and federal government. His political responsibilities include respecting the courts and established laws; supporting fire protection, law enforcement, public schools, city utilities, and other public services;

accepting jury duty when called; studying local and national issues; voting intelligently in accord with his personal convictions; electing capable men and women to office; expressing his views to elected representatives; and serving in public office when qualified. In addition to study of these topics through instruction in civics, political science, government, and the problems of democracy, the school's goal of education for active and informed citizenship can be furthered through student development of local citizenship codes, sound disciplinary policies and procedures, student body elections on appropriate local school issues, elected student representatives on policy-making boards, responsible student councils, and student participation in civic improvement programs.

Today's concept of successful group living must go beyond our national boundaries. Americans have been too slow in accepting responsibility for international welfare and progress. The twentieth-century world is highly interdependent; both moral and practical considerations force us to give greater attention to our role in the international community.

Our schools should be educating world citizens—citizens with increased knowledge and understanding of world history, international geography, cultural anthropology, world economics, national political systems, foreign languages, world religions, regional literature and fine arts, and sociological and psychological characteristics of other cultures. We must engender attitudes of interest in and appreciation of other cultures, enthusiasm for international friendships and genuine understanding of other peoples, and a desire for individual and national service to the world community. Our youth must develop the skills to communicate with citizens of other nations, to live harmoniously in other countries, to participate in the work of international agencies and organizations, to share the best of American culture with the rest of the world, to enrich the American way of life with the best of other cultures, and to work with individuals from all lands toward a better world for all.

THE SCHOOL'S ROLE BASED ON LEARNING PRINCIPLES

The school's role in maintaining and improving American culture is determined by the present characteristics of that culture and the cultural changes we as a people desire. In performing its complex functions, the school must necessarily be guided by the nature of the learner and the learning process. Even if all educators agree on the specific content of the curriculum, little learning will be achieved unless learning experiences are organized in terms of the facts established on how man learns. Basic principles of learning must be recognized and utilized in planning and conducting educational experiences.

Each Learner Is a Unique Individual

Each individual human being is unique. The way in which he learns is not exactly like that peculiar to any other individual. Individual variations in learning are as great as in physical dimensions, visual acuity, or food preferences. Since American schools must educate all the children of all the people, they are typically concerned with large groups of learners. It is important that individual differences be given careful and continuous consideration in the organization and conduct of the curriculum.

Modern schools have found various means of individualizing instruction. Flexible grouping permits relatively homogeneous groups of learners in terms of the specific learning task and facilitates variations in group size as required by different types of learning activities. School schedules that allow a significant portion of time for independent study and breadth in elective learning opportunities help to accommodate individual differences. Guidance programs with complete testing facilities and staffs of competent educational and psychological specialists can give realistic counseling to individual learners and effective assistance to students and to the teachers who work with them. Teachers who understand the importance of gearing instruction to individuals learn to identify specific learning difficulties; to seek additional professional help when required; to direct students to textbooks and other educational materials selected according to their needs; to use varied presentation techniques designed to reach more students with better results; to vary class assignments for individual class members; and to differentiate among learners in planning field trips, projects, and small group activities.

The Child Learns as a Whole Individual

We have long known that there could be no neat division of an individual into several separate and precise categories. The whole of man is an entity; he functions effectively only as a total person. All of his being is in some measure participant in any action he performs. Whatever he learns, he learns as a total individual.

In school learning situations, we are frequently concerned with specific knowledge objectives. But we must keep in mind that our primary concern is the total child. What he learns will reflect his general physical health and the degree of his momentary physical well-being. What he learns may be limited by preoccupation with conflicts at home or an important athletic contest. What he learns will be colored by his opinion of his teacher and by his feelings toward his classmates. He learns through all his senses, using both muscle and nerve cells, and with his autonomic as well as his voluntary nervous system.

Recognizing these facts, the school must concern itself with the whole child. The school environment must provide the essentials for his physical comfort and well-being. The individual teacher is responsible for needed adjustments in classroom physical conditions and for establishing and maintaining in his classroom a psychological environment conducive to sound mental hygiene. He should help to reinforce learning by presenting key instructions and facts through a combination of oral presentation, visual aids, individual reading assignments, and through student practice of any motor skills involved.

Supervision of students on the playground, in the lunchroom, in the corridors, on the school bus, during athletic contests, at school parties and other special events should be adequate for prompt attention to incipient behavior difficulties and interpersonal conflicts. Disciplinary practice and other personnel policies should be reasonable, consistent, and educationally sound. School administrators, social workers, counselors, and guidance specialists should work closely with families, with local social agencies, and with the members of the instructional staff to know the child as a whole individual and to help him to be a happier total person and a more successful learner.

Learning Is an Active Process

One does not learn simply by exposure to knowledge. Learning requires the active participation of the learner in the process of his own learning. The learning of a motor skill demands actual performance and practice of the skill. Active participation is an obvious requisite for learning to use a hammer, to make a buttonhole, to catch a football, to type, or to play a trumpet.

But the learner must also be actively involved in the process of learning knowledges. He must make his own applications of facts that are presented. He must use knowledges in differing circumstances and in varied combinations to make them part of his learning. He must discover their relevance in the solution of problems.

Attitudes are not learned by reading about them or hearing adults explain why certain ones are desired. The child develops attitudes in situations in which he must make value judgments. Attitudes grow out of experience resulting from his own behavior choices. Attitudes frequently stem from strong emotional experiences. The learner is likely to be even more deeply involved in the process of learning attitudes than in learning skills or knowledges. *All* learning is an active process in which the individual learner is an active participant.

If the school is to increase the amount of learning that occurs under its auspices and improve the quality of the knowledges, skills, and attitudes learned, it must maximize student participation in planned learning situations. The problem-solving approach must be emphasized, with careful selection of problems to permit active student involvement, and with provision for student choice of appropriate problems. Each lesson should include, in addition to a motivating introduction and an organized presentation, opportunities for students to make immediate application of the new materials through discovering relationships to previous learnings, utilizing them in simple class exercises, and searching for their significance in solving long-range problems. Techniques involving overt student activity, such as discussions, buzz sessions, panels, debates, role-playing, projects, surveys, field trips, and laboratory experimentation, and guided skills practice should be used liberally.

The Individual Learns in Terms of His Maturity, His Experience Background, and His Own Purposes

The child cannot learn what he is not ready to learn. Physiological growth follows the same general developmental sequence in all children, though individual rates of growth vary widely. Physiological maturity does not necessarily correspond to chronological age. All five-year-olds are not ready to skip, nor is every six-year-old mature enough to read, nor is a seven-year-old automatically ready for cursive writing.

The physiological maturity of each individual child establishes a minimum age before which it is not realistic to expect him to achieve a specific learning objective. Educators cannot control individual physiological growth rates. But the child's experiential background is also a factor in his readiness for learning. The first-grade girl who has played ball with older brothers will be ready for more advanced ball skills than the girl who has not been encouraged in similar play. A seventh-grader reared in a bilingual home may be an apt foreign language pupil, but he may not be ready for advanced English composition. The high school youth who has discussed basic electronics with his physicist father will be ready to learn more difficult scientific concepts than most of his classmates.

Educators are able to stimulate readiness for certain learnings by providing appropriate background experiences. Fortunately, we need not be satisfied with biding our time until the individual child is ready for an important learning. We can shorten this time period by arranging key experiences that most children have had, but which he has not yet known, by encouraging him to explore interesting related materials, by introducing appropriate "readiness" materials in combination with learning activities in which he already finds success and pleasure.

The individual learns in terms of his maturity and his experience; he also learns in terms of his purposes. Efficient learning is purposeful. The child learns in terms of his felt needs; he does not learn that which he feels no need to learn.

Ideally, the individual student establishes worthwhile goals and learns desired knowledges, skills, and attitudes because they lead him toward his goals. Frequently, however, vital goals and the genuine long-range values of certain learnings are beyond his present comprehension. Then it is the teacher's responsibility to identify purposes that are currently meaningful to him and which can be guided toward long-range educational goals; to encourage student development of new, more foresighted goals; and to motivate interest in important learnings by clarifying relationships to current interests. Thus, in determining placement of curriculum content, although the school must wait for appropriate physiological maturity, readiness for learning can be stimulated by identification and guidance of individual student purposes as well as by thoughtful building of experience backgrounds.

2

Principles of Curriculum Development

No American public school curriculum should be a haphazard collection of traditional subject matter. The selection and organization of learning experiences for the children and youth of the community is a vital function and should be guided by sound principles. No school is justified in repeating uncritically a curriculum established for a previous generation. On the other hand, a curriculum organized to include every promising new subject will be a piecemeal kaleidoscope at best. Furthermore, no curriculum whose content is determined solely by the convictions of a few educators is soundly conceived. Building a curriculum is a highly complex and exceedingly important process. Curriculum development in the public schools of the United States should follow consistent guiding principles.

Before considering these basic principles of curriculum development, a few definitions are needed.[1] We have been using the term "curriculum" in its broad sense to mean the total of all experiences in which the learner participates under school auspices. It includes both the formal curriculum and the informal curriculum. The *formal curriculum* consists of the organized learning experiences conducted in classrooms, shops, laboratories, gymnasiums, and playing fields, that part of the curriculum commonly known as the course of study. The remainder of the child's school experiences constitutes the *informal curriculum*. Guidance and extraclass activities are its major aspects.

The informal curriculum in physical education has particular signifi-

---

[1] The definitions used here are based on those used by Harold C. Hand, *Principles of Public Secondary Education* (New York: Harcourt, Brace & World, Inc., 1958).

cance, since it rates very high in student interest and consequently affords extensive learning opportunities. It includes the *intramural program* of activities conducted with members of the same student body, such as sports clubs, school track meets, and interclass basketball tournaments; and the *extramural program* of activities engaged in with students from other schools, such as varsity interscholastic athletics, playdays, sportsdays, telegraphic and postal meets, and workshops and clinics.

The term "curriculum development" encompasses the planning, organization, conduct, and improvement of both the formal and informal phases of the curriculum. As stated above, sound curriculum development is guided by certain basic principles.

DETERMINING OBJECTIVES

Curriculum objectives must be directed toward the fulfillment of basic human needs, the realities of social circumstances, and the achievement of democratic ideals.

The achievements of the school are necessarily shaped by its goals. Thus, the problem of selecting objectives is of crucial importance. The history of education has spanned many centuries and numerous proposals for determining educational objectives. Since it is manifestly impossible to accomplish all the worthwhile goals that have been suggested, selection is a key task.

Sound educational objectives lead to the satisfaction of basic human needs. Universal needs have been variously classified; Murphy lists four main categories of inborn needs:

1. Visceral needs—that is, needs directly related to the vital organs. These include, among others, needs for food, water, air, etc.; needs related to the reproductive system; needs related to protection of the body from extremes of cold and heat.

2. Activity needs. These include the need to explore and manipulate and the urge to "keep going" . . .

3. Sensory needs. These include needs for color, tone, rhythm; the need to orient ourselves to the environment; the need to escape confusion; the "urge to perceptual clarity."

4. The need to avoid or escape attack, injury, threat, shock, or unbearable disturbance, as exemplified by fear, disgust, rage, and many other "emergency responses." [2]

Curriculum objectives may lead directly to the fulfillment of the above needs. For example, the objective "to be able to throw a playground ball" is directly related to the need to explore and manipulate. On the

[2] Gardner Murphy, *Human Potentialities* (New York: Basic Books, Inc., 1958), pp. 60–61.

other hand, most curriculum objectives lead to meeting basic needs indirectly through various derived needs. As an example, "to understand techniques of water purification" is an educational objective directed toward a need derived from the basic need to furnish the body with sufficient amounts of water. Curriculum objectives are sound only if they can be expected to lead to acknowledged basic or derived needs.

Educational objectives serve no function if they are unrealistic under contemporary social conditions. Water safety and motor vehicle safety are much more appropriate objectives for American schools today than safety in the use of kerosene lamps. Typing is a more valuable skill than making soap. Knowledge of the physiological effects of cigarette smoking is a more important objective than knowledge of the course of typhoid fever. The realities of our present social circumstances dictate more emphasis on such educational objectives as development of moral values, understanding of other cultures, physical fitness, utilization of electronic computers, linguistic skill, realistic evaluation of consumer goods, and critical thinking ability.

Educational objectives in a democracy must be directed toward the optimum development of all the children of all the people. The future of American democracy depends upon maximum utilization of all our resources; our greatest resource lies in the total fitness of our citizens, in their individual creativity and their combined productivity. As stressed in Chapter 1, optimum individual development requires genuine self-realization in intellectual power, in personal resources for "re-creation," in moral and spiritual well-being, and in physical and mental health. Educational objectives must be directed toward the optimum self-realization of every individual student.

Education in a democracy is concerned with the development of individuals who are capable of helping to determine and achieve cooperative group purposes. Curriculum objectives must be consistent with this aim. No matter how great the achievements of our schools in developing individual talents and abilities, our nation cannot fulfill a world leadership role unless our citizens can function effectively in family units; in local occupational, recreational, and civic groups; in state and national professional and political organizations; and in international committees, agencies, and informal social situations. The school curriculum should be directed toward the achievement of successful democratic group living.

Educational objectives in a democracy must, in addition, lead to the development of reasoning ability, and of attitudes supporting reason as the method of settling differences. One of the basic tenets of democracy is its reliance upon reason, rather than violence or force, in the solution of social problems. Problem-solving is the democratic method. Selection of objectives in accord with the criterion of potential achievement of democratic ideals requires acknowledgment of faith in reason as a basic characteristic of democracy.

In addition to meeting the above criteria, curriculum objectives must be capable of reduction to behavioristic terms. Learning involves changes in behavior. If an educational objective is to have any real meaning for those responsible for its achievement, they must know what specific behavioral changes are desired. "To perform accurately the basic arithmetical skills of addition and subtraction of whole numbers" clearly indicates specific behavioral expectations. On the other hand, "mental discipline" does not. The objective "to practice good sportsmanship" does not provide a sufficiently clear guide to behaviors desired. This objective, however, can be reduced to behavioristic terms through rephrasing such specific objectives as "to admit when tagged," "to accept officials' decisions without complaint," and "to refrain from offering alibis for poor performance."

All subject-matter areas must contribute effectively toward the school's selected objectives. Unless a given subject makes a significant contribution to the over-all objectives of the total school, its inclusion in the curriculum is not justified. Physical education, in common with other subject fields, earns its place in the program through its potential for achieving important educational objectives.

SELECTION OF SUBJECT MATTER

Curriculum content should be selected and organized in terms of significance to the solution of important social problems.

The wealth of accumulated knowledge is so great that selection of the most significant content for the public school curriculum is an awesome task. Without some guiding principle for selection and organization of curriculum content, it would be an impossibility. The writers hold an "interactive" view of educational purpose, maintaining that the schools must serve the needs of the social group while serving the needs of individual pupils. In accordance with this view, content must be selected and organized in terms of usefulness to the individual in the solution of important social problems.

The selection of content in terms of important social problems should not be construed to indicate any lack of attention to the needs of individuals. Social problems will, of course, be solved by persons, working as individuals with common concerns. Curriculum content must be meaningful in terms of individual needs. Students' needs determine the meanings found in subject matter. The individual certainly needs knowledges, skills, and attitudes that have value in his society; he feels no need for that which has no significance in the world in which he lives. A number of proposals for curriculum organization have been based on this concept. Partridge proposed major areas of living as a pattern for curriculum design.[3] Havighurst and associates identified series of developmental tasks of people in our culture.[4] Stratemeyer and associates defined persistent life situations that learners face.[5] In order to acquire learning that can be utilized in helping to solve important social problems, the individual learner must study curriculum content that has meaning for him and significance for his society.

Some critics of this theory of content selection have expressed concern for possible neglect of the established organized fields of knowledge. Such concern is unwarranted. Learnings from the established fields of knowledge are required for intelligent solution of all important social problems. It is for this purpose that we need these knowledges. Organized knowledge that serves no function in dealing with any important social problem can be eliminated from the curriculum without loss. But we need not fear the neglect of the established arts and sciences, using this criterion. On the whole, scholars have organized traditional fields of knowledge because of the need for these knowledges in dealing with recurrent problems of living.

The significance of content to the solution of important social problems implies long-range relevance. It would be a serious mistake to allow immediate interests to outweigh long-term values in selecting curriculum content. Misinterpretations of progressive education theories in the 1930's led to numerous instances of overemphasis upon superficial interests of children as a basis for selecting content. Justifiable criticism of this practice led to similar objections to the social problems criterion. The important point to keep before us is that thoughtful selection of curriculum content in terms of genuine long-range value for solving truly important social problems should lead beyond superficial knowledge and the satisfaction of transient interests to sound curriculum organization.

The relative significance of specific curriculum content may vary, however, among differing local communities. The curriculum in a small centralized school in the Middle Atlantic region should vary in certain key respects from that of a large Midwestern suburban high school. Essential content in an area almost completely dependent upon the aircraft industry cannot duplicate the most meaningful content in a region distin-

---

[3] Deborah C. Partridge, "Guidelines for Curriculum Design," *School Executive*, LXVIII (December, 1948), 29–30.

[4] Robert J. Havighurst, *Human Development and Education* (London: Longmans, Green & Co., Ltd., 1953).

[5] Florence B. Stratemeyer, Hamden L. Forkner, Margaret G. McKim, and A. Harry Passow, *Developing a Curriculum for Modern Living* (New York: Bureau of Publications, Teachers College, Columbia University, 1957).

guished by its predominantly agricultural and small retail business economy. Caution in this regard is important, however. Curriculum planners must not lose sight of the great mobility of our population or the increasing nationwide and worldwide scope of modern living. The criterion of long-range significance should always take precedence over relatively minor and rapidly shifting local interests and problems.

Selection of content must be based upon a concern for improvement of society. The school cannot perform its role in our society effectively if content is selected only in terms of maintenance of the status quo. The solution of important social problems necessitates cultural change; it requires identification of potential improvements in our social arrangements; it demands knowledges, skills, and attitudes that our citizens do not now have in sufficient abundance or of satisfactory quality. Therefore, curriculum content must be selected in terms of its significance for facilitating desired cultural change. This is a prerequisite to solving many of our most urgent social problems.

SEQUENCE OF MATERIALS

Sequence of curriculum materials should be based upon knowledge of the maturation, experiential background, mental age, and interest of the learners; and of the usefulness and the degree of difficulty of the material.

All learners meet the same developmental tasks in the same general sequence. But each individual grows at his own pace. As discussed in Chapter 1, readiness for given curriculum materials varies according to level of maturity, native abilities, past experiences, and present interests. Educators must consider the continuity of learning experiences in terms of the individual learner instead of relying upon subject-matter logic as the basis for determining curriculum sequences. If we plan toward the development of key concepts rather than a logically organized presentation of specific facts, there is more flexibility for meeting individual needs within sequences of curriculum materials. Sequences of large units organized around major areas of living or persistent life situations offer greater probability of developing continuity for the individual learner. Such organization also permits teachers to guide students in terms of concurrent sequences, not in terms of a single series.

Sequence of curriculum materials should be based upon knowledge of the learners, but it must also give recognition to considerations of usefulness and difficulty of the material. In general, we prefer to arrange learning materials in order of degree of difficulty, following the principle of proceeding from the simple to the more complex. But certain skills, because of their immediate usefulness, are taught as early as possible without undue pressure on the child. Skill in reading constitutes such an advantage in achieving other educational objectives that it is given considerable priority in the curriculum. Usefulness, rather than degree of difficulty, determines the sequence of most of the "tool" subjects.

Usefulness is the primary criterion for grade placement of many curriculum materials in another sense. Driver education, for example, is most frequently offered at tenth-grade level because most students reach the minimum age to apply for motor vehicle operator's licenses at this level. The decision as to grade placement for social dance is usually based on its usefulness as a recreational and social skill in the local cultural pattern.

Educational economy is an important consideration in planning curriculum sequences. Facing steadily mounting pressures upon the time available for essential school experiences, we can ill afford to waste instructional time. Insofar as possible, all curriculum materials should be offered to children at the time when they can be learned most economically. Economy of learning in the physical education curriculum dictates an emphasis in the early years on movement exploration and the development of fundamental movement skills. Such an emphasis at this stage of the child's developmental pattern is apt to be most efficient in terms of long-run achievement of the total outcomes desired from his physical education experiences.

Children of seven have demonstrated that they are able to learn intricate square dance figures. But the educational wisdom of stressing this objective so early in the sequence of rhythmic activities is certainly open to question. Some boys of eight can achieve considerable baseball skill. But we must raise the question of whether practice in a wide variety of ball-handling skills would not be more economical in the ultimate achievement of all physical education objectives. Undoubtedly, nine-year-olds can learn the fundamentals of badminton; but is this the best sequential placement of the activity in a twelve-year physical education curriculum?

The allotment and distribution of instructional time must depend upon judgments of the relative importance of the objectives to be met and the time required to achieve these objectives. The time devoted to the major content areas should be proportional to the importance of key concepts to be learned. This statement offers a general guide. In practice, we know that each learner has realistic limitations. He requires a given minimum time for achievement of each learning goal. If we do not allot this minimum amount, it may be useless to encourage him to try to reach the objective at all. Thus, judgments concerning time allotments must consider the relative importance of objectives in relation to the estimated minimum learning time each requires.

PRINCIPLES OF CURRICULUM DEVELOPMENT

Another factor in distributing instructional time is the need for repetition in achieving many learning objectives. In many cases, a single exposure is not enough to assure learning. The sequence of experiences must be planned to provide practice opportunities in a variety of situations, possibly at several different curriculum levels.

Decisions concerning sequence, grade placement, and time allotment should be based upon research evidence. Recent curriculum experimentation in mathematics lends support for striking changes in the traditional mathematics sequence. Studies in the teaching of foreign languages indicate considerable success with earlier grade placement than has been customary. Research evidence now available strongly suggests the need for more flexible time allotments, school schedules, and pupil groupings. Curriculum planners should study and utilize current research evidence in planning better local school programs.

Educators should make use of available research evidence in making relevant decisions concerning the local curriculum. They should also initiate local studies to determine applicability of research findings in the local setting and to seek answers to specific problems facing their own schools. Any new curriculum organization to be tested; any major innovation considered; any planned change in sequence, grade placement, or time allotment should allow for adjustments to deal with individual differences among students and teachers.

SELECTION OF METHODS

Teaching methods should use the best current knowledge concerning the nature of the learner and the learning process.

Four key principles of learning have been discussed briefly in Chapter 1. A few major implications for teaching methods resulting from the nature of the learner and the learning process are noted in the following paragraphs.

Educational experiences must be developed as unified "wholes." The first step in learning a new activity is to establish a concept of the whole to be learned. As a learning unit progresses, pupils will concentrate on specific facts, skills, and attitudes; but interrelationships among specifics and the significant relationships of specific learnings to the whole must be continuously clarified and emphasized. The learner should always be able to understand the relationship of a specific task to his over-all goal. The concept of the whole will be expanded and refined as he achieves daily objectives and perceives interrelationships.

A wide variety of learning experiences must be provided to meet individual differences. The wide variability of individual differences has been amply documented. If all children are to benefit from the educational experiences offered in the public schools, it is self-evident that a tremendous variety of experiences must be available to meet their individual needs, to be appropriate to their differing abilities, capacities, levels of maturity, and background experiences.

Pupils must participate actively in the planning, conduct, and evaluation of educational experiences. Since the first impact of John Dewey on American education, there has been widespread agreement that the child learns by doing. Although the principle is frequently ignored in classroom practice, there is no doubt that the active involvement of the student is an essential element in learning. Pupils should actively participate in planning long-range group goals, in setting weekly and daily objectives leading toward major goals, in establishing individual purposes within the class framework. Students should play active roles in the actual conduct of instruction through the assumption of leadership responsibilities, working as committee members on class projects, carrying out individual assignments to further established group goals, and accepting responsibility for individual learning and achievement. Unless pupils share actively in the evaluation of educational experiences, significant portions of the available learning opportunities are lost. Pupils learn through participation in the evaluation process; they contribute toward more accurate and more effective evaluation.

Emphasis must be placed upon the development of reasoning and problem-solving skills. It is manifestly impossible for anyone to master every learning for which he will someday have need. The research evidence on transfer of learning has been disappointing to any hopes that a well-selected core of required content could prepare the student with necessary learnings for the widely varying demands of modern living. We are unable to predict the future accurately enough to estimate the specific knowledge or skill requirements of the successful adult. Under these circumstances, the best preparation that schools can give to future citizens is the ability to reason and to solve problems, along with the basic tools for seeking knowledge and for communicating, and such subject-matter content as we judge to be of significance to the solution of important social problems.

A variety of teaching techniques and resource materials should be utilized. Variety in techniques and materials increases the potentialities for meeting individual needs of the pupils. The many desired learnings that require repetition and practice can be made more interesting to the student, thus increasing his motivation. The use of different techniques and materials in a variety of situations provides better opportunities for the student to develop generalizations and key concepts.

Knowledge of group structure and group dynamics should be employed.

Most school learning takes place in groups. A group of persons is more than the sum of the individuals who compose it. Teachers need to understand general principles of group dynamics and specific facts about the structures and working dynamics of the groups with which they work. Such understanding permits the teacher to assist the individual in learning effectively in the group situation; to manipulate the social environment of an individual learner when desirable and feasible; and to guide the group in helping individuals, in strengthening its working procedures, and in improving its output.

Continuous evaluation is essential. Evaluation is a vital aspect of the learning process. Learning procedures and outcomes should be evaluated continuously in order to identify successes and shortcomings, to determine specific changes needed and areas for additional work. Better education can result only if the results of instruction are evaluated thoroughly and continuously by all concerned.

BROAD PARTICIPATION IN CURRICULUM DEVELOPMENT

Curriculum improvement requires participation by the lay public and by pupils as well as by the entire professional staff.

In the United States, the schools belong to the citizens. With increasing centralization in government and expanding federal aid, the people express a strong disposition to keep the control of the public school in the local community. Americans see the school as their agent for transmitting their values and beliefs to the next generation, for giving their children the opportunities they most desire for them, for making them into the kinds of citizens they want them to become. Everyone has a stake in public education and a concern for the outcomes of the school curriculum. These circumstances demand broad participation in the process of curriculum development.

Curriculum change is action research in that changes result as school personnel test the effectiveness of new ideas on the job. Research processes are used to study and improve practices. The action research cycle in curriculum development is described by Smith, Stanley, and Shores:

> The group will survey the specific situation to identify the difficulties together with the forces and conditions that must be dealt with in order to overcome the difficulties. It will devise ways of dealing with the difficulties, and after critically evaluating these plans, it will try them out to see whether or not they work as anticipated. The group will secure data bearing on the success, or failure, of the plans as tried out. If the plans do not work out according to anticipations, they are then revised. Thus, the process of action-research continues until a satisfactory solution is found.[6]

[6] B. Othanel Smith, William O. Stanley, and J. Harlan Shores, *Fundamentals of Curriculum Development* (New York: Harcourt, Brace & World, Inc., 1957), p. 446.

Action or cooperative curriculum research has been subject to much criticism on the basis of comparisons with other types of research. It should be remembered that the aim of action research is the direct improvement of instruction. Teacher involvement and professional growth are expected outcomes. McNally and Passow make the significant point, "Whatever the resulting contribution to general theory of education, there is little doubt that action research can make a contribution as an in-service procedure for curriculum improvement." [7]

Curriculum improvement requires changes in people. All curriculum improvement projects are directed toward changes in individual pupils. No attempt to improve instruction can be considered successful unless it has the desired effects on the pupils. For this reason, it is sound practice to give pupils a larger role in curriculum development. Pupils play an important role from day to day as they plan and carry out learning experiences with their teachers. But beyond this, they should be invited to contribute to long-range planning and systematic evaluation through questionnaires, interviews, opinion surveys, follow-up studies of graduates, and the participation of their representatives on curriculum committees.

The teacher is the key participant in curriculum improvement, since he is the person in direct control of most of the learning experiences and the chief agent for carrying out curriculum decisions. Curriculum changes can be effected only as individual teachers change, and can guide changes in pupils in their individual classrooms accordingly. Teachers must be active workers on curriculum committees and play an active role in curriculum development at all levels, including determination of objectives, planning of procedures, testing new approaches in the classroom, and evaluation.

Administrators and other professional personnel not directly involved in the teaching play vital roles in curriculum development. Administrators should assume leadership in stimulating local curriculum evaluation, the in-service growth of teachers, and the planning and conduct of action research. They are responsible for establishing and maintaining a school environment that facilitates the daily work of teachers in carrying out sound curriculum decisions. They must interpret the local curriculum to the public and guide and coordinate the participation of lay citizens in evaluation and improvement of the local schools. Supervisors and consultants provide assistance to the teaching staff by providing training in appropriate research techniques, guidance in the development of effective human relations procedures, and resources for increas-

---

[7] Harold J. McNally, A. Harry Passow, et al., *Improving the Quality of Public School Programs* (New York: Bureau of Publications, Teachers College, Columbia University, 1960), pp. 95–96.

ing scholarly and technical competence in subject-matter specialties. Professional associations and governmental agencies contribute to curriculum improvement through research projects of regional and national scope, yearbooks and other publications, consultative services, workshops, clinics, institutes, and conferences. Smith, Stanley, and Shores have summarized the spheres of professional leadership in curriculum changes as follows:

> The leadership function of the profession is limited to four spheres of knowledge and skill: technical skills and knowledge of education, knowledge of intellectual disciplines, knowledge of social and educational values, and knowledge and skill in educational engineering.[8]

Although professional education personnel should assume the major leadership responsibility in curriculum development, lay participation is vitally important. Citizens of the community are significantly affected by curriculum policies and programs and are entitled to share in shaping them. Furthermore, widespread participation in planning changes in school practices provides some assurance that new programs will be understood and supported. Lay citizens are partners in the educational enterprise. Intelligent leadership from the education profession can make them helpful and constructive partners.

Lay participation in curriculum development should not be limited to serving as resource personnel in areas of specialization. When a parent or a businessman is invited to meet with a group of students to enrich learning opportunities or to meet with a group of teachers and administrators to share an expert opinion, he is essentially a professional consultant; he has been asked to contribute to curriculum improvement as a professional in a given field. Such utilization of local citizens as resource personnel should be encouraged. But, more than this, citizens should participate in curriculum improvement through sharing in the determination of the goals of the school and in the evaluation of the degree to which the local schools are serving the needs of the children, youth, and adults of the community. The individual citizen can exercise his role in curriculum change through the board of education, citizens' committees, the legislature, special interest groups, foundations, and lay publications.

Curriculum improvement should not be limited to major projects undertaken within a specified time period or to annual inventories of revisions currently needed. Curriculum evaluation and change should be continuous. Evaluation of both the curriculum development process and actual changes in the quality of instruction should be an integral part of planning the next modifications. Educators must work with students and citizens of all segments of the population in the on-going cooperative process of curriculum development.

[8] Smith, Stanley, and Shores, *op. cit.*, p. 454.

3

Curriculum Patterns and Physical Education

The previous chapter has discussed the basic foundations of curriculum development and has described fundamental principles that guide curriculum improvement. This chapter will analyze three major types of curriculum organization; namely, the *separate-subjects* curriculum, the *broad-fields* curriculum, and the *core* curriculum. Each of these patterns will be discussed in terms of its general description; the role of subject matter; provision of scope, sequence, and grade placement of learning experiences; teaching, learning, and evaluation; and the role of physical education in the pattern. The chapter will conclude with brief references to other curriculum patterns.

THE SEPARATE-SUBJECTS CURRICULUM

Historically, the American public school curriculum has long been organized on a separate-subjects basis. Discrete areas of study commonly called "subjects" are selected by the decision-making authorities in the school or school district and are assigned to each grade. The so-called three R's—reading, writing, and arithmetic—were the separate subjects that constituted the major portion of the public school curriculum in the nineteenth century. Gradually, other subjects were added to the school curriculum at different grade levels. Some subjects are continued in a sequence of difficulty in several grades; and occasionally a subject is required in all grades of an elementary school, or junior high school, or high school, or in sequence between two or three of the above educational levels.

CURRICULUM PATTERNS AND PHYSICAL EDUCATION

As an example, physical education is required by state law of all children in California schools on a daily basis in grades one through twelve. The activities assigned to a particular grade level receive a prescribed allotment of time within the confines of the total daily or weekly time schedule of the school. Traditionally, most school subjects received an equal time allotment and were taught daily, at least for one semester, and in many cases for an entire school year. Over the years, a newer concept developed, whereby varying lengths of time were assigned to different subjects based on the criterion of relative importance of the subject to the child's educational development and on teacher experience and research evidence concerning the optimum length of time conducive to best learning results, which may differ in the various subject-matter fields. In recent years, even greater flexibility has been introduced into the scheduling of separate subjects. The rationale for such practices, several practical suggestions for flexible scheduling in physical education, and an evaluation of these practices are described at length in Chapter 10.

A typical separate-subjects curriculum pattern for the sixth grade in an elementary school is as follows:

9:00– 9:05	Flag salute
9:05– 9:45	Arithmetic
9:45–10:05	Spelling
10:05–10:15	Recess
10:15–11:10	Reading (3 groups)
11:10–11:45	Geography
11:45–12:45	Lunch and recess
12:45– 1:15	History
1:15– 1:45	Language
1:45– 2:10	Physical education
2:10– 2:40	Science
2:40– 3:15	Music (M.,W.,F.)
2:40– 3:15	Art (T.,Th.)
3:15	End of school day

A separate-subjects curriculum for a college preparatory student who is a junior in high school is as follows:

8:00– 8:50	English
9:00– 9:50	History
10:00–10:50	Physical education
11:00–11:50	French
11:50–12:30	Lunch
12:30– 1:20	Chemistry
1:30– 2:20	Art
2:30– 3:20	Free period

The Role of Subject Matter

In the separate-subjects curriculum, the subject matter or content is basically composed of the accumulated knowledge and experience of the culture. In fact, in many societies, this function is considered to be the chief purpose of the school. A thorough mastery of selected subject matter in each of the separate fields is an essential element of this curriculum. All students are given a certain basic subject content to learn thoroughly, despite wide individual differences, interests, and learning abilities. Physical education in many schools of the country is still taught in this manner.

One feature of the separate-subjects curriculum is that much of the content is predetermined for the child. Sometimes the individual teacher or a committee of teachers in a subject field may plan the content and the sequence of course material for each grade level. Sometimes the school district, through consultants and supervisors, publishes curriculum guides that specify the subject content to be included at each grade level in each field. Textbooks are relied upon heavily as the source of subject matter to be learned by the students at each grade level. Many texts are written in series for several grades, and teachers follow these textual materials almost without question. State curriculum guides and curriculum recommendations from professional associations often provide guidance in the selection of common learning materials in specific subject-matter fields.

Scope, Sequence, and Grade Placement

Because the school obviously cannot instruct the pupils in the sum total of human knowledge and experience in each subject field, selection and grade placement of content is an essential feature of this type of curriculum. Until recent times, subject-matter content was chosen according to the various types of authorities and sources indicated in the previous paragraph. It is interesting to note that until very recently teachers and so-called educationists primarily were the persons who took leadership in the development of subject-matter content selection and grade placement. The scholars of academic disciplines in the universities and in advanced centers for the study of the natural sciences and the behavioral sciences rarely contributed directly to this essential educational task. A great change has taken place within the past ten years. Now, many learned societies and national and international authorities in subject-matter fields have taken an intense interest in the selection and organization of curriculum materials for the public schools and have devoted their time and services to national projects for this purpose. The School Mathematics Study Group is an excellent example of the development of new curriculum materials in mathematics prepared jointly by scholars, public school teachers, and administrators. Similar notable curriculum studies currently in progress involve scholars and national authorities from academic fields working hand in hand with educators in the fields of chemistry, physics, biology, and the foreign languages, just to cite a few examples. Philanthropic foundations have granted large sums of money to support this pioneer work and to test these new curriculum materials in classrooms and to evaluate their effectiveness in terms of pupil learning outcomes.

In physical education, which is a so-called "practical" field, there is not such a notable difference in the designation of certain members of the profession as scholars and others as teachers or practitioners as is the case in other subject-matter fields. The leading authorities and experts in physical education frequently also are regarded highly as the leaders in administration, methods of teaching, and in teacher education, as well as in research and publication. Therefore, in physical education, the joining together of the so-called scholar and the educational practitioner in the development of the content of the special-subject type of curriculum has long been a fact in being. Some physical educators have noted with concern the seeming lack of individuals in the field who can be identified primarily as scholars of physical education. Staley, for example, makes the point that college departments of physical education should:

a. Appoint as teachers only individuals who have some appreciation of scholarship.
b. Appoint one or two teachers who are qualified scholars.
c. Include some scholarly activity (quality reading, writing, lectures, and discussion) in all courses.
d. Include a few courses that are basically scholarly in type, such as history of sport, history of dance, history of exercise, sports in American culture, etc.[1]

Staley also notes that the physical education profession ". . . like other respected professional groups, must nurture researchers and scholars and foster research and scholarly activity."[2]

Subject matter, which is to be required of students in more than one grade, must be organized in a sequence. This becomes a matter of the professional judgment of the people who are charged with curriculum development in the particular school or school district. One of the bases for determining curriculum sequence in a given subject field has to do with the internal structure or logic inherent in each subject field. At the same time, the experience of teachers and data from research studies give guidance to the proper sequential development and grade placement of the content of the field. The scope and sequence of physical education, as in any other field, need continual evaluation and revision in

[1] S. C. Staley, "Graduate Study in Physical Education and Scholarship," *College Physical Education Association Annual Proceedings,* 1961, pp. 56–58.
[2] *Ibid.*, p. 57.

order to improve the curriculum and make pupil learning more effective. Theoretical considerations and practical suggestions for carrying out this process are suggested in later chapters.

Teaching, Learning, and Evaluation

Teaching methods in the separate-subjects curriculum emphasize the personality and activity of the teacher. The teacher continually explains, tells, describes, and raises questions to which the children respond in terms of the information and ideas he has given them previously; he assigns homework and tests in such a manner that learning material is reproduced and returned to him for grading. The teacher must be particularly well informed with respect to his subject and should know the literature in the field that contributes the knowledge and ideas relevant to the topics selected for learning at the grade level he is teaching.

In conservative schools using the separate-subjects curriculum, pupils make little or no contribution to the selection and stating of student objectives for each course; these objectives are predetermined by the experts and by the teacher. There are teachers, however, who believe that it is appropriate for pupils to be involved in the planning, active conduct, and evaluation of the learning material used in the separate-subjects curriculum. The degree of pupil involvement is not limited by the inherent characteristics of this type of curriculum pattern but, rather, depends upon the educational philosophy of the school administration and the teachers.

Teaching methods emphasize learning materials, such as textbooks; workbooks; written assignments; and audio-visual aids, such as diagrams, blackboard explanations, motion pictures, and tape recordings. Teachers assign reading, homework, and workbook tasks for the purpose of reviewing learning materials presented in class and also to clarify and enlarge upon the basic content taught during the class period. The written homework projects are assigned in order to give the student practice in utilizing the knowledge gained in the classroom and in homework.

Periodic testing and evaluation characterizes teaching methods. Teachers construct their own tests, utilize standardized tests available from commercial sources, or use tests provided in teacher manuals that sometimes accompany textbooks. Frequently, these tests are of the objective type, which elicit responses from the student by way of designating or writing out a "correct" answer that the student presumably has memorized in the course of studying the subject in the classroom and in his homework. Excellent teachers will also emphasize the development of skills of reasoning and logical analysis, utilizing basic subject matter learned in the course.

Physical Education in the Separate-Subjects Curriculum

Physical education has long been organized typically in elementary and secondary schools in the pattern of the separate-subjects curriculum. Even today, in elementary schools and junior high schools that emphasize a core curriculum and in high schools that have the broad-fields curriculum, physical education usually is scheduled as a separate subject. Rarely is it used as part of a core curriculum program. In some schools, it is combined with health education to form what might be identified as a modified broad-fields curriculum. However, most elementary schools, junior high schools, and high schools schedule physical education for the length of the normal period of the school day for a set number of times per week, thus following the basic premise of the separate-subjects curriculum.

Elementary schools typically schedule physical education for twenty or thirty minutes daily, in addition to recess periods and noontime. Junior and senior high schools schedule physical education for the length of a normal period in the school day. The number of physical education periods scheduled per week varies in different schools and states throughout the United States. Probably more schools schedule physical education for two or three periods per week than any other pattern. Sometimes schools will allot a daily period that alternates physical education instruction and health education. For example, California requires a daily period of physical education for all pupils in grades one through twelve, except those excused for medical reasons, for a period equal in length to the regular period of the school day. The Illinois School Code provides that pupils enrolled in all grades of the public schools shall participate in a daily instructional period in health and physical education. Regulations of the New York State Commissioner of Education specify a minimum of 120 minutes per week of supervised physical education activities in elementary schools; in the secondary schools, the minimum requirement is 300 minutes per week of directed physical education activity, at least 90 minutes of which must be devoted to purposeful class instruction. Chapter 10 examines the issues involved in physical education scheduling and offers suggestions for the more effective utilization of available school time for the scheduling of physical education.

In summary, it is evident that physical education is organized typically as a separate-subjects curriculum in the majority of the nation's schools and that the general comments above, which describe the nature of this type of curriculum, apply to the present status of the organization and teaching of physical education in America.

The traditional separate-subjects curriculum developed weaknesses, which soon became apparent to perceptive educators. Critics pointed out that the separate-subjects curriculum resulted in fragmentation of subject matter and departmentalization to an extent that almost resulted in isolation between departments and faculty members. One outcome of this situation was the lack of cohesive, energetic educational programs bound together with a common purpose and organizational frame. Thus, it was felt that fullest intellectual development was not being realized. Another criticism was that pupil interests and needs were not being met. The lack of teacher concern for pupil interest and for individual pupil readiness to learn new materials based on previous learnings and experience, plus intense concentration on learning principles involving repetition and drill, seemed to many critics to result in inefficient learning. These teaching methods and emphases involved extensive use of extrinsic motivational devices and rewards. Many observers believed that students might be learning undesirable attitudes or even developing a dislike for a particular subject, due primarily to the types of learning activities forced upon them and the direction of the motivational incentives utilized to promote learning. As educational leaders, interested parents, and lay leaders became more and more concerned over the weaknesses of the separate-subjects curriculum, many schools began to modify their curriculum patterns in an attempt to overcome these deficiencies. Several other curriculum patterns thus evolved. Two of them will be discussed in more detail in this chapter, namely, the broad-fields curriculum and the core curriculum. Brief reference will be made to other patterns less commonly employed.

THE BROAD-FIELDS CURRICULUM

The broad-fields curriculum evolves from the dissatisfaction discussed above. Its beginning, in approximately 1910, was in the colleges; and it soon spread to elementary and secondary schools throughout the country. In addition to the influences listed above, this curriculum pattern also was encouraged as a solution to the continuing problem of the pressure for introducing more and more separate subjects into the school curriculum. There were not enough periods in the school day to assign a full period to each of the new subjects that many so-called "pressure groups" forced into the school curriculum by means of passing state legislation, or by other pressure exerted upon state boards of education and local school boards. The combination of closely related subjects into so-called "broad fields" seemed to be a promising solution to this dilemma, which in these days is called the "curriculum squeeze."

Early phases of the broad-fields curriculum consisted of condensing subject content from two or more closely related courses and essentially trying to make them into one subject. Typical examples include a high school general science course developed by selecting some subject matter from a variety of scientific fields, such as chemistry, physics, zoology, botany, astronomy, and geology. Another notable example is social studies, composed of history, geography, economics, and civics. The curriculum builders, the textbook writers, and teachers worked for the systematic organization of subject matter and study, which usually was centered upon major topics or problems related to the facts, understandings, and insights from several of the separate subjects that combined to make up the broad field. It was an attempt to develop a unified view of the knowledge of a "broad" or comprehensive field. Emphasis was centered on the development of new relationships among elements of subject matter and upon broader generalizations that might be applicable among and between related fields.

The Role of Subject Matter

The broad-fields curriculum retained some characteristics of the separate-subjects curriculum in that objectives were predetermined by authorities, textbook writers, supervisors and curriculum specialists, and teachers, with little or no pupil involvement. Also, subject matter was selected, planned, and organized in the same manner. Therefore, in these two respects, this new curriculum pattern did not improve significantly upon the traditional separate-subjects curriculum. The role of subject matter was extended in this curriculum to permit more understanding and development of relationships between allied fields and the utilization of broader generalizations applicable among subject fields.

Scope, Sequence, and Grade Placement

Again, the broad-fields curriculum made little or no significant contribution to curriculum improvement with respect to the sequence and grade placement of subject matter compared with the traditional separate-subjects curriculum. The descriptive remarks in the previous section on the separate-subjects curriculum apply equally to the broad-fields curriculum in this respect except, of course, that a considerable expansion of scope of subject matter selected was a new feature of this pattern.

Teaching, Learning, and Evaluation

Teaching methods employed in the broad-fields curriculum are very similar to those described above for the separate-subjects curriculum. The teacher is active as he tells, describes, explains, and illustrates logically organized knowledge, ideas, and generalizations. Student activities emphasize recording what the teacher has said, studying textbooks, and doing homework lessons that repeat the material given in class. Textbooks for each grade level play a large part in this type of teaching and must be written differently from those in the separate-subjects fields, because of the necessity of relating knowledge and generalizations from two or more fields that make up the broad field. One difficulty is placing the material as to proper grade level in the textbooks according to difficulty and according to pupil ability to learn. Also, textbook authors must have greater competence and wider knowledge and understanding in more than one field. One way of meeting this situation is the use of co-authors, each of whom has a specialty in one of the fields discussed in the textbook.

Some of the weaknesses of this method of teaching seem to be (1) that the subject matter may tend to become too broad and too generalized so as to be almost meaningless, (2) the related problem of "watering down" the subject matter in the process of trying to select topics from a variety of fields, and (3) difficulty in establishing a logical framework within which to develop a systematic structure of the so-called broad field.[3]

Although the broad-fields curriculum pattern exists in many elementary and secondary schools in such areas as the social studies, the language arts, general science, and health and physical education, there is considerable agitation in several quarters for a return to the separate-subjects pattern. Oftentimes, this recommendation is made by scholars and academic leaders in various separate fields or academic disciplines. Many school-board members are sympathetic with this recommendation; and some school districts have now abandoned the broad-fields approach and have returned to the separate-subjects curriculum, preferring to teach separate courses labeled history, geography, and economics instead of a course called the social studies, for example.

Physical Education in the Broad-Fields Curriculum

Many schools teach health education and physical education as one single broad field, changing instruction in these two fields on alternate days throughout the week. Some schools also include safety education, outdoor education, and driver education. In other schools, these subjects are organized, scheduled, and taught as separate subjects. The extent of the involvement of the physical education teacher as a teacher of a separate health course is subject to great variation in the schools throughout the country. In one state where health education and physical education now are taught as separate-subject fields, there are strong lay public

[3] G. Wesley Sowards and Mary-Margaret Scobey, *The Changing Curriculum and the Elementary Teacher* (Belmont, Calif.: Wadsworth Publishing Co., Inc., 1961), pp. 154–56.

and professional education sources advocating the combining of health education and physical education into one broad field to be taught by the physical education teachers. The California Association for Health, Physical Education, and Recreation is strongly opposed to this recommendation and is on record with a detailed explanation of why it considers health education and physical education to be separate disciplines that should remain separate in the organization of the curriculum.[4]

It is difficult to forecast the type of curriculum pattern in the fields of health education and physical education that will predominate in the coming years. On the one hand, there is the pressure of the "curriculum squeeze," whereby school administrations are attempting to find ways to make room for the teaching of additional subjects in the school day that leads them to advocate the combination of health education and physical education as one broad field. On the other hand, the intense interest and support of the President's Physical Fitness Council's recommendations seem to emphasize the necessity for a daily physical education program plus the scheduling of separate formal health education courses. This pattern results in the separate-subjects curriculum.

THE CORE CURRICULUM

A core curriculum, which began to develop in the 1920's, resulted from dissatisfaction with the existing curriculum patterns, which is the genesis of most curriculum changes. Many critics felt that the separate-subjects curriculum and the then developing broad-fields curriculum did not sufficiently motivate and interest pupils to learn subject matter by the formal teaching methods employed. They felt there were other ways in which learning content could be made much more interesting to the students and, at the same time, result in greater and more efficient learning. The idea was that the core curriculum would be a way to unify and interrelate subject matter from several different fields of knowledge in a more meaningful manner, going far beyond the limited interrelationships attempted by the broad-fields curriculum that still retained too many of the criticisms of the separate-subjects curriculum.

Another void in the separate-subjects and broad-fields curricula, which the proponents of the core curriculum felt should be filled, concerned the role of the school in making a greater contribution as an institution of society. It was believed that schools should not restrict their role merely to the psychological foundation of promoting mental learning,

[4] Harold J. Cornacchia, "A Critical Issue: Are Health Education and Physical Education Separate Disciplines?" *CAHPER Journal*, XXIII, No. 4 (March–April, 1961), 4, 5, 9.

but that the schools also should take a much more active role as an agency for the development of democratic ideals and practices. Hence, the schools were urged to build their programs not only on psychological foundations but also on social and philosophical foundations with respect to curriculum organization and development. Thus, the school would include in its ever-increasing responsibilities a program to meet one of the great needs and challenges of American life in those times. The core curriculum emphasized the development of human values and education for desirable human behavior and conduct; it provided a heavier emphasis on the teaching of values than any previous curriculum pattern. This increasing emphasis in turn had a notable effect upon the nature of subject matter and also influenced teaching methods. In essence, the core curriculum was devoted to developing closer relationships of school experiences to life in American society.

The Role of Subject Matter

In the core curriculum, the subject matter is concerned with basic human activities and pupil interests related to these activities. There have been several attempts to organize basic human activities as the structural framework within which to teach the core curriculum. The following list by Dr. Paul Hanna of Stanford University illustrates an interesting and useful framework that has gained wide acceptance in recent years.[5]

1. Protecting and conserving life, resources, and property.
2. Producing, distributing, and consuming goods and services.
3. Transporting people and goods.
4. Communicating ideas and feelings.
5. Providing education.
6. Providing recreation.
7. Organizing and governing.
8. Expressing spiritual and aesthetic impulses.
9. Creating new tools and techniques.

It is evident from a perusal of the above list that it does describe activities that closely follow life as children and adults are living it in American culture today. This framework would seem to assist in meeting one of the purposes of the core curriculum, namely, to help relate life in society to the school program and to use it as the basic framework for studying the cultural heritage and learning essential knowledge.

Fundamental knowledge from the basic academic disciplines representing the storehouse of human knowledge can be related to these basic human activities and taught as essential elements of subject matter.

[5] From a project of the integrative-core curriculum prepared by Paul R. Hanna, School of Education, Stanford University.

However, in this type of curriculum, the emphasis is different from that found in the separate-subjects and broad-fields curricula, because in the core curriculum human activities are regarded as the central point in the development of the learning process rather than the subject matter per se. The proponents of the core curriculum believe they have evidence to indicate that pupils learn subject matter more efficiently. Thus, subject matter becomes a means for the realization of pupil goals, rather than being an end in itself, such as is the case in the separate-subjects and broad-fields curricula.

Finally, the core curriculum stresses the transmission of the cultural heritage that is inevitably bound up with the basic human activities that form the structure of the core curriculum. The transmission of the cultural heritage is regarded by most authorities as one of the essential purposes of the public school, and the advocates of the core curriculum believe that this pattern is a very effective way of achieving this purpose.

Scope, Sequence, and Grade Placement

The scope and sequence of the curriculum in the core pattern come from studies and authorities in a variety of fields, such as sociology, anthropology, history, education, and other fields of human knowledge and behavior. From evidence available in these fields of knowledge, educational and subject-matter experts plan the broad framework of the core curriculum in advance. In some instances, classroom teachers who specialize in a particular field of knowledge are involved in this advance planning. In other situations, curriculum experts, textbook writers, and similar authorities develop the over-all framework of the core curriculum; and the school district prescribes it to the teachers. This broad framework based upon the organization of basic human activities serves as a guide to the individual teacher. It does not specifically prescribe all of the learning experiences and subject-matter content that the individual teacher should cover in a particular grade but, rather, serves to guide the teacher in a general way in order to provide a basis for most efficient teaching and learning in a given classroom according to the teacher's individual personality traits and teaching abilities. This over-all preplanned framework also provides a reasonable basis for the articulation of instruction from grade to grade and even between the elementary school and the junior high school, and the junior high school and the high school in some fields.

In the early elementary grades, the curriculum is based on the common experiences most children in a particular school are judged to have had in the first five or six years of their life. Learning is based on subject matter related to basic human activities in a restricted geographical sense to the nearby localities, such as the home, the neighborhood, the school, and possibly the town or city. Gradually, there is an expansion, both in the complexity of the human activities studied and in the geographical range involved in succeeding grades, to cover state, national, and international boundaries. And now we find the latest extension of the curriculum to considerations of outer space and other planets. Thus, it can be seen that the core curriculum provides experiences that build gradually on the previous experiences of the pupil and hence depends for its success to a greater extent upon pupil interest and readiness than do the other two types of curriculum patterns previously discussed.

For a more detailed exposition of the core curriculum, the reader is referred to the analysis found in Sowards and Scobey, *The Changing Curriculum and the Elementary Teacher*, which shows a marked preference for the core curriculum. These authors conclude that "a great deal of our thinking about curriculum for the elementary school is heavily influenced by the core curriculum pattern."[6]

As far as grade placement is concerned, it is interesting to note that today the core curriculum pattern is found predominantly in the elementary schools and to some extent, at least to a modified degree, in some junior high schools. There is very little evidence of the core curriculum pattern in American high schools today, although it originally began in the high school.

Teaching, Learning, and Evaluation

It was indicated above that the core curriculum is based on an over-all framework preplanned by experts and authorities with little or no pupil participation. However, this curriculum pattern does permit extensive teacher-pupil planning and development of specific learning units within the over-all framework. This teacher-pupil planning emphasis is more extensive than that usually associated with the other curriculum patterns previously described. Teaching methods, by and large, are based on evidence available from psychology and education concerning the nature of the learning process, the motivation of pupils, and growth and development characteristics as well as other individual differences. Problem-solving methods are stressed in this curriculum rather than the lecture-textbook reading-recitation-objective testing cycle typical of the other two curriculum patterns. There is a continual emphasis on the value of problem-solving as well as its techniques. Problem-solving is supplemented by strong teacher support and assistance through the more traditional teaching methods of explanation, illustration, use of audio-visual aids for explanatory purposes, and other traditional teacher-

---

[6] Sowards and Scobey, *op. cit.*, p. 171.

dominated procedures typical in the other curriculum patterns. The teacher remains in complete control of the class but utilizes characteristics of the individual pupils and principles of teaching and learning that presumably result in more effective learning and understanding and establishment of desirable attitudes and values.

Teaching and learning materials and experiences are broader and more varied than those presented by the typical textbooks and blackboard lectures used by the traditional teacher. The core curriculum teaching materials and methods also employ community resources; visits away from school to specific human activities related to the unit of study; the invitation of authorities and experts to come to the school to discuss the subject at hand with the students; and the use of a greater variety of educational materials in order that children may manipulate, see, construct, dissect, and take apart these materials in order to utilize all of the human senses as media for learning.

Finally, the teaching of values receives constant emphasis in this curriculum and is regarded by its proponents as one of its major strengths.

The core curriculum emphasizes the psychological principle of "readiness" as a basis for the presentation of a new and more complex learning experience. Also, the psychological principle of pupil interest is utilized to promote effective learning. Another advantage of this pattern seems to be that not only are common areas of learning for all children organized as part of the basic framework of the curriculum, but that, in addition to these common learnings, provision is made for individual pupil differences based on specific needs and interests as they become evident. The teacher is continually alert to manifestations of these needs and interests and provides learning experiences that are extensions of the basic learning units providing the opportunity for expanding the pupils' learning according to their individual differences.

The evaluative process in the core curriculum is more extensive than that normally associated with the broad-fields and separate-subjects curricula. Evaluation is not restricted to written objective or essay tests that emphasize memorization of subject matter. In addition to such tests, evaluation includes the use of other instruments such as attitude scales, interest inventories, sociometric techniques, and on occasion even uses certain projective-type techniques. This assessment is in keeping with attempts to apprize the extent to which the broader purposes of the core curriculum are being achieved. Teacher judgment of pupil progress and development necessarily is broader and also more subjective. Finally, the teacher has an added responsibility of not only evaluating individual pupil progress, but also of making a rating description of the class and of predominant subgroupings of pupils within the class. The teacher attempts to utilize modern knowledge of educational evaluation techniques.

In summarizing the characteristics and purposes of the core curriculum, it might be safely stated that the central area of controversy concerning the strengths and weaknesses of this curriculum is the issue of whether or not the school curriculum should be centered around so-called "social problems" and whether or not it is appropriate, particularly for elementary school children, to begin the study of complex social problems at such an early age.

Physical Education in the Core Curriculum

It will be recalled that earlier in this chapter the suggested list of basic human activities by Hanna included the specific activity of "providing recreation." Similar lists of basic human activities include items with respect to the worthy use of leisure time, protecting the individual's health, and other descriptions of activities that are directly related to the purposes and programs advocated by physical education leaders. In a review of recent publications concerning curriculum patterns in the elementary and secondary school wherein fundamental work in health education and physical education is advocated at every grade level in the core curriculum, detailed descriptions by the authors rarely, if ever, propose the organization and teaching of physical education in the manner typically describing the teaching of other basic human activities. There are excellent chapters concerning physical education to be found in general elementary and secondary curriculum books. However, when carefully analyzed, the descriptions and recommendations for program and teaching methods contained in these chapters follow the typical pattern of separate-subjects curricula. Even the strong proponents of the core curriculum, who recognize the necessity for daily programs in physical education, do not present a method of organizing and teaching physical education that varies from the traditional separate-subjects methodology. Perhaps some elementary schools and junior high schools have developed techniques for organizing and conducting physical education in the core curriculum according to the patterns established for other basic areas of human activities. Oberteuffer presents a detailed explanation of the possibilities of the core program concept being used in physical education and indicates by several examples how physical education can contribute to the enrichment of core units concerning other basic human activities.[7] The authors agree with Oberteuffer and others that the core curriculum concept has not been adequately developed in physical education. Apparently because physical education has long been thought of and conducted as a special subject, most teachers and

---

[7] Delbert Oberteuffer and Celeste Ulrich, *Physical Education* (3d ed.; New York: Harper & Row, 1962), pp. 347–57.

administrators seem reluctant to change from that pattern and experiment with promising innovations available in the core pattern. In this connection, the point of view of the authors concerning new curriculum designs for physical education will be presented at the end of this chapter and will be elaborated upon in considerable detail in later chapters.

OTHER CURRICULUM PATTERNS

In addition to the three major types of curriculum patterns discussed above, there are others frequently reported in educational literature. Two of these may be identified as the activity curriculum and the correlated curriculum.

The activity curriculum utilizes as its basis for organization the interests and activities of children rather than formal subject matter. Thus, this curriculum is child centered rather than subject centered. Subject matter is considered to be a resource for learning. As the child pursues his interest and seeks to solve problems that confront him, he is taught to scrutinize the cultural heritage or the organized subject matter of one or more fields that concern the topic or problem. Continuously in this process, the child learns many fundamental skills of study and educational development that enable him to deal with the problems and situations with which he is confronted. Also, subject matter, rather than being organized logically and chronologically, is studied in a psychological order of content. For example, in arithmetic, rather than learning addition and multiplication tables by rote memory, pupils learn necessary arithmetic concepts as the need arises to utilize them in problem-solving and in pursuing interests. The framework of the curriculum is not organized in advance as in other patterns, but rather develops or emerges from week to week and month to month in the educational development of the child. Teacher-pupil planning is very evident and results in statements of problems to be solved. Hence, teaching methodology is rooted in the problem-solving process. Learning materials also are considered as resources for learning rather than material to be learned in its own right. Many techniques of evaluation are utilized, such as interest inventories, sociometric techniques, and attitude scales; sometimes projective instruments are used, and a teacher descriptive evaluation is required.

From this brief description of some of its major components, it is easy to understand that the activity curriculum soon was the object of considerable opposition and criticism from a number of sources. It seemed to be too unorganized, too superficial, and did not deal with academic subject matter in an organized, disciplined way. Others felt that too much emphasis was placed on children's interests and needs, and that the children had too much responsibility for selection of learning experiences and learning materials. Another interesting criticism was that, although the psychological foundations of this approach seemed to be quite strong, it had very little basis in sociological principles. It will be noted that this criticism is the opposite extreme from one of the chief characteristics eventually developed in the core-curriculum pattern.

Physical education in the activity curriculum was important to elementary school children in the sense that play was considered to be a major phase of a child's life and was an important source of interest and fun. Upon reflection, it seems safe to say that physical education in the activity curriculum emphasized the so-called recreational objective of physical education and utilized physical education and play as a medium for self-expression. However, the activity curriculum did not appear to give sufficient stress to other important objectives of physical education, such as the development of organic power and vigor on a systematic basis; the teaching of specific sports, exercises, and rhythmic skills; and the social development objective that many people feel is one of physical education's strongest contributions.

Another curriculum pattern frequently mentioned is the correlated curriculum. Some writers discuss this as a separate pattern, while other authorities prefer to describe it as one of six types of the major curriculum pattern labeled "core." Alberty lists six categories or types of core curricula: [8]

(1) The core consists of a number of logically organized subjects or fields of knowledge, each one of which is taught independently.

(2) The core consists of a number of logically organized subjects or fields of knowledge, some or all of which are correlated.

(3) The core consists of broad problems, units of work, or unifying themes which are chosen because they afford the means of teaching effectively the basic content of certain subjects or fields of knowledge. These subjects or fields retain their identity but the content is selected and taught with special reference to the unit.

(4) The core consists of a number of subjects or fields of knowledge which are unified or fused. Usually one subject or field serves as a unifying center.

(5) The core consists of broad, preplanned problem areas, or resource units from which are selected learning experiences in terms of the psychobiological and social needs, problems, and interests of students.

(6) The core consists of broad teacher-student planned units of work or activities in terms of the expressed wishes or desires of the group. No basic curricular structure is set up.

[8] Harold Alberty, "Designing Programs To Meet the Common Needs of Youth," Chapter VII of Fifty-Second Yearbook of the National Society for the Study of Education, Part I, *Adapting the Secondary-School Program to the Needs of Youth* (Chicago: University of Chicago Press, 1953), pp. 119, 120.

It is evident then that the word "core" is used appropriately by various authors to indicate quite different arrangements to refer to that part of the curriculum that is common to all students. Thus, category number two in Alberty's list above is the same as the so-called correlated curriculum.

As far as physical education is concerned, it is obvious that there are many ways in which this subject-matter field can be correlated with other subjects in the curriculum. In order that physical education can make its fullest contribution to the curriculum in any school, it is believed that all teachers on the staff must be aware of the possibilities for correlating relevant physical education learning experiences with their own subjects. At the same time, it is the responsibility of all physical education teachers to make known to the other members of the faculty the ways in which physical education can be appropriately correlated. Also, physical education teachers need to be constantly alert for opportunities in their own teaching that enable them to correlate with important learning areas in other phases of the school curriculum.

Several examples of physical education correlated with other subjects are offered by Knapp and Hagman.[9] These authors indicate how physical education can be correlated with health education, safety education, recreation, camping and school outdoor education, and other subjects as well. Several examples of specific ways in which teachers have provided correlation with the above subjects are described. We are all aware of plans for correlation existing in most schools wherein the music department furnishes the school band for entertainment at athletic contests, where the art department cooperates in the preparation of posters, and where the wood and metal shops help to construct physical education and athletic equipment and apparatus. Also, that phase of the school newspaper or other student publications that relates to the athletic department is another example of the correlated curriculum.

Humphrey,[10] and Halsey and Porter [11] describe in detail the nature of integration in the physical education curriculum. It would appear from their discussion and actual examples of integrating physical education with other subjects in the curriculum that these authors are using the term "integrated curriculum" somewhat synonymously with the Knapp and Hagman terminology of the "correlated curriculum." However,

[9] Clyde Knapp and E. Patricia Hagman, *Teaching Methods for Physical Education* (New York: McGraw-Hill Book Co., Inc., 1953), pp. 80–84.
[10] James H. Humphrey, "The Nature of Integration in Physical Education," Chapter VI of *Elementary School Physical Education* (New York: Harper & Row, 1958), pp. 97–111.
[11] Elizabeth Halsey and Lorena Porter, "Integration," Chapter VII of *Physical Education for Children* (New York: Holt, Rinehart & Winston, Inc., 1958), pp. 128–45.

Halsey and Porter point out that integration, as defined by them, may be carried out between physical education and other subject matters in any form of curriculum organization. Humphrey continues with several chapters indicating in detail how physical education can be integrated with arithmetic, the language arts, science, the social studies, and finally with health and safety.

Finally, the general literature uses several other terms to talk about specific varieties of curriculum patterns, such as the fused curriculum, the integrated-core curriculum, and the experience curriculum. It is beyond the scope of this book to attempt detailed explanations of these additional types of curriculum patterns.

As we consider the curriculum patterns and actual examples of school programs used in the organization and teaching of physical education in grades one through twelve throughout the United States, it seems fair to conclude that the separate-subjects approach predominates over other curriculum patterns. Even in schools that emphasize other curriculum patterns, physical education usually is taught as a separate or "special" subject. In fact, the terminology "special subject" is now in very common usage in referring to physical education as something separate from, and different from, the so-called "academic" subjects. It is true that many schools throughout the country are attempting to improve their physical education offerings by adapting their curriculum patterns in some way to those that have been described herein and to other variations of their own origin; but, traditionally, physical education seems to have been slow in moving from the separate-subjects approach and in experimenting with newer curriculum patterns.

One of the purposes of this book is to suggest curriculum changes that the authors hope will result in more effective achievement of the objectives of physical education.

4

Influences Toward Change in the Physical Education Curriculum

It is evident from the preceding chapters that curriculum development that successfully results in changed pupil behavior is a highly complicated, continuous process. There are many influences on curriculum development as it ultimately affects a class of students or an individual student in the classroom. The literature reveals considerable differences of opinion concerning the relative weight of influence various agencies and individuals should have and do exert in curriculum improvement. Basically, however, there seems to be agreement that the teacher is the key factor in the total process. In order to understand the teacher's role more clearly, this section deals with a review of the general framework of sources and types of influences upon curriculum development that relate in various ways to the teacher's functions. The teacher must be aware of the multitude of forces that continually create pressures upon his own teaching field, as well as upon public school curricula in general.

NATIONAL INFLUENCES

It is not possible to list all so-called national sources of influence that in some way may have a bearing on curriculum development in any local school system in the United States in the field of physical education. However, some notable examples follow as illustrative of the sources and nature of influences that can emanate from the national level.

The National Education Association

Many offices, departments, commissions, and other organizational entities of the NEA continually exert strong national influence on public school curricula in general, and upon specific subject-matter fields in particular, both directly and indirectly.

The periodic statements of the Educational Policies Commission are well known to all educators. Examples of recent publications that have important implications for curriculum development in physical education are cited.[1,2,3] It seems safe to say that every statement of the Commission has important implications for the physical education curriculum. One publication of the EPC deals specifically with one phase of the physical education curriculum, namely, the athletic program,[4] and has been very instrumental in providing sound curriculum guidance to school districts throughout the country.

The Association for Supervision and Curriculum Development of the NEA

This organization is also very active in continually guiding and influencing curriculum development throughout America by means of publications, conferences, and workshops. General curriculum materials of direct relevance to the physical education teacher, as well as specific publications concerning physical education, are available from ASCD and are a fruitful and influential source of curriculum guidance in many schools throughout the country. Also, the opportunity for the field of physical education to "work across the board" with specialists in other subject fields, as well as with general supervisors and curriculum coordinators and administrators, is one of the big contributions of ASCD. It is obvious that no field can stand in isolation; it must be part of the total curriculum team. There must be close interrelatedness, continual interchange of ideas and interpretations, and cooperative development of general educational goals and of plans and processes for achieving objectives. Perhaps many physical education teachers can be criticized for failing to see the importance of "joining the team" in curriculum revision in their own school or school district. Particularly in states where a legal provision guarantees a specific time allotment to physical edu-

[1] *The Central Purpose of American Education* (Washington, D.C.: The Educational Policies Commission of the National Education Association, 1961).

[2] *Contemporary Issues in Elementary Education* (Washington, D.C.: The Educational Policies Commission of the National Education Association, 1960).

[3] *Education and the Disadvantaged American* (Washington, D.C.: The Educational Policies Commission of the National Education Association, 1962).

[4] *School Athletics—Problems and Policies* (Washington, D.C.: The Educational Policies Commission of the National Education Association, 1954).

cation, some physical educators are prone to rest on this edict and thus fail to serve as full-fledged members of total school or district curriculum projects.

The American Association for Health, Physical Education, and Recreation

This professional organization is a department of the NEA and not only serves many essential professional purposes, but also provides important services to its members and to many other phases of American public education as well as to the lay public. The AAHPER makes its influence felt on the local teacher and school district in a variety of ways. It has many publications such as periodicals, workshop and conference reports, books, and pamphlets, which are very significant sources of information directly relevant to good curriculum planning in any school in any part of the United States.

The AAHPER National Conference held yearly is a rich source of information and ideas for curriculum improvement. Also, the AAHPER sponsors or co-sponsors numerous national conferences on topics vital to the physical education field. These conferences not only provide a fertile opportunity for the exchange of thinking among the participants but, in most instances, result in the formal publication of the deliberations and agreements reached at the conference for the benefit of all physical educators and other interested persons throughout the country. Some of these reports are particularly significant as influences in the development of the physical education curriculum in a local school or school district.[5]

Furthermore, the AAHPER makes available highly qualified consultants from its staff to work with groups interested in curriculum change. These staff members are highly knowledgeable about curriculum trends throughout the country and are experienced in the role of curriculum consultants so that they are effective in making a maximum contribution to a curriculum project.

Another essential role of the AAHPER in curriculum development, as well as in other areas of concern, is the liaison function with other educational, legislative, medical, and similar organizations that have an influence on the physical education field. There are many examples of this coordination and liaison with other groups, and the importance of this role cannot be exaggerated.

The Project on Instruction of the National Education Association

Another example of NEA influence at the national level that ultimately may have decided effects on local school systems is the recently author-

[5] Ruth Abernathy and Ben W. Miller (eds.), *Report of the National Conference on Interpretation of Physical Education* (Chicago: The Athletic Institute, Inc., 1961).

ized Project on Instruction.[6] This Project is under the direction of a fourteen-member national committee composed of public school teachers, school administrators, professional educators, a college president, and a representative of a state education association. The purpose of the Project is to improve the quality of the school program, and it has two focal strands. One effort will involve "deciding what to teach" and will result in a publication that will make recommendations on issues such as the making of curriculum decisions, the proper utilization of recent research on learning and the structure of knowledge, the effective use of recommendations from major curriculum studies in so-called academic subjects, the development of an effective school curriculum for all members of the school population, the central responsibility of the school, and a discussion of priorities and balances in the school curriculum. Many specific problems will be discussed under these broad issues. The second strand of the Project involves "planning and organizing for teaching." It will culminate in a publication that will discuss such vital topics as the major problems and decisions in curriculum planning, more effective organization of the curriculum, improved school organization, improved organization in the classroom, and instructional resources. Again, many specific issues will be analyzed within these broad topics. The Project will culminate with a handbook containing recommendations for school-board members and the general public. It is evident that this Project may have a highly significant long-range effect on curriculum change at the local level.

Although the national committee will be augmented by a large number of writers and members of reviewing committees representing academic disciplines, research agencies, college and university departments and administration, teachers, school administrators, and professional educators, a perusal of the list of these contributors indicates that the field of physical education is not directly represented in the Project. If this is the case, the AAHPER, other professional organizations in physical education, and physical educators who know members of the Project have an essential responsibility for keeping currently informed of the work and progress of the Project. It will be important to maintain close liaison with Project members to see that physical education is interpreted properly and that it is represented when the field is discussed directly, as well as when it comes into deliberations indirectly in other contexts.

United States Office of Education

The United States Office of Education, in the Department of Health, Education, and Welfare, has long given high-level leadership to curric-

[6] *Project on Instruction—A Preliminary Report* (Washington, D.C.: National Education Association, November, 1961).

ulum revision in physical education through studies, publications, and consultative service throughout the country. Two staff member specialists in physical education, a man and a woman, have provided influential leadership in many ways; and the results of their work and the support of the United States Office of Education have had considerable influence on curriculum decisions in physical education at state, school district, and local school levels.[7,8]

President's Council on Physical Fitness

The President's Council on Physical Fitness, established by President Eisenhower and continued with increased vigor and support by President Kennedy, has been a powerful influence in stimulating many elementary and high schools in America to step up time allotment for physical education and to emphasize vigorous activities. As a result of publications,[9,10,11] numerous personal school visitations by the staff of the Council, the most intensive peacetime program of public interpretation of physical education through press, radio, television, and advertising media, and vigorous personal support from President Kennedy, the Council has been a powerful force in introducing its major recommendations into thousands of schools throughout the United States in the past few years. These recommendations include periodic health appraisals for every student; the identification of the physically underdeveloped pupil through school screening tests that measure strength, agility, and flexibility; a special program of progressive physical development for all pupils who fail to reach passing standards in the screening test; an adapted physical education program for pupils whose health precludes normal, vigorous activity; and the re-emphasis on physical development of all pupils by provision of a daily program of at least fifteen minutes of vigorous physical activity. The Council, while not having mandated authority to prescribe health and physical education requirements for any school, does have sufficient prestige and influence to bring about the acceptance, by school boards, school administrators, and physical education staffs, of comprehensive "suggested elements of a school-centered

[7] Simon A. McNeely and Elsa Schneider, *Physical Education in the School Child's Day*, Bulletin No. 14 (Washington, D.C.: U.S. Office of Education, Federal Security Agency, 1950).

[8] Elsa Schneider, *Physical Education in Urban Elementary Schools*, Bulletin No. 15 (Washington, D.C.: U.S. Office of Education, Department of Health, Education and Welfare, 1959).

[9] *Youth Physical Fitness: Suggested Elements of a School-Centered Program* (Washington, D.C.: President's Council on Youth Fitness, 1961), Parts I and II.

[10] *Physical Fitness Elements in Recreation* (Washington, D.C.: President's Council on Youth Fitness, 1962).

[11] *Adult Physical Fitness* (Washington, D.C.: President's Council on Physical Fitness, 1963).

program," [12] which are carefully spelled out in the publication cited above.

It is interesting to observe how powerful an influence an organization such as the President's Council can be on curriculum revision in a particular field. President Kennedy, at periodic conferences of state governors, stressed his own concern for the state of physical fitness in American citizens and the need for improved programs of physical education in the schools as one means to bring about improvement so urgently needed. Governors are being urged to bring this essential matter of national concern to the attention of their departments of education and to their state legislatures. As a result of such stress from the President himself, many states have accepted the challenge and have directed the implementation of the Council's recommendations in their schools. Some state legislatures have recently passed state laws requiring an expanded school program of physical education, and improved school facilities, and have issued other legal mandates to carry out the Council's suggestions. The student of the profession of physical education and the thousands of teachers and administrators working in this field every day should not overlook the tremendous influence on local curricula of such a source as the President's Council. It is of special interest to note the by-line article by John F. Kennedy in *Sports Illustrated Magazine*.[13] This direct expression of concern for one major curriculum area in the public education program of the United States was a most unusual act by a president-elect.

American Medical Association

Another national influence favorable to the promotion of physical education in the school curriculum was the action of the House of Delegates of the American Medical Association in passing a resolution strongly advocating regular programs of health education and physical education for all pupils from grade one through college.[14] Although the exact degree of influence such an action has on improving a specific physical education program in any given school can never be assessed precisely, it is the weight of professional judgment among physical educators involved in curriculum interpretation and change that this positive support by the AMA is indeed beneficial. The added weight this resolution gives to other types of influences listed in this section, nationally and at other

[12] *Youth Physical Fitness, op. cit.*, pp. 7–9.
[13] John F. Kennedy, "The Soft American," *Sports Illustrated*, December, 1960, pp. 15–17.
[14] "Resolutions on School and College Health and Physical Education," passed by the House of Delegates of the American Medical Association, Miami Beach, June, 1960, *Journal of Health, Physical Education and Recreation*, October, 1960, p. 1.

levels, seems clearly to entitle us to conclude that here is another type and source of national influence on physical education curriculum that should be recognized by those concerned in local schools.

Another sphere of influence contributing directly to curriculum improvement in health and physical education by the AMA is the Health Education Bureau and the publications [15,16] of the professional staff consultants in that bureau. Also, these staff members exert national influence in their role as consultants to schools, professional organizations, medical groups, and other related agencies having a direct concern for health and physical education programs.

The Council for Public Schools

This organization is of such recent origin that its probable effects upon public school curriculum revision in physical education are unpredictable at this time. This council was formed in 1962 as an outgrowth of the Massachusetts Council for Public Schools, which had notable success in developing a television course in French for elementary schools. The council states that its purpose is "to promote, develop, and produce new courses for the public schools curriculum." [17] It is reported that initial projects will be concerned with Spanish and geography in our elementary schools and with the teaching of English as a second language in foreign countries. There was no available statement of interest in physical education at the time of the formation of the council.

The council has a national advisory committee of impressive stature, including leading scientists, university administrators, national magazine publishers and authors, a prominent educator, and others of national reputation in their fields. Teachers of physical education should be alert to policy pronouncements and projects that may develop in the future and that have direct relevance to health education and physical education.

The Council on Basic Education

This national group, composed of scholars of so-called "academic disciplines" and noted figures from various phases of American public and professional life, has held a narrow and restricted view of the place of physical education in the public school curriculum. In attempting to assess its views about physical education and athletics as objectively as possible, one must conclude that the influence of this organization and

[15] W. W. Bauer and Fred V. Hein, *Exercise and Health—A Point of View* (Chicago: Bureau of Health Education of the American Medical Association, 1958).
[16] Fred V. Hein, "Not Just Exercise," *Hygeia*, December, 1957, pp. 1–8.
[17] "While School Keeps," *Saturday Review*, September 15, 1962, pp. 64, 65.

its members is a negative one with respect to implications for curriculum development. Physical education teachers should be aware of this council and its views, because local members and representatives in many communities appear at school-board meetings and elsewhere to promote the views of the council.

STATE ORGANIZATIONS

Another category of organizations that have potential power to contribute to curriculum change in a local school district conveniently can be labeled as state organizations, of which several notable examples are cited below. These organizations, being closer to local schools, may exert even more direct pressure on curriculum change than national organizations discussed in the previous section. Another factor in this direct force is that more individual teachers and administrators have the opportunity to come into personal contact with the spokesmen and leaders of the state organizations at conferences, workshops, and similar types of meetings than is the case at the national level.

State Department of Public Instruction

Obviously, the State Department of Public Instruction, or Department of Education as it is called in some states, is in a strategic position of first magnitude to affect local curriculum decisions. The Superintendent of Public Instruction, elected by popular vote in some states, and appointed by the Governor or State Board of Education in other states, may make public pronouncements in his own right that may prove highly effective in persuading local school boards to adopt specific curriculum recommendations. These pronouncements may be made in speeches, articles in professional publications, or (on occasion) even in public news media. Perhaps a notable example in the physical education field is the following recommendation made by Dr. Roy E. Simpson, who at the time was Superintendent of Public Instruction for the State of California. In the state's leading educational journal, he commented about time allotment for physical education in the California public schools:

> I believe the recommendations on the deletion of some form of physical education for students in the first three grades unwise, also the proposal to make physical education in the eleventh and twelfth grades elective. In an increasingly indoor, urban world, physical education is more important than ever before.[18]

[18] Roy E. Simpson, "Days for Decision," *California Schools*, XXXII, No. 1 (January, 1961), 5.

It seems plausible that this unequivocal statement by the most influential educational leader in that state may well be highly effective evidence in future debates in the state legislature, or in deliberations of the State Board of Education, or in local school districts, in the event the question of time allotment for physical education in the curriculum, as prescribed by state law, becomes a controversial issue. In fact, the influence of this statement on curriculum decisions in other states that have not experienced the outcomes of daily physical education requirements for all students may be important in lending weight to such decisions on this problem.

In addition to the curriculum recommendations of the Superintendent of Public Instruction speaking from his own personal beliefs and basic educational philosophy as the educational leader of his state, another powerful influence on local curriculum change is the educational philosophy of the State Department of Education. Within the official statement of the philosophy of the department, one usually will find direct and indirect references to health and physical education as vital objectives in the broad educational program for all youth. These official departmental statements of educational philosophy and policy take many forms. Sometimes official publications are issued that are all-encompassing, thus providing a basic document that attempts to state explicitly the broad educational philosophy of the state department. It is probable that most states have such a document in public print. In some states, this publication is considerably more detailed than in others. An example of a very detailed statement of educational philosophy, which is the official policy of a state department of education, is the California Framework for Public Education.[19] Physical education as an essential subject in the school curriculum is explicitly emphasized in this Framework statement as indicated by the following excerpt:

Experience should be provided for the learner to develop and maintain a satisfactory degree of physical efficiency for daily living and to enjoy a variety of wholesome physical recreational activities, some of which can carry over into adult life. The learner should also have an opportunity to develop the useful skills related to locomotion, those related to work and safety, those related to individual and team sports, with full recognition given to the responsibility he has to conduct himself in socially acceptable ways, exemplifying a spirit of sportsmanship and fair play. Each child or youth who is found to have handicapping defects, whether remediable or not, should be encouraged to participate in a modified program of activities designed to meet his individual needs.[20]

---

[19] *A Framework for Public Education in California,* Bulletin of the California State Department of Education, XIX, No. 6 (1950).
[20] *Ibid.,* pp. 13, 14.

In most states, a variety of official publications of the State Department of Education directly or implicitly deal with the subject of physical education, even if the title or topic of the document is general in nature, and at times even when other specific subjects are featured. Hence, official policy statements by State Departments of Public Instruction may have considerable bearing on curriculum decisions made at local levels, not only in general curriculum problems, but in special fields such as physical education.

Department or Bureau of Physical Education

This is one agency of the state department that has a particularly crucial and highly strategic role to perform in suggesting curriculum improvement in physical education. Again, it is not possible to list here all the various titles given to these offices in the several states; but, generally speaking, responsibility for the over-all supervision and coordination of health education and physical education is delegated to highly trained and broadly experienced professional personnel in such offices who act as staff representatives to the Superintendent of Public Instruction. Oftentimes these departments have responsibility for school recreation and interscholastic athletic programs as well. Unfortunately, not all states have a separately established Bureau of Health and Physical Education in the State Department of Education. In some states, supervisory responsibility for health, physical education, athletics, and recreation is an additional duty that rests with a general coordinator or supervisor, or his assistant, who has other duties and assignments. This arrangement is not conducive to the proper supervision and leadership deemed necessary in physical education throughout the state and is not in keeping with strongly held professional recommendations from the organized physical education profession. Happily, however, with the increased recognition of the fundamental need for regular physical education programs for all public school pupils and with the urging of the President's Council on Physical Fitness, there are indications that several states are now establishing, or making studies prerequisite to establishing, separate departments of health and physical education in the state agency for public education.

The Director of Health and Physical Education in the State Department of Education and his staff have tremendous opportunities and challenges with respect to providing curriculum guidance and leadership at the "grass roots" level throughout the state. Some of the most obvious vehicles for providing such curriculum influence are the publications of the bureau; conferences and workshops conducted by the state department; surveys and research studies and consequent recommendations;

speeches; panels and discussions at local and regional meetings by state department representatives; liaison work with other educational, medical, and lay organizations concerned with public education; and by consultative services provided to local schools, school districts, county schools offices, colleges, and universities. Some examples of these contributions by the Department of Health and Physical Education follow, from which it should be apparent how teachers of physical education may be influenced directly, or how they and their administrators may be guided more indirectly toward better physical education programs and practices.

Virtually every bureau of health and physical education periodically publishes official state curriculum guides for teachers of physical education and provides these guides free of charge as a state service to every school administrator and every teacher of physical education. There are several ways of organizing these guides according to educational level. Typically, there will be a guide for elementary school physical education, which covers grades kindergarten through six; a junior high school guide for grades seven, eight, and nine; and perhaps two guides, one for girls and one for boys, in the senior high school. These guides give primary emphasis to the philosophy of physical education held by the State Department of Education for the relevant grade levels and then spell out in detail the selection of activities, grade placement, and sequential teaching progressions. Usually included are other details of evaluation; pupil grouping; organization of classes; teaching methods; and equipment, facilities, and supplies. These curriculum guides for teachers constitute perhaps one of the most important influences on the individual teacher when he considers changing his program, or becomes involved in a departmental curriculum evaluation and revision project.

Bureaus of health and physical education continually publish many other types of material related to curriculum change in local schools. This information is made available in many forms: ditto reports, mimeographed statements, pamphlet and booklet forms, manuals, professional magazine articles and reprints, cloth-bound books, illustrated posters and summary reports, and so on. Generally speaking, it is the policy of the state to make free distribution of such materials at least to every department of physical education in the public schools of the state and, if possible, to teacher education institutions. When funds permit, an attempt is made to see that every individual teacher of physical education receives a personal copy of most important publications, such as teacher curriculum guides, statewide tests, and similar material. It is unfortunate that oftentimes the mechanics of such distribution through normal educational channels break down to the extent that large numbers of teachers fail ever to receive personal copies of such publications. These materials frequently are made available for distribution to teachers attending conferences and workshops at which state bureau staff members are present. Meetings are held regionally to interpret and explain such publications and to clarify state department views and to answer teacher questions about implementation at the local level. All of these activities have an accretion of effect upon ideas and motivation for curriculum change in individual schools. Research and survey studies at the state level are an occasional and important source of information, insights, and ideas that may result in significant program changes in a particular school or school district.

State department supervisors of physical education exert tremendous influence upon individual physical education teachers, as well as upon teacher education personnel and school administrators, by presentations they make at conferences, workshops, and similar meetings. These persons are highly respected, and their recommendations concerning physical education program standards are seriously considered. Undoubtedly, many a school or school district has improved its physical education program as a direct result of hearing a state department specialist speak at such a meeting.

The liaison responsibility of state department personnel in physical education cannot be overlooked, although its influence upon the individual physical education teacher might be more indirect than in several of the examples listed above. Nonetheless, the importance of this role to the programs in local schools, and ultimately to the activities of individual teachers, must be emphasized. For example, in one state, a Citizens Advisory Commission on Public Education to the Joint Committee on Education of the state legislature seemed to be split in its deliberations concerning time allotment it might recommend for physical education in the public schools. Appearances before this citizens commission by the Chief of the Health and Physical Education Bureau, plus the efficacy of research and professional judgment evidence presented most effectively by him to the commission, undoubtedly was highly significant in stemming the tide of a possible recommendation on reduction in time allotment for physical education. There are numerous other examples of effective liaison work by state department physical education supervisors with educational, medical, legislative, and lay groups too numerous to mention here. The essential importance of this task, however, seems self-evident and should be recognized by the physical education teacher as he contemplates his own program and the factors that ultimately affect it.

The personal, consultative role the state supervisor of physical education performs with individual teachers, departmental staffs, school faculties, school district supervisors and coordinators, school and district administrators, and school boards is perhaps the single most important facet of the myriad of duties befalling the state office. In most states, a professional staff member of the Bureau of Health and Physical Education makes these consultative visitations upon the request of the local school district transmitted through official channels to the State Department of Education. In the capacity of a consultant, the state representative is very effective in most cases in giving guidance to curriculum evaluation and revision. Although usually he has a built-in advantage to begin with because some person or official group in the school or district already has an interest and a desire to become involved in physical education curriculum revision, the state consultant still has a most crucial role to fulfill. His ability, forcefulness, tact, and powers of persuasion will determine the extent to which he can motivate the local group to give careful, detailed consideration to their problems and evolve a sound set of recommendations for curriculum improvement. Parenthetically, it might be noted that the state representative, as any other consultant, does not always enter a local situation upon invitation where the atmosphere of the majority of the group concerned is entirely favorable to the assignment he has been given. An official invitation may well have been extended to the consultant from a superior administrative authority. The school administrator may have assigned the physical education department or the interschool teacher committee to undertake a curriculum revision project by edict. The consultant must enter this type of potentially hostile situation with great care. Techniques for consultant behavior in such situations are detailed in other literature.[21,22]

Unfortunately, the policy of consultant visitation to local schools only upon prior invitation leads to serious gaps in the stimulation and encouragement of local curriculum revision by the state consultants. Schools having an interest in program improvement are the ones seeking further assistance. It is probable that in most cases such enlightened schools holding a positive attitude toward the desirability of curriculum improvement already have programs that are better than the average programs in schools throughout the state. On the other hand, schools with ineffective programs, or with teachers who prefer the status quo to the hard work and pleasurable rewards of curriculum revision, may be less likely to request state consultative assistance, for which they, more than other schools, have greater need.

---

[21] K. Wiles, C. Brown, and R. Cassidy, *Supervision in Physical Education* (Englewood Cliffs, N.J.: Prentice-Hall, Inc., 1956).

[22] Ruth Evans and Leo Gans, *Supervision of Physical Education* (New York: McGraw-Hill Book Co., Inc., 1950).

State Boards of Education

Many states are organized in the field of public education so that, in addition to the State Department of Education composed of professionally trained and experienced educators, there is a small statewide representative State Board of Education. The most common pattern is for this board to be appointed by the Governor with specific numbers of members holding staggered terms of office to insure continuity of experienced members on the board and to give new Governors during their tenure of office an opportunity to have some members of their choosing placed on the board. These boards vary in number of members with the majority being comprised of eight to twelve persons. Members are lay citizens supposedly selected as statewide representatives of broad segments and interests of the citizens of the state.

In theory, the State Board of Education is non-political in nature and function. There is considerable prima-facie evidence that, in the years since the launching of the first Russian sputnik and the suddenly aroused public and governmental interest in education with its accompanying critical reassessment, there has resulted a much more significant and dynamic leadership role for the State Boards of Education than previously was the case. It is also apparent that some of this activity has become beclouded with political twinges. Governors are now seeing the political advantages to be gained from emphasizing the achievements of their states on the educational horizon. Aspiring young politicians and legislators are introducing state legislation in the field of education, which, while we are willing to grant the inherent good intentions of the sponsor and the content of the proposed laws, nonetheless serves a useful concomitant purpose in bringing favorable public attention to the individual legislator, to the majority political party of the state, and to the Governor himself. Obviously, the greatest concern among thoughtful educators and lay citizens is that public education in general and specific subject fields and related student learning experiences do not become "political footballs" to be kicked around in an attempt to win political advantage.

The foregoing remarks about state boards of education are offered by way of clarifying how great the power and influence of these groups can be with respect to affecting curriculum changes in any given field of study. Physical education seems to be one of the subjects frequently discussed by these boards, and again the importance of constant liaison with board members by representatives of the physical education profession is of utmost urgency. This liaison role and formal and informal interpretation endeavors usually are performed in the physical education field by the specialists in the health and physical education department of the State Office of Education and by responsible leaders of state professional health and physical education organizations.

The functions and powers of state boards have assumed greater importance and authority than ever before. In most states, the State Board of Education has the delegated legal power to issue state regulations that are mandatory upon local school districts and schools. The line of demarcation between powers of a state legislature to pass laws in the field of public education and the delegated powers of the state board to issue regulations in the same area frequently are not clearly delineated. For example, a recent study comparing state laws and state regulations on the topic of time requirement and allotment for physical education in the elementary, high school, and junior college curriculums vividly demonstrates how inconsistent these powers delegated to state boards are and how difficult it is to determine specifically what the criteria are by which a state board regulation may be issued under some general legal grant of authority from the state legislature. With the increased importance of state board leadership, as described in previous paragraphs, it is apparent that several of these boards are becoming more aggressive than ever before and are taking more leeway in announcing board regulations with which school districts must comply.

The explicitly delegated legal authority from the state legislature to the state board and the implied powers state boards seem willing to accept for themselves combine to make the State Board of Education today a powerful influence in curriculum revision. Physical education teachers should be fully aware of this source of power and authority. Boards usually call upon the State Department of Education and upon interested professional and lay citizen organizations for testimony and official recommendations concerning the subject of discussion, prior to establishing a statewide regulation. It is at this point in the process that the curriculum field has its formal opportunity to interpret its objectives and programs and to recommend its professional beliefs and to present its evidence in support of those basic beliefs.

State legislatures are passing more laws pertaining to public education than ever before. A recent trend seems to be that, rather than attempt to spell out detailed implementing steps in the law itself, the legislature passes a provision that delegates to the State Board of Education authority to establish policies and procedures to carry out the general intent of the state law. Again, this is another example of the rapidly increasing importance and influence of the state board upon curriculum improvement on a statewide basis, as well as at local school district levels.

Citizens Advisory Committees

Another source of influence on curriculum development, both statewide and in local school districts, that is coming into more prominence than ever before is the Citizens Advisory Committee. There seems to be a definite trend for school districts to appoint such committees. Normally, these advisory committees are composed of invited lay citizen representatives from the community, selected teachers from the schools or grade level concerned, school administrator representatives, and possibly a school-board member. One city school district set up a series of such advisory committees for each of the major subject-matter areas of the school curriculum. These committees eventually made formal reports, which contained recommended curriculum revisions for the subject under consideration, to the school board. Occasionally, these advisory committees will have the paid assistance of a curriculum specialist in the subject field, usually a professor in the subject from a nearby college or university.

Some districts employ as consultants a team of subject-matter scholars from nearby universities to make a curriculum survey and a final report of curriculum recommendations to the board of education. It is possible that such a committee will not have a trained specialist in physical education, in which case curriculum recommendations in these areas may be entered by professors who do not have professional qualifications in those fields.

COLLEGE AND UNIVERSITY CONSULTANTS

Subject-matter specialists and professors of education from colleges and universities make important contributions to curriculum change in local schools through appointment as curriculum consultants. Several of them from various subject-matter fields may be employed as a team to recommend total curriculum revision for a school district; or they may be employed as consultants individually to work on a curriculum revision project in one subject area with a selected group of teachers and administrators, and possibly lay citizens. Frequently, the final detailed report of the committee is written by the consultant and is presented orally to the district curriculum committee and to the school board by the consultant. Sometimes the consultant serves as a resource person to the curriculum committee and acts as a full-fledged partner and member of the committee. In other studies, he may be designated by the superintendent of schools to conduct a curriculum evaluation and then to submit a consultant's report of recommendations for change and improvement. In this case, the consultant usually functions with a teachers' committee to assist him and to clarify school policies and procedures for him, in order to supplement school visitations he makes. Also, these teachers present to him their views and those of their colleagues in the district concerning desirable policies and practices that they would like to see promulgated. However, in the final analysis, the consultant is responsible for the recomendations he submits to the superintendent and the board under this particular plan of curriculum revision.

Cassidy,[23] as well as other writers in physical education, gives an excellent description of how curriculum revision should proceed under the first set of conditions listed above. In the second situation, where the consultant alone has final responsibility for submitting his evaluative judgment and recommendations for action to the superintendent and the board, little help is found in existing literature. If the consultant has the final responsibility for submitting an evaluation and recommendations for curriculum change, he can be most helpful to the teachers in the district by not only submitting his own views, but also acting as spokesman for changes the teachers themselves may have been advocating for a long time. Sometimes the superintendent or the school board will accept the recommendations of the consultant that, in effect, are the same recommendations that have been submitted previously by the teachers or supervisor within the district. The dynamics of such a situation are not clear, but this role of "carrying the ball" on the part of the consultant is most important in inducing administrative decisions that, in turn, facilitate curriculum improvement in a particular school and even in a specific teacher's class.

In some cases, the consultant's recommendations are not necessarily a direct reflection of the consensus of the teachers on the advisory committee, but rather represent the consultant's firm conviction of how the curriculum can be improved in the district or the school. If the school administration is persuaded favorably, resultant decisions can affect markedly the local physical education program.

One of the most important consequences of the utilization of an outside consultant for a specified period of time in a curriculum study is the possibility of developing teacher enthusiasm for long-range improvement so that teachers' groups themselves will continue the study and will set up long-range plans and procedures, which are self-directing on the part of the teachers and which will operate over a long period of time.

For example, the entire faculty of the boys' and girls' physical education departments of one high school agreed to the suggestion of one of their colleagues that they form a curriculum committee of the whole staff

[23] Rosalind Cassidy, *Curriculum Development in Physical Education* (New York: Harper & Row, 1954), p. 339.

to continue the work that a university consultant, under contract with the district, had initiated with them. Upon expiration of the contract of the consultant, these teachers set up plans and procedures to implement the recommendations of the study and to continue with curriculum evaluation on a long-range basis. They agreed to meet one morning per week from 7:00 to 8:00 A.M. before the start of the first period of the school day. Thus, these teachers volunteered to perform this important curriculum revision function on their own time, in addition to their full-time work, because of their own personal belief in the desirability of improving their program. This curriculum study was coordinated with their own principal, with the district supervisor of physical education who met regularly with the teachers' committee, and with the assistant superintendent of instruction. This school moved rapidly ahead in improving its physical education program.

Concerning the above situation, it should be pointed out that school administrations are becoming more and more aware of the necessity of providing time, as a scheduled part of the teacher's regular load, for the important curriculum committee work. Schools are finding ways to provide released time for teachers on such committees by employing substitute teachers for regular teachers who have committee assignments and by employing teachers to report for duty a week or two before school begins in the autumn or to remain on duty after school is over in the spring. Until public school teachers have loads requiring not more than eighteen to twenty hours of classroom teaching per week, with resultant freedom of time to work on such assignments as curriculum revision as part of their regular duties, curriculum revision and full teacher participation will not progress as rapidly or effectively as it should. Further consideration is given to teacher assignment and professional duties in Chapter 9.

COUNTY SCHOOL OFFICE AND DISTRICT CONSULTANTS

Local school physical education programs can be affected greatly by the influence of physical education specialists from the local county superintendent of schools office and from the school district central staff. These specialists have various titles, such as supervisor, director, coordinator, and consultant. Sometimes they are specialists in physical education only; sometimes they are responsible for such diverse areas as physical education, health education, safety education, school recreation, outdoor education and school camping, and even driver education.

The modern view of the role of these consultants is that, having been successful master teachers in their field with many years of teaching experience, they are now highly qualified to provide guidance and advisory services to the teachers in the district or county. These specialists basically serve as resource persons to teachers and administrators. They need to have a thorough understanding of human relations and need to be experts in group dynamics. They must possess inspirational leadership qualities and abilities in order to assist teachers in reaching their own highest potentials. The literature on the general subject of supervision in schools and on physical education supervision is abundant and should be referred to for a greater understanding of the roles of these specialists.

The county schools physical education supervisor serves strictly in an advisory capacity. He has no direct authority over any teacher and cannot "order" any curriculum change in a local school or district, even if it were desirable to do so. Typically, county school supervisors devote a majority of their time and attention to physical education in the small city and rural elementary schools in the county, from grades one through eight. Some time is reserved for working with large elementary school districts and with junior and senior high schools. The reason for this distribution of time is that larger elementary schools are more likely to have a trained physical educator on their staff, or available to them, or to have a classroom teacher or administrator in the school with professional preparation in physical education, or that larger districts will have their own physical education consultant, and that junior and senior high schools generally have their own departments of physical education staffed with professionally trained faculty members. In other words, county consultants try to provide service and guidance in schools and areas most in need of such assistance due to lack of qualified physical education specialists in those schools.

The county consultant, as in the case of the state director, visits only schools where he has received an official invitation from the administrator of the school. He conducts in-service education workshops for teachers, leads demonstration lessons in physical education with a class of pupils, acts as consultant to the school principal and interested faculty with respect to curriculum improvement, provides resource materials for curriculum and suggestions for facilities improvement, and in every possible way assists local schools in improving their programs.

In addition, the county consultant will organize countywide workshops, clinics, demonstrations, and other types of in-service education opportunities for interested teachers and administrators. Frequently, these activities are carried on with the assistance of the state director, or his representative, and with a consultant from a nearby college or university. All in all, a capable county consultant can wield far-reaching influence in shaping physical education curriculum improvement in a local school.

The school district consultant in physical education serves on the staff of the superintendent of schools in the central office. He is a staff member in the line and staff organization. His channels of authority, both vertically and horizontally in the organization, are clearly delineated. Sometimes his duties are not so clearly defined. A recent informal study by one of the authors concerning the duties and functions of school district supervisors in the home state indicated a dismaying variety of related, and often unrelated, duties befalling the so-called physical education supervisor and his staff. One of the conclusions of this study was that the physical education supervisor's office sometimes is regarded as a "catch-all" for the many miscellaneous responsibilities delegated by the superintendent that do not have an obvious "home" in existing supervisorial offices. It is not within the scope of this book to discuss this problem in detail, but it is mentioned here in order to illustrate the possibilities that exist for the district physical education supervisor to be influential with regard to curriculum matters both directly and indirectly throughout his district. It is obvious that, regardless of the less-related duties assigned him, this supervisor devotes his major attention to curriculum problems, both from the point of view of districtwide policy and procedures and with respect to specific problems in any local school.

Although in theory the district supervisor is regarded as a resource person who gives guidance and assistance at the request of teachers and administrators in schools within his district, it should not be overlooked that this supervisor has a much more direct influence on the destinies of the physical education teachers in the district than does a county supervisor in relation to teachers in schools within the county.

No longer is it the duty of the district supervisor to rate the job performance of all physical education teachers in the district, as was the case in the early days of school supervision. Now, the principal, being the chief administrative agent of the school, has the responsibility for rating his teachers. However, the indirect power of the district supervisor to affect the professional advancement of at least some of the physical education teachers should be emphasized, even in today's era of a philosophy of supervision that presumably envisions the supervisor as the teacher's advisor, a professional friend and leader, and a consultant and guidance expert. For example, if a new high school is about to open and the superintendent and the newly appointed principal of that school are deciding on department heads and faculty members for the new school, it is likely that the district supervisor of physical education will be asked for recommendations concerning superior teachers in the district as potential candidates for such positions. Thus, it becomes clearly evident that, in fact, the supervisor is directly evaluating individual teacher performance on the job and, as a result, can influence the professional advancement of teachers, at least within his own district. By the same token, he can submit influential recommendations to administrators outside the district who may be considering the employment of a teacher from the district.

Another very important function of the district supervisor is the so-called "staff" function relating to districtwide policy decisions in physical education that are made by the superintendent in his administrative capacity, or by the school board in its over-all broad policy-forming role. It is the empirical conclusion of the authors that by and large the school districts with the most successful physical education programs are districts with supervisors who function particularly well in the role of "staff" representative to the superintendent and board. The whole area of properly interpreting the purposes of physical education and the role of physical education in the curriculum, the planning and recommending of a comprehensive program of physical education to meet those objectives, and the staff studies that clearly indicate the personnel and logistical support required to do the teaching job effectively is most crucial among the many roles of the district supervisor. Again, an elaboration of the many duties of the district supervisor and his staff is not possible in this volume; but these comments are included to illustrate the highly important role the supervisor can play in giving proper direction to curriculum improvement in his district and in local school situations.

COLLEGES AND UNIVERSITIES

It seems safe to assume that a majority of public school teachers attend classes, workshops, clinics, demonstrations, and conferences sponsored by colleges and universities, at least in a somewhat consistent manner over the years. Motivations for such attendance may be several. Many salary schedules are keyed either to the attainment of baccalaureate, masters, and doctoral degrees, or to the attainment of specified numbers of matriculated graduate credit in order for teachers to qualify for salary raises additional to increments granted merely for longevity in the district. This incentive obviously impels many teachers to return to graduate school somewhat regularly in summers, or to night and Saturday morning classes in nearby areas. Colleges and universities cooperate with this built-in demand by scheduling classes at convenient times specifically for experienced teachers. In addition, many colleges establish extension courses taught in centers of population that do not have institutions of higher education. Thus, teachers in such an area can enroll in a night or Saturday morning course in their own area, an obvious convenience to them.

Some colleges make arrangements for individual study or independent study for matriculated graduate students. Under this system, a teacher can propose a problem for study, or a topic that he may desire to study in depth in recent professional and academic literature. He and his college advisor agree upon the nature and scope of the assignment and the number of graduate units to be awarded upon completion of the assignment. Then the student does most of the work independently, on his own initiative, and in his own geographical area. Arrangements are made for periodical checkups of student progress with the professor, either by correspondence or by travel to the college campus at stated intervals. The professor provides the necessary over-all guidance and assistance throughout the course of the project.

Some colleges and universities sponsor summer tours for groups of teachers who have an interest in a common field. Several physical education oriented trips to European and Middle East countries have been sponsored in recent years by well-known colleges. These tours are conducted by professors representing the sponsoring institution. The best tours are those that set forth specific educational objectives to be achieved and that have organized instructional experiences built into the tour, using local facilities and local specialists at each stop. These tours carry regular graduate credit applicable toward advanced degrees in that institution, or toward salary increment standards in local school districts.

It is not unrealistic to note that an individual teacher on such a tour can be influenced by what he sees and studies in a foreign country to the extent that he will introduce some new activity, or teaching method, or equipment to his own class upon his return, and hence will improve his own program. It is the contention of the authors, both of whom have served in educational programs in several countries overseas, that the physical education curriculum in American schools should be much more responsive than it now is to the possibilities for developing desirable attitudes in pupils toward international relations and understanding. Sports and dance are media for international communication and goodwill. Teachers who have had an opportunity to study and observe abroad almost unanimously agree with this viewpoint and are active in improving their own physical education programs on the basis of their experiences in other countries. Hence, overseas assignments and tours are becoming more and more an influential source of stimulation for curriculum change in American physical education.

In addition to regular course offerings for matriculated graduate students, many colleges and universities offer other forms of in-service education for interested teachers on a non-matriculated basis wherein formal admission requirements are waived. There are countless examples of coaching clinics, workshops, demonstrations, conferences, symposiums, seminars, summer encampment programs, and similar arrangements that teachers attend yearly throughout the United States and in foreign countries, covering a wide variety of topics pertinent to the teaching of physical education in the schools. Sometimes non-matriculated credit awarded to the participant is acceptable in certain school districts for salary increment purposes.

In summary, it seems fair to conclude that the experiences a teacher has in connection with educational opportunities provided by colleges and universities may be very important in developing an attitude and motivation toward general curriculum improvement at his own school, plus providing a source of specific suggestions as to how such improvement can be implemented. The teacher may be under more influences than he realizes as he talks with colleagues in and out of class, as he interacts with professors and other instructors who are specialists in the subject matter, as he reads recent literature and research, as he crystallizes his own thinking in debate with others and in the preparation of projects and term papers, and in other similar ways. One note of criticism might be interjected at this point, namely, that many of these in-service experiences for teachers are predominantly based in methodology. While proper method certainly is one of the prerequisite tools of the successful teacher, particularly in a "practical" field such as physical education, it may be observed that too much of an imbalance in the direction of "how to do it" is a mistake in the judgment of the authors. Physical education also is a subject-matter field involving much substantive "content." In-service courses for teachers should insure a balance of substantive content along with attention to newer methods and techniques.

COLLEAGUES

As we conclude our discussion of several sources of powerful influence upon the individual teacher who is concerned with curriculum revision in his school, it seems fitting to return to the teacher's immediate everyday environment. Can we possibly estimate the influence his own colleagues have upon his thinking, his attitude, and his motivation, with respect to curriculum improvement in his own school? The other teachers in his department have innumerable opportunities to persuade him to many points of view. The process probably is going on continuously in both implicit and explicit ways as all staff members interact with each other throughout the year. The authors have noted some of the most effective curriculum changes resulting from the inspirational leadership and personal example of one person in a department who was able to raise the interest of his colleagues, to "spark" them to higher personal conviction, and hence lead them to desirable action, to improve the program. If a department has two or more individuals who possess these traits, then, obviously, so much to the good. It is seldom that enthusiastic, creative, imaginative teachers resent other teachers of similar bent; rather, they enjoy the inspiration and the association; and each benefits from the contributions of the other. It is the teacher "in the rut," satisfied with the status quo, afraid to "rock the boat," or just plain lazy who resents the new proposals, the hard work, the drive and the desire to improve the program, to elevate the sights of the staff, to become a superior teacher of boys and girls through the medium of physical education.

A teacher's colleagues in other fields and other departments in the same school can serve to stimulate and encourage desirable curriculum change in physical education, and the alert physical educator can make a similar contribution to other fields. The physical educator's colleagues in his field in other schools in the district and in the local geographic area also are sources of ideas, motivations, and insights that may move the teacher in the direction of providing desirable program improvement. Some schools now have a policy that permits teachers a certain number of days each year to visit colleagues in other schools in order to observe their program and to discuss with them what they are doing, how they do it, and why they are doing it. This is a very worthwhile trend that we hope will continue to expand in coming years.

Colleagues in administration and in guidance and health services may be helpful to the physical education teacher as he considers program improvement. The principal and the superintendent and his curriculum staff specialists may exert great influence and in some cases pressure, informal or formal, upon an individual teacher, which will result in curriculum change. This relationship has been discussed in greater detail on previous pages.

Fellow teachers with whom a physical education teacher associates at conferences, workshops, clinics, and college classes probably constitute a very significant source of influence upon the teacher relevant to his thinking about curriculum matters. One of our most natural impulses as teachers is to ask other teachers, "What activities do you have in your program," "What tests do you give," "How do you classify your students," "How do you grade in physical education," and many other questions central to the teaching and organization of the physical education program. It seems highly probable that many curriculum innovations in a particular school have been "borrowed" or adapted from a successful program in another school. While this chain of events does not account for the origin of the idea or of the practice in the first place, it nonetheless seems to be an accurate appraisal of what happens, operationally speaking, when curriculum improvement influences are carefully considered. While this process of using what seems to be "good" or "effective" from other schools has certain values, it should by no means be the primary source of ideas and suggestions for curriculum improvement. In addition to the spreading of "good" practices, we urgently need the development of new goals, new programs, and new methods in order to improve the effectiveness of desirable changes in behavior of children who engage in the physical education learning environment under our direction. One of the main purposes of this book is to present some relatively new and some original proposals as to (1) program elements that might be added to physical education curricula, (2) a more effective way of classifying and grouping pupils so that instruction can be individualized to a greater extent to better achieve objectives, (3) organization of learning experiences for greater effectiveness, (4) the best utilization of professional and subprofessional personnel to teach physical education, (5) arrangement of time allotment for physical education for improved learning, and (6) the best method of using supplies, equipment, and facilities to support the proposals listed.

5

Role of the Physical Educator in Curriculum Change

Physical education should always be an integral part of the total school curriculum, concerned with achieving the over-all aims and objectives of public education. Thus, curriculum change in physical education always takes place within the framework of curriculum change in the school as a whole. Efforts toward improvement in physical education must always be directed toward goals accepted by the community and by staff specialists in other areas. Curriculum development requires interdisciplinary cooperation, the use of knowledges from many interrelated subject fields, and a constant concern for the whole child and his total curriculum experience. At the same time, teacher specialists contribute most effectively to curriculum improvement by studying problems in terms of their individual areas of expertness and by offering potential solutions in the fields that they have studied and experienced in depth. Since this text is addressed primarily to physical education specialists, the focus is upon physical education curriculum change within a framework of schoolwide and systemwide curriculum development.

CURRICULUM CHANGE AS PROBLEM-SOLVING

The process of curriculum change is a problem-solving process. All curriculum study, every curriculum project, and each proposal for curriculum research is directed toward the solution of some problem of improving the quality of instruction. Problem-solving skill is a requisite for leaders of curriculum change.

Problem-solving has been analyzed and described in detail by many psychologists. The process is usually presented as a cycle of several steps: (1) identification or definition of the problem, (2) collection of data, (3) selection of a potential solution, (4) testing the solution, (5) evaluation of results, and (6) redefinition of the problem, further collection of data, and/or selection of a new hypothesis, etc., until the problem has been satisfactorily solved. Problem-solving behavior may be individual activity or it may be engaged in by a group of persons concerned with common problems. The modern concept of curriculum change conceives of it as group problem-solving.

All teachers need to develop problem-solving skills. The key role of the individual teacher in curriculum change has been stressed repeatedly. No teacher is adequately prepared for his role in curriculum development unless he has achieved competence in problem-solving. Since he is in daily contact with the learners, his function in helping to identify significant curriculum problems is primary. He will be a key participant in collecting data and testing selected hypotheses. No evaluation of the results of instruction or the process of curriculum improvement can be considered complete without his active and conscientious contribution.

DEFINING PROBLEMS

Curriculum modifications have characterized American schools since their beginnings. Actual study of the process of curriculum improvement is a relatively modern feature, however; planned programs for curriculum development have become a part of the educational scene since World War I.[1] Building upon the experiences of the past four decades, we are now able to take a systematic approach to curriculum change.

If we view the curriculum with a broad concept of its nature, we must recognize that curriculum change is social change. Program improvement requires study of the factors that affect the learning environment as well as the content included in the approved course of study. Curriculum development must be based upon a thorough diagnosis of the local school-community situation.

A systematic approach to curriculum change is directed toward changes in people, changes in the structure of the school as a social institution, and changes in human relationships within local groups. It will include well-organized plans for broad involvement. Its evaluation will be anticipated with carefully devised criteria for determining status, estimating progress, and assessing next steps for further improvement.

[1] Harold J. McNally, A. Harry Passow, *et al., Improving the Quality of Public School Programs* (New York: Bureau of Publications, Teachers College, Columbia University, 1960), pp. 28–33.

Schoolwide and Subject-Field Approaches

Every school system with a dynamic curriculum development program has established an institutional pattern for facilitating continuous curriculum improvement. In most instances, the curriculum development function is officially assigned to a member of the administrative staff designated as an assistant superintendent, curriculum director, instructional supervisor, curriculum coordinator, or director of instructional services; and to a committee of teachers and administrators called the steering committee, coordinating committee, curriculum committee, or instructional council. Typically, these individuals are assigned responsibility for stimulating program improvement and for coordinating suggestions and contributions from individual departments and staff members.

The identification of problems for intensive study may be approached primarily on a schoolwide basis. The steering committee or the curriculum director may take the leadership in identifying problems of general concern to the school as a whole. Individuals may present to the committee or the director problems with systemwide implications. In either case, the process of selecting and refining problems and the structure for systematic study of these problems will be centralized, and "across-the-board" studies will be emphasized. Schoolwide approaches are advantageous in identifying general school problems that should receive priority, in ensuring selection of problems that are significant in view of over-all curriculum objectives, and in coordinating staff efforts for intensive study of a limited number of problems. Their chief weakness lies in the quality and degree of involvement of all the professional personnel.

On the other hand, subject-field approaches may be emphasized in identifying local curriculum problems. Each department may be given major responsibility for program improvement in its area. Individual staff members are expected to identify problems, discuss possible solutions with their colleagues, and initiate procedures for improvement. This organization is less centralized, but normally functions with a coordinating committee and under a designated administrative leader. In schools that stress departmental channels for identifying curriculum problems, coordinating committee membership may consist chiefly of department chairmen. Primary responsibilities of the committee and the curriculum coordinator will be screening projects, steering group studies toward over-all school objectives, coordinating efforts of the various departments, and maintaining balance in the total curriculum development program. "Broken-front" approaches have greater potential for identification of problems that are meaningful to pupils and individual staff members and for active involvement of the total faculty in curriculum improvement. Regrettably, subject-field approaches present difficulties in achieving coordination, balance, and consistent direction in local curriculum change.

Both schoolwide and subject-field approaches have merit. The most effective curriculum development program probably uses both. Whichever approach is emphasized, the individual staff member sees possible improvements from the viewpoint of his own specialty. He has a continuous responsibility toward the solution of curriculum problems in his own subject area as they become evident in his daily work with students. In schoolwide curriculum study, he is charged with applying general criteria to improvement of learning experiences in his own field and with contributing the concepts and skills of his discipline to the solution of broader school problems. In this volume, the authors consider curriculum improvement primarily from the point of view of the physical education specialist.

Identifying Problems Through Curriculum Development Principles

A systematic study of a given school's curriculum demands specific attention to each of the principles of curriculum development. Careful application of these principles in the local situation undoubtedly will focus attention upon definite problems for consideration by all concerned with program improvements. Examples of problems identified by physical education specialists, using this approach, are suggested below.

We have stated that curriculum objectives must be directed toward the fulfillment of basic human needs, the realities of social circumstances, and the achievement of democratic ideals. Evaluation of local curriculum objectives against this criterion highlights certain significant problems. The development of kinesthetic perception is a basic human need toward which physical education should make a significant contribution. Are we giving this objective sufficient emphasis in planning our programs? Are we guided by satisfactory specific movement education objectives? Do adults in the community who are not physical education specialists understand the importance of improving our programs to achieve this objective?

Are our physical fitness objectives realistic in terms of the physiological demands of modern living in our culture? Are they possible to achieve without guided out-of-school activities? Have we selected the most significant aspects of physical fitness for emphasis?

Will the achievement of our stated objectives actually further democratic ideals? Have we given enough attention to determining our objectives in the area of teaching democratic values? Do we know which values should receive instructional priority? Can we reduce these objectives to behavioristic terms?

The principle of content selection stresses the selection and organization of curriculum content in terms of significance to the solution of important social problems. Which important social problems will physical education help to solve? Will the learning of folk dances of different countries be more significant than other types of rhythmic experiences? Will experiences in decision-making in stress situations contribute more than experiences that encourage self-testing and the setting of higher levels of aspiration for individual performance? Will co-educational movement activities provide skills and/or understandings for solving any important social problems?

Can we allow available facilities to determine program content—or will we insist that facilities must be adapted to utilization of significant content? Do we know enough about individual differences among our pupils to vary curriculum content appropriately? Can we select content with high potential for teaching democratic values as well as for optimum physical fitness?

The principle of sequence helps to identify such problems as the following. At what point in their growth and development can most children learn to swim with maximum economy? At what age level is interest in team sports highest among American girls? Can we agree upon stunt sequences on various pieces of apparatus based upon progressively increasing levels of difficulty? What constitutes a sound progression in basic movement activities? Can the teaching of attitudes of responsibility be broken down into a specific sequence of learning experiences? Can we improve physical education programs by developing more experience-oriented units?

How can we achieve greater continuity in twelve-year physical education programs? What learning experiences are needed to provide better articulation between elementary school and secondary school movement experiences? How can junior high school teachers improve the continuity of the individual pupil's physical education experiences?

Shall pupils be grouped according to grade level, physical fitness test scores, sports skills performance, or some other classification criterion? What constitutes optimum class size? Is a short daily period preferable to a longer, less-frequent class period? Do these factors vary for pupils of varying skill levels and for different types of movement activities? Should the total amount of time in aquatic experiences be less than, equal, or exceed that allotted to basketball activities? How much repetition of softball-type games will result in best learning? At which levels should these games be used?

A fourth principle states that curriculum methods should use the best current knowledge concerning the nature of the learner and the learning process. Consideration of this principle suggests many problems that might well be subjects of curriculum study by physical educators. How can we provide for more individualization of instruction? Can we create new devices and techniques for encouraging self-testing and stimulating more individual practice? How can we utilize television as a more effective teaching aid? Are we using pupil-teacher planning procedures to best educational advantage? Can we provide for better learning through improved evaluation procedures?

What constitutes a learning "whole" in physical education? Are we providing sufficient experience in problem-solving? Do our programs sacrifice depth and meaningful movement experiences for superficial breadth and variety of activities? Can we learn more effective techniques for guiding interpersonal relationships among our students? Which teaching methods are most appropriate for the teaching of democratic values? How can the differing talents and interests of individual staff members be used to achieve optimum learning results? What types of facilities are needed for utilization of the best methods to realize physical education's potential?

Our fifth principle of curriculum development emphasizes that curriculum improvement requires participation by the lay public and by pupils as well as by the entire professional staff. Studies in this area could be directed toward a variety of problems. How can we guide pupils more effectively in setting meaningful individual goals? Which administrative organization is most conducive to active involvement of all physical education teachers in curriculum change? How can criticisms of faculty members in other departments be channeled into responsible participation in physical education curriculum improvement?

How can we interest the community in the less glamorous aspects of the physical education program? Which procedures will develop more effective partnerships with parents in achieving physical fitness objectives? What leadership techniques can be directed toward winning lay concern for movement education and citizenship goals? Are varsity athletic contests, physical education demonstrations, and PTA campaigns satisfactory vehicles for stimulating constructive lay participation in physical education curriculum development?

Many more examples could be given of the identification of curriculum problems using principles of curriculum development as criteria. The above examples should suffice to illustrate the possibilities of approaching curriculum development in this manner. Actual improvement of learning outcomes depends upon intelligent analysis of the principles as they apply to local situations.

Studying Both Product and Process

In curriculum improvement, both the product and the process are important. We have tended to evaluate our programs in terms of the product, neglecting evaluation of the process. If the process is poor, the product may lack stability or constructive achievements may be negated by undesirable by-products.

Thus, we must be concerned with identifying problems relating to the process of curriculum development as well as those dealing with the product. As we plan for curriculum improvement, it is always necessary to clarify objectives. If we are satisfied with our statements of objectives, we begin asking ourselves how these objectives can be realized more completely. Have our pupils discovered the deeper meanings in human movement? Do individual learners achieve and maintain satisfactory levels of physical fitness? Do participants in our extraclass activity programs display evidence of good emotional health? Is the daily behavior of our students consistent with the democratic values we are attempting to teach? All of these questions are concerned with the product. They open up many potential curriculum projects, for they identify areas of important problems demanding better solutions than we have yet found.

Process problems also require attention, however. Perhaps the key factors in significant improvement of the local curriculum are problems growing out of the particular curriculum development processes in operation. What are the forces working against adoption of the proposed student body code of ethics? Do all physical education instructors have sufficient scientific and technical knowledge to teach basic principles of human movement successfully? How can we minimize the threat that individual teachers feel in the introduction of television as a teaching aid in physical education? Have each of the appropriate community groups been represented in planning the local youth fitness program? How should curriculum committees be organized for greatest productivity? Such process problems often block desired curriculum improvements more surely than problems concerned primarily with the product. Identifying and solving process problems pose a tremendous challenge to all curriculum workers.

Techniques for Defining Problems

Many techniques have been employed successfully in identifying and defining local curriculum problems. Probably the most frequently used techniques are those that solicit individual opinions in a variety of ways. These include questionnaires, interviews, surveys, and the problem census. The structure may be quite informal or may utilize a mass-produced, printed instrument. They can be adapted to securing opinions of pupils, teachers, administrators, parents, professional consultants, or lay citizens. Sociometric and projective techniques can also be used to gain additional information about the individuals involved in curriculum development.

Another group of techniques useful in problem definition includes those that deal with the study and analysis of local data relevant to educational concerns. Studies of the school population bring out facts on "I.Q." status, socioeconomic backgrounds, participation in extraclass activities, uses of guidance services, and hidden costs of school attendance. Follow-up studies of graduates and of pupils who dropped out before graduation can be very valuable in identifying curriculum problems. Analyses of test scores on standardized achievement tests will pinpoint other types of problems. Case studies of individual students in special categories may highlight important problems when compared with representative case studies of "typical" students.

A third technique that is used extensively for identifying problems, and often used in combination with other techniques, is the group meeting. Individuals can share their ideas regarding curriculum problems and stimulate each other's thinking in refining problems through committees, departmental meetings, faculty meetings, conferences, professional association meetings, university extension classes, in-service seminars, professional institutes, and workshops. Such meetings may be sponsored by the local school district or by other professional groups. They may take place in the local school building or in a completely different setting.

Problems can also be identified through observation techniques. Policies that encourage parent observation of learning activities, adult attendance at school-sponsored activities, and demonstrations of actual classwork present opportunities for local citizens to identify problems by actual observation of practice. Teachers may be assisted in recognition and refining of curriculum problems through visitation in other classrooms, professional convention attendance, demonstrations of new teaching techniques, instructional materials, and teaching aids. Such experiences can be provided by local in-service programs, university field services, commercial interests, foundations, or statewide experimental curriculum projects.

Many of these different techniques can be used in combination. Whichever techniques are used to identify local curriculum problems, careful selection of problems for intensive study is essential. McNally and Passow have suggested the application of three criteria for problem selection: significance, involvement, and scope and time.

. . . problem significance should be judged in terms of (1) its potential for involving individuals both intellectually and emotionally; (2) its meaningful relationship to classroom activities and to teaching tasks; and (3) its possibilities for being resolved. . . . Individuals who are to be involved in the solution of a problem should participate in its definition. . . . Problems must be so refined that they are of manageable size in terms of the personnel resources available and so that there is promise of tangible results with a reasonable expenditure of time and effort. . . .[2]

COLLECTING DATA

Once the problem has been identified and carefully defined by those concerned with its solution, the next step is to collect relevant facts and to gather all data useful in solving the problem. In many cases, the problem can be further refined and more clearly defined through the data-collection process. Sources for relevant data are unlimited. We seek applicable facts by studying both related disciplines and past experience in physical education.

Study of Related Disciplines

Research in many organized fields of knowledge has established facts important to the solution of physical education curriculum problems. Accurate knowledge of human anatomy is basic to planning sound movement experiences. Studies in human physiology underlie our selection of activities for developing physical fitness, our planning for active adult recreation, and our rules governing participation in athletic contests. Kinesiology is the stock in trade of the physical educator. Medical research is constantly offering new insights that can be applied in the improvement of physical activity programs.

Study of the social sciences can be just as profitable in gathering information for dealing with curriculum problems. Philosophy is an important source in determining our objectives. History provides the perspective of time for studying current problems. Anthropology offers the perspective of other cultures, so helpful in determining the influence of specific environmental factors upon motor performance. Sociological research has produced a wealth of evidence describing different aspects of group life, the operation of the class system in our society, and the influence of various status and prestige symbols.

Psychology is continually enriching our resources for curriculum improvement. The facts of child growth and development offer guidelines for all educators. New knowledge of the process of human learning should be applied in all subject fields. Research in educational psychology dealing with such topics as readiness, method, value formation, skill

[2] McNally, Passow, *et al., op. cit.,* p. 77.

learning, and personality development has direct application in the physical education curriculum. Deeper insight into the field of testing, measurement, and evaluation is helpful in any curriculum study.

Sources of data in related disciplines should be sought in determining solutions for physical education problems. Experience in our own field should always be studied in relation to other organized fields of knowledge. Curriculum workers should be alert to new findings in other disciplines while investigating the resources of the physical education profession as a whole for solving local problems.

Physical Education Methods Research

Much of the research completed by professional physical educators contributes data relative to teaching methods. The literature includes studies concerned with whole-part learning, motivation techniques, skills practice procedures, kinesthetic approaches to learning, and the use of a wide variety of specific presentation and practice techniques such as television, athletic conditioning routines, weighted basketball shoes, and underwater speakers. Much professional research has also been directed toward the development and validation of skills tests and other evaluation techniques.

Research on Organization of Physical Education

A number of physical education research workers have studied and compared different plans for grouping students for physical education learning. Many investigators have compared learning achievements of students in heterogeneous class groups with those grouped homogeneously on the basis of motor ability, physical fitness, or skill achievement. The relative success of students in learning groups of different sizes has been studied. Many research problems have dealt with such time allotment problems as the length of skill practice periods, length of intervals between practice periods, distribution of time within the physical education class period, length of the instructional period, frequency of instruction periods, and flexible scheduling procedures. Researchers have also attacked problems of grade placement of physical education learning materials and the development of specific skill progressions. Some contemporary investigators are interested in staff utilization studies.

Human Relations in Physical Education

Researchers have studied human relations in physical education classes, in informal sports groups, and in athletic team organizations. Investigators have considered the relationship of athletic skill to social status, the significance of personal acquaintance scores in physical education classes, characteristics of leaders in sports clubs, and techniques of leadership. Much interest has been shown in analyses of interpersonal relationships among athletic team members.

Research on Physical Education Attitudes

Studies of attitudes toward physical education have been numerous; these studies extend over the whole period of physical education research and reflect attitudes of participants of both sexes and all age levels. Some of them attempt to pinpoint specific aspects of the program considered valuable, worthless, or harmful; in some instances, specific sources of dissatisfaction and enjoyment have been identified.

Surveys of voluntary participation in physical activities during school years and after leaving school are of considerable interest to those studying the physical education program. Participation studies attempt to determine who participates in active sports for recreation, which sports are most popular, when individuals participate, how often and under what conditions, and how much they spend. Information from these studies provides additional knowledge of adult recreational patterns and of the extent to which activities in the physical education curriculum are selected for voluntary participation.

Physical education literature also includes a number of studies of the opinions of experts toward various aspects of the program. Most of these have been concerned with philosophy of physical education and the determination of objectives for the curriculum.

Current Practices in Physical Education

Information on the status of physical education is available from the appropriate governmental agency. Most state departments of education have divisions staffed by physical education specialists. These individuals can usually provide information on legislation, qualifications of employed teachers, scheduling practices, facilities, in-service education programs, and plans for supervising physical education in elementary school districts. State departments offer assistance with curriculum problems through official publications; consultant service; and lending libraries for books, films, recordings, and other professional aids.

The United States Office of Education offers similar services on a national scale. Reports of research studies undertaken by the staff to secure data not readily available in local situations are often especially helpful. United States Office of Education personnel are oriented toward broad professional problems, have access to information essential in identifying problems of national import, and possess resources for studying these problems and providing leadership in their solution.

Information on current physical education practices is also available through the professional organizations. In addition to encouraging, sponsoring, and reporting research studies exemplified in preceding paragraphs and organizing working conferences directed toward the solution of major contemporary problems, the American Association for Health, Physical Education and Recreation publishes current statistical information on many aspects of physical education. The Association conducts numerous national surveys and makes the findings available through a wide variety of publications. Many state associations conduct studies and publish reports that focus on local data and statewide problems.

Curriculum guides constitute an excellent source of information on current physical education practices. Some states publish detailed curriculum guides and bulletins; programs and procedures suggested by agencies of the different states can be studied and compared. Many individual school districts are now publishing curriculum guides locally. The primary purposes are to provide guidance, assistance and in-service education to local teachers, and to furnish information to local citizens. In most cases, however, such curriculum materials are available upon request to other professional persons; studying the specific solutions that others have used can be of immeasurable help when facing comparable problems.

Professional Conference Reports

Major problems of common concern to professional workers in physical education and related fields frequently become topics for working conferences called to study possible solutions. Such conferences are sponsored by governmental agencies, professional associations, higher education institutions, and private foundations or business organizations. Often they are sponsored jointly by a number of interested groups. Plans for such conferences normally include distribution of published reports and recommendations at minimum cost. Recent conferences have led to publication of reports on a wide variety of subjects of special interest to physical education curriculum workers. Examples include youth fitness, competitive athletics for elementary and junior high school children, values in sports and athletics, professional preparation in physical education and related fields, planning facilities, international physical education, and interpretation of physical education.

Services of Private Business

Certain other groups represent valuable sources for specialized data. The sporting goods manufacturers and other firms with commercial interests allied to physical education can supply much helpful information. Many companies maintain their own research departments to test fabrics, experimental materials, and new products. Facts provided by such studies are frequently shared with professional leaders. Such sources of information can be highly beneficial, provided the physical educator uses them in a context of data collected from a variety of authoritative sources. It it not unusual for a manufacturer with a new piece of equipment to provide teaching aids, suggested activity progressions, and recommended patterns of organization. The physical educator must accept the responsibility for evaluation of this material; much of it proves to be educationally sound if used with reasonable caution by qualified persons.

The professional contributions of the Athletic Institute should be noted in this connection. The Institute is a non-profit organization of athletic equipment producers that aims to strengthen the development of sports and recreation. In the quarter-century since its founding, it has promoted and financed professional conferences, produced teaching films and manuals, conducted surveys and field services, and distributed sports information widely.

Solutions to problems encountered in planning or improving facilities usage often require highly technical assistance. School plant planning laboratories have been established by certain educational institutions, with the cooperation of appropriate governmental agencies and construction and building supply firms. These laboratories are designed to improve curricula through developing educationally sound school plants; expert consultant service in solving local problems is an essential part of the concept. The value of such work has been recognized on the national level in the organization of programs for research and experimentation with creative designs for educational facilities.

Other Sources of Data

The sources of data for solving physical education curriculum problems are unlimited. This discussion has attempted only to highlight those that have proved particularly useful in a variety of curriculum development projects. A rich source that has received insufficient attention is the work of colleagues in other school departments. In addition to building upon the foundation work in related disciplines and past experience in the physical education profession, it is important to study educational research in other subject-matter fields, to read reports of experimental curricula in other areas, and to talk with and observe the work of local colleagues who are seeking solutions to problems similar to those faced in physical education.

It should be recognized, in addition, that many of the techniques previously discussed as procedures for identifying problems can also be utilized in the collection of data. These aspects of problem-solving are closely interrelated. The identification, definition, and refining of a problem normally requires the gathering of facts and the collection of data. Collecting data to solve a problem may lead to restatement of the problem or result in the definition of new subproblems.

Several examples of the use of techniques already mentioned in collecting data follow. The survey, interview, or questionnaire technique may be used to gather information on local attitudes toward swimming in the elementary school curriculum, number of pupils who would require instruction at beginning and intermediate levels, and available resources in personnel and facilities to support the program. Administering standard physical fitness tests to the entire school population can serve not only to pinpoint fitness problems, but also to suggest possible curriculum modifications. Scores can be analyzed to secure comparisons between student participants in athletic programs and non-participants, between groups of students enrolled in courses in different activities, and between those students receiving supplementary classroom instruction in the development and maintenance of physical fitness and those receiving none. Group meetings can be structured to provide for the sharing of information needed in solving curriculum problems as well as to encourage recognition and identification of problems. Observation of demonstrations and learning situations in progress is clearly a means of gathering applicable data for solving specific curriculum problems.

SELECTING AND TESTING SOLUTIONS

The collection of data relevant to problem solution usually leads toward more than one potential solution. The curriculum worker must weigh all available alternatives in light of the information that has been gathered and select the one that, in his best judgment, is most likely to lead to the solution of the specific problem that he hopes to solve. In contemporary curriculum work, this judgment becomes a group decision growing out of the interaction of individual convictions.

Sometimes tentative solutions can be discarded on the basis of additional information before they have actually been put to the test of practical application. In certain instances, curriculum workers may have the opportunity to study a proposed solution by observing its effectiveness in another situation; the proposal can then be partially tested with the investment of a minimum of time, energy, expense, and dislocation to the local curriculum. But in most cases, it will be necessary to test the selected solution by actual application in the practical situation, by action research at the local level. Only by actual use can the effectiveness of the solution be adequately tested.

Since the selection of a potential solution must be based upon human judgments and frequently upon insufficient data, it is inevitable that the alternative chosen will sometimes fail to solve the problem. When this happens in curriculum change as in any other type of problem-solving, the problem must be redefined, additional data must be gathered, and another solution selected and tested. Sometimes many alternative solutions must be tested before a problem is satisfactorily solved.

Although curriculum development takes place at all levels, current emphasis is upon problem-solving by the individual teacher. Organizational structure for solving curriculum problems necessarily varies. Effective patterns provide for the involvement of professional staff, students, and lay citizens; for the emergence of leadership at all levels; and for adequate communication among the various individuals involved. Good organization ensures a variety of curriculum improvement activities and the coordination of the various activities in progress. Useful procedures include committees, study groups, workshops, seminars, clinics, institutes, visitation, supervision, curriculum libraries, cooperative studies, and experimentation. The structure must facilitate the development of group problem-solving abilities; research competences; and such curriculum development skills as demonstration and other means of communicating to various groups, working with consultants, and using resource specialists. In planning professional schedules, sufficient time must be allotted for these diverse curriculum improvement activities.

Curriculum change should be a creative process directed toward the solution of local problems, guided by local leadership. Specific procedures for selecting and testing solutions to physical education curriculum problems should be developed in the local situation. Descriptions of such procedures are included in some detail in following chapters.

EVALUATING RESULTS

Evaluation occurs throughout the problem-solving process but is accentuated as each potential solution completes a testing cycle. Evaluation of the results of testing a solution in action determines whether another solution will be attempted or whether the major emphasis of curriculum study will shift to identification of a different problem. In some instances, achieving a satisfactory solution clearly pinpoints the next problem to be attacked. In any event, the evaluation and the entire cycle of curriculum change should be continuous.

Genuine curriculum improvement demands built-in plans for continuous evaluation. Best results cannot be achieved unless adequate provisions for evaluation are built into the basic curriculum development organization. Plans for evaluation must include procedures for before and after appraisals of the product. We cannot demonstrate progress resulting from our efforts unless we have some record of where we started. Tests that can be used to compare status at different points in a physical education curriculum study include motor performance tests, physical fitness tests, sports skills tests, and knowledge tests. Other evaluation devices include inventories, opinionnaires, surveys, interviews, school records, checklists, rating scales, personality tests, sociometric techniques, and systematic observation.

Evaluation procedures should also include appraisals of local curriculum development processes. The effectiveness of the organizational pattern can be evaluated on the basis of the degree of involvement of personnel, facilitation of leadership, and open communication channels. Techniques used can be appraised in terms of clarification of individual responsibilities, interpersonal relationships within working groups, diversity of approaches, resources used, coordination of activities, and distribution of results to all concerned. Every curriculum improvement program should be evaluated frequently for consistency with the basic principles of curriculum development.

THE TEACHER AND CURRICULUM DEVELOPMENT

It cannot be emphasized too strongly that the teacher is the key factor in curriculum development. He must be highly motivated and have deep conviction that curriculum change is necessary and can be accomplished. He must be ready for action and must have accepted the challenge as his own personal goal.

Once he is ready and determined to act, he must decide *how to act*. How can he present his ideas and gain acceptance for them so that actual curriculum change will result? There seem to be at least three alternatives available. He can do nothing at the moment, beyond organizing and clarifying his ideas and his implementing recommendations, while he waits for someone else to initiate action. After the principal, or the superintendent, or the supervisor, or the school faculty has set in motion some type of curriculum review process, he submits his proposal at the most propitious time. At best, this is a timid approach that most likely will not produce results very quickly and risks the possibility that very little if anything will be done at all.

As a second alternative, the teacher may attempt to integrate his proposal into some presently existing project of relevance, or make use of an existing school or district policy for the introduction of his recommendations for consideration by the proper authorities. This course of action seems highly desirable when policy structure exists that permits such action by the teacher as an approved, worthwhile, encouraged procedure. If the policy structure is such that a physical education curriculum proposal emanating from an individual teacher can be introduced as a routine, relevant procedure, then the project is at least assured of a smooth beginning and the teacher proceeds from there. Schools and school districts that genuinely desire to promote continuous curriculum review and improvement will have existing policies and procedures within which an interested teacher may proceed as indicated.

In the event proper machinery is not present in the school or district policy labyrinth, the physical education teacher who is sufficiently "ready" to act must then intuitively seek the best means available to him for introducing his proposals. This becomes a matter of properly estimating the situation and depends upon his knowledge of the manifold interrelationships and feelings that exist among the persons most likely to be involved in the project, either at its inception, or later in the discussion and evaluation phase of the curriculum change process.

In order to improve the possibilities of gaining acceptance of his proposals, the teacher must take the time and effort to prepare a careful presentation. The proposal must be clearly described. This description should be in writing, accompanied by such diagrams, charts, and illustrations as will serve to make its meaning perfectly clear. Sufficient copies should be provided so that all concerned can have their own copy for review and analysis. After presenting the proposal, there should be an explanation of the reasons, and the evidence supporting those reasons, favoring the adoption of the proposal. The ultimate criterion in spelling out the reasons and presenting supporting evidence is the predicted change in behavior that it is expected will result in the children to be affected by the change.

Then follows a description of how the change is to be integrated into the present program. What part of the present program does it replace, or modify? Can it be added without eliminating other desirable facets? The whole complex problem of selection and arrangement of learning materials and experiences on a priority basis comes into focus here. The case for the new proposal must be made in the light of utilizing available time most effectively. It is not sufficient to believe that some new idea is "good" or has merit. It must be judged to have greater merit than some other phase of the program that it might replace.

It is usually highly desirable to have an opportunity to present the proposal orally to those who will consider it and those who are charged with authority to approve or disapprove it. The oral presentation can be used to supplement the written proposal and to respond to questions that arise concerning it. The teacher should take notes of the comments and suggestions he receives from others concerning his proposal. Chances are that the proposal will go through a process of one or more revisions, and he should be prepared to incorporate the best thoughts of his colleagues as he steers the proposal along through the sometimes devious channels major curriculum revisions require.

The teacher who presents a proposal for curriculum change should continually bear in mind that such change ultimately takes place in the learning experiences of the pupils under his leadership, or that of other teachers. All else—plans, strategy, hard work, and personal hopes—are for naught if this desired change in pupil behavior is not accomplished. Curriculum development too frequently fails when a sincere effort of curriculum revision on paper culminates with the publication of an elaborate Course of Study Guide for Teachers. Sometimes these guides are expensive because they make extensive use of photographs, charts, stick figures, and tables; and they even have elaborate high-cost cloth or plastic covers. Perhaps the new course of study is approved by the superintendent and then by the school board and congratulations are handed down to the teachers. But further investigation reveals that the teachers continue to teach the same activities they had in their program before the revision, and that they teach them in the same old way. In other words, the children have not benefited at all. True curriculum revision has not occurred.

Good teachers know that student needs are the central point in curriculum redirection. Teachers interested in curriculum change should systematically assess pupil needs relevant to physical education experiences. These needs should be described clearly in writing so that they may be communicated to others. Then proposed changes that are likely to meet those needs more effectively than present practices should be defined.

After a teacher has introduced a suggestion for curriculum change in one of the three ways described above, he frequently faces the problem of gaining full acceptance and approval of the recommendation. What strategy should he use in order to obtain this acceptance?

The carefully written detailed description of the proposal is the first essential. A proposal that is poorly constructed and not clearly understood has less chance for adoption than a clear-cut recommendation. When accompanied by a careful verbal explanation, the proposal may be well on its way to successful adoption.

If opposition is anticipated or actually encountered, the advocate of the proposal may seek the backing of influential persons in positions of authority or high status. For example, the teacher may try to obtain the approval of his department chairman, or the principal, or the district physical education supervisor. He may try to find allies among the senior teachers on the faculty or other teachers held in high regard by their colleagues. It is hoped that these persons will announce their support of the proposal to those who are in opposition. This technique may bring about at least a favorable majority vote, if not a unanimous approval of the proposal.

If opposition still persists among one or more teachers or administrators involved at the decision-making level, the advocate of the proposal has several alternative courses of action open to him. He must use good judgment and common sense as he selects his course of action. He may have to change from one course of action to another as the process evolves and he evaluates what is happening. One suggestion is to find a way to involve personally the person who seems to have some objection to the new plan. Perhaps he can be assigned to a committee that has been appointed to review the proposal. The dissident member could be given a subcommittee job of looking into some specific aspect of the recommendation or gathering specific facts about it. His own personal involvement in reviewing the project may result in a change of interest or attitude, as he learns more about it, as he hears the opinions of others, and as his own objections seem to be met. Sometimes the proposed plan can include a specific assignment or duty for the skeptic, one that requires the utilization of certain special interests or strengths he may have. If he can be shown that favorable participation on his part is an essential element in the over-all plan, he may more willingly accept the total proposal. Most of us have seen examples of the melting away of personal opposition to a new teaching method, a new activity, or a new testing procedure when a person who opposed it originally became personally involved in it.

Sometimes there is sufficient opposition to a recommended change that it cannot be completely overcome. In this case, after sufficient effort, it may be necessary to scale down the scope of the project. In effect, this would be agreeing to a compromise suitable to the proponents and opponents. Sometimes it is better to make changes slowly and steadily, to make progress in small steps, rather than to hope to make "a great leap forward" all at one time. If compromise is necessary, but changes still lead toward the ultimate goal, then perhaps this is the most judicious strategy. Some proposals that are viewed with great skepticism initially demonstrate merit when put into action on a limited basis. In such cases, the strength of the original opposition may melt away and vanish. Sometimes it is desirable to introduce a new activity on a trial basis, rather than to include it for all pupils in a certain grade. Try it out on a class of forty-five students for a block period and evaluate the results. Then the proposal can be considered for extension to the remainder of the classes, or for adaptation, or for total elimination from the program, depending upon the trial results.

The total atmosphere of mutual respect and confidence among teachers and administrators is often another aspect of the problem of obtaining approval of a curriculum proposal. This spirit is constantly under development and test in all of the working and social relations of the day, every day, month in and month out. As a result, the generalized feeling each faculty member has for the other may well serve as the basis for the extent to which a proposal from a colleague is sympathetically received. This is not intended to mean that faculty members should accept each other's proposals without serious reflection and analysis of the merits. However, when an air of mutual respect and confidence exists, there is more likelihood that a sound proposal will be accepted, or at least given a trial.

Sometimes it is effective to use the appeal of a higher authority or a leader with high status, from a source outside the school or the district. The influence of the State Director of Physical Education, or the consultant from the university or from the national professional organization, has been mentioned previously. However, there are additional sources of influence that can be valuable allies to the individual teacher who proposes a significant curriculum change. For example, the statements of President John F. Kennedy,[3] the Resolution of the House of Delegates of the American Medical Association,[4] the statement of Dr. James Conant,[5] and others may prove to be very valuable.

Finally, when the opposition seems too strong to overcome by the above means, the teacher who firmly believes in his proposed plan must decide whether to abandon it or to continue to a final showdown against the opposition at the decision-making level. There are many examples of high school teachers, individually, or in small groups, on a staff who felt certain that the physical education program in their school could and should be strengthened considerably. These people were so convinced about this matter that they engaged in open conflict with other teachers who were opposed to such extensive changes.

The authors are firm supporters of serious minded, enthusiastic teachers who hold high standards and a strong personal commitment to the values of a good physical education program. They hope that curriculum development can proceed on an orderly basis in individual schools by

[3] John F. Kennedy, "The Soft American," *Sports Illustrated,* December 26, 1960, pp. 15–17.

[4] "Resolutions on School and College Health and Physical Education," passed by the House of Delegates of the American Medical Association, Miami Beach, June, 1960, *Journal of Health, Physical Education, and Recreation,* October 1, 1960, p. 1.

[5] James B. Conant, speech to the American Association of School Administrators, February, 1960, Atlantic City, New Jersey.

use of one or more of the techniques and processes suggested above. When opposition is not overcome in this manner and the teacher or teachers decide to push the revision proposals to a showdown, we would still fully support them. However, we should point out that when the situation reaches this type of crisis, the advocates of change must realistically assess the consequences of the drastic action they will elect to take. They must decide how they will react to the possible alternative outcomes of their endeavor; and they must be willing to live personally and professionally with the consequences, whatever form they may take. In order to illustrate this seemingly dire warning, two examples of actual cases that reached such a critical state are cited below. Particular attention should be devoted to the consequences both as to (1) improvement in the physical education program per se and (2) the professional future of the individual teachers involved.

A new high school was opened in a growing urban area. A physical education teacher with twenty years' experience in the old high school was appointed as department chairman in the new school. Within three years, the school had grown so rapidly that the staff in the boys' department had added four new teachers, each having less than five years' teaching experience. The chairman had introduced a "throw-out-the-ball" type of program with a minimum of teacher responsibility and instruction involved. This sterile program did not meet the standards of the young teachers. They worked for two years to try to persuade the department chairman to undertake a departmental curriculum revision study in order to plan and implement a sound, instructional program of physical education for all pupils. The chairman would not permit such a study and would not change the program or regulations that he had originally introduced to the school. The young teachers abided by the proper channels and followed professional and ethical standards and procedures in attempting to promote curriculum change. Finally, they gave up and decided that they would fight this battle to its conclusion in another way. They were fully aware of the possible consequences of this decision, but they agreed to stand or fall together and to undertake the challenge.

In effect, they formed their own four-man curriculum committee and planned a program and teaching procedures that they all agreed to follow in the classes they taught. They spent countless hours in planning the program, on their own time, in the evenings and week ends, meeting at individual homes. They did not use school time or school facilities and supplies for this purpose.

Eventually, they had their plans fully drawn and proceeded to organize and teach their classes in the way they had agreed. Before long, this change became apparent to the department chairman. He asked them to cease the new practices and to return to the old routines he had decreed for the department. They refused; they kept on teaching their classes in the new way. The department chairman brought this matter to the attention of the school principal. The principal had already noticed the change. Also, he had heard about it from approving students and from parents who carried reports to him that their children brought home. He did not enter into the conflict immediately. He let the situation develop and proceed for the remainder of the school year.

The upshot of the situation was that the principal was so impressed with the fine physical education program the young teachers were giving that he requested the district office to reassign the department chairman to a teaching position in another subject, in order to provide the physical education department with a chairman who was sympathetic to the new program and who would give it full support. As an aside, the deposed chairman fought the transfer all the way to the school board, which finally reaffirmed the transfer. The chairman resigned from the district after having been employed in it for more than twenty years.

This school continues to have one of the finest physical education programs in the state and one of the original young teachers is now chairman. This particular situation had a happy ending for the curriculum improvement advocates involved, and even more important, an educational improvement for the pupils in the school. It may be that the circumstances eventually were favorable to the resigned teacher because it is reported that he now is a highly successful and wealthy businessman.

In another school, some elements in the situation were similar to the above example, but the outcome was quite different. This was a well-established city high school that had been in existence for more than thirty years. One year it just happened that three vacancies in the staff of the boys' department occurred at once. These positions were filled by three young men, each of whom had not more than three years' previous teaching experience. Again, the department chairman had been teaching in the system for more than twenty years and had been chairman for ten years. The physical education program had not seen marked revision for many years. There seemed to be a satisfaction with things as they were and little or no desire to seek self-improvement. In their first year of teaching in this school, the three new teachers followed the regular procedures but soon began to build up a feeling of dissatisfaction and a belief that the program could be considerably improved. They attempted to make suggestions to the chairman who responded cheerfully but did little to change the situation. The teachers were permitted some slight flexibility in how they conducted their own classes. At the start of the second year, the three young teachers, as in the previous example, decided that they would not progress far in bringing about significant changes by using methods and channels available to them. They enlisted the support of a fourth member of the department who was in agreement with their philosophy; and, again, these four teachers met on their own time and formed their own *ad hoc* unofficial curriculum revision committee. They agreed on new activities they wanted to introduce to their classes and to improved instructional methods that they desired to follow. They then announced their plans and desires to the department chairman and told him they were going to teach their classes in this new way henceforth. The principal soon became involved in this delicate situation. The chairman recommended to the principal that the teachers be permitted to continue to teach in the way they desired for the remainder of the year. However, the principal made it very clear to these teachers that they had violated administrative channels and had acted in an unauthorized manner. It is to the credit of the principal and the chairman that they both recognized the sincerity and desire implicit in the actions of the teachers and did not regard the indiscretions of the teachers as personal assaults, but as genuine strongly held desires to improve the curriculum.

In this case, however, unlike the previous case, the principal felt that the teachers had acted in an inappropriate manner that he could not condone. He told these teachers that they were not subject to reassignment in his school for the following year, much as he appreciated their sincerity and professional desire to improve the program. These teachers knew in advance that such administrative action was one of the consequences that might result from their activities, and they were prepared to accept such judgment without remorse or a feeling of personal vindictiveness.

The three young teachers were advised to terminate their employment in that district and to seek employment elsewhere. It is to the credit of the principal and the chairman that they both wrote favorable recommendations for these teachers concerning their abilities as teachers and their ambitions to become associated with programs based on the particular philosophy of physical education that they held. It was also believed that these teachers were educable enough that they would learn from their errors in judgment, and that they could learn to work cooperatively in the total context of a school situation. The fourth teacher, who already had tenure in the district, was reassigned to another school. Follow-ups revealed that all three young teachers successfully found employment in the same general area and are now doing fine jobs, as predicted.

At the school in question, the philosophy and practices of physical education held by the chairman continued to prevail; and the school goes along today with an undistinguished program. In this example, perhaps the teachers who went through this experience benefited; at least they report they did. However, it is doubtful if any long-range value accrued to the pupils in the school. It is even possible that the field of physical education suffered a lowering of prestige in the eyes of that particular principal and the central district office administration, as well as among teachers on the staff of the school.

After all reasonable effort has been expended to bring about changes through normal, ethical channels of administration, the final course of action open to teachers who strongly desire curriculum improvement, but who meet with opposition that cannot be overcome, is to resign. Many unsatisfied teachers resign every year. There are countless examples of those who subsequently find employment in another school that provides the very opportunity that they seek.

Curriculum revision, and the role of the individual teacher in the process, is difficult but usually highly rewarding work. There are innumerable sources of pressures and influences, continually being exerted on the individual teacher, either explicitly or subtly and implicitly. The teacher sifts and synthesizes these influences as he attempts to crystallize his own basic beliefs and, finally, as he attempts to make specific recommendations for curriculum improvement in the practical everyday job context. When a teacher sincerely desires curriculum change, several alternative courses of action are available to him. It is important that he analyze carefully the possible consequences of each course before making his selection.

CHALLENGES FOR PHYSICAL EDUCATION CURRICULUM CHANGE

Curriculum change should be initiated on the local level. Nevertheless, certain problems are of general concern to the physical education profession as a whole. These problems stem from our common human nature, a shared cultural heritage, the universal contemporary crisis, and similar traditional education patterns.

Physical education in these United States today faces many significant problems, urgently demanding solutions. Some of the most challenging of these are the following:

1. What constitutes the basic core of movement education, the essential content of physical education?
2. How can continuity be achieved in twelve-year physical education curricula?
3. How can physical educators teach democratic values more effectively?

4. By what means can we individualize physical education more successfully?
5. How are the individual talents of professionally qualified physical education personnel used to best advantage?
6. Which scheduling patterns facilitate optimum achievement of physical education objectives?
7. What adaptations in facilities and instructional technology will expedite attainment of physical education goals?

These problems have concerned many individuals with varying responsibilities in widespread geographical areas and in exceedingly diverse local situations. They have been approached by physical educators in different school systems in many unique ways. Each of them represents a major area of consideration in curriculum development and warrants further analysis and illustration in the following chapters. Only in this way is it possible to view local curriculum problems in terms of the over-all goals and the total concept of curriculum change.

Part II

CURRICULUM CHANGE AND EDUCATIONAL PROBLEMS

6

Content Selection and Organization

Chapter 3 analyzed three major types of curriculum organization: the separate-subjects curriculum, the broad-fields curriculum, and the core curriculum. The relationship of physical education to a total school curriculum organized according to each of these major patterns was discussed. In this chapter, attention will be focused upon the selection and organization of curriculum materials within the physical education program itself. Common patterns for organizing physical education content in both elementary and secondary schools are described. Actual examples of modern physical education curricula are included to illustrate good principles of curriculum planning and organization.

STANDARDS FOR ORGANIZING PHYSICAL EDUCATION CURRICULA

Curriculum planners in physical education should be guided by the principles of curriculum development discussed in Chapter 2. These principles apply to the development of the total school curriculum, including the physical education aspects of both the formal and informal curricula. Whichever over-all curriculum pattern is used in the local school (e.g., separate-subjects, broad-fields, or core), the following standards should characterize physical education.

1. *A regular program of physical education should be provided in all grades.* Most authorities agree that physical education should be a daily program from grades one through twelve. The President's Council on Youth Fitness (now the President's Council on Physical Fitness) has

recommended: "For grades 1–6, one period per day, 5 days each week, minimum 30 minutes, exclusive of recess and time spent in dressing and showering. For grades 7–12, one standard class period per day, 5 days per week."[1] On the other hand, some educators are experimenting with the scheduling of physical education in longer, but less frequent, blocks of time in the upper secondary school grades. Some of these proposals are discussed in Chapter 10. Although consideration should be given to all reasonable proposals for modification of the daily pattern, ample evidence is available to support the necessity of regular physical education for children and youth in all grades of the public schools.

2. *The regular physical education program should be an instructional program, directed toward specific educational objectives.* Recess periods, after-school activities, and intramural and extramural opportunities can be used as laboratory experiences to supplement the regular instructional program but should never be considered an adequate substitute for physical education instruction. Instruction should be planned to achieve varied educational goals. Objectives need not be limited to those concerned with physical fitness but should include the development of kinesthetic perception; health and safety; and intellectual, social, emotional, and recreational objectives.

3. *Physical education should provide for vigorous, developmental activities.* Although physical education can and should contribute toward many educational objectives, its unique contributions lie in the development of deeper, significant human meanings and values through kinesthetic perception and in improved physical fitness. In order to serve its unique purposes, the physical education curriculum must emphasize vigorous activities of a developmental nature.

4. *The physical education curriculum core of key movement concepts and fundamental movement skills should integrate sport, gymnastic, aquatic, and rhythmic experiences.* Physical education should emphasize key movement concepts at all grade levels. Specific learning activities should be selected to promote continuous integrated movement education. Instruction in sports, gymnastics, aquatics, and dance should highlight common fundamental movement principles and skills. The authors maintain that essential movement learnings can be reinforced and progressively more advanced movement concepts and skills developed through all facets of the physical education curriculum. In order to achieve its objectives, the program in movement education must include activities selected from several major areas of physical education experiences. An approximate distribution of class time among these areas is suggested in Table 6–1; but attention should consistently be focused

[1] *Youth Physical Fitness* (Washington, D.C.: President's Council on Youth Fitness, 1961), p. 11.

upon core movement learnings, irrespective of the particular activity unit in progress.

5. *The scope and sequence of activities should be defined according to individual student needs.* Chapter 8 is devoted to the subject of individualizing instruction in physical education. Several major approaches to this problem are discussed. Provision of opportunities for some student election from among activities offered in the physical education curriculum should not be overlooked.

6. *Intramural and interscholastic programs should offer additional opportunities for voluntary participation in physical education activities.* In addition to the required class instruction, extraclass exeperience in physical education should be available to all students. An intramural program should supplement the class program through voluntary laboratory experiences in activities stressed in classes and by introduction of additional activities not included in the required curriculum. Gifted students in physical education and those with specialized interests in particular activities need the more intensive participation opportunities

TABLE 6–1

Recommended Time Allotment to Major Program Areas

Activity Areas	Grades					
	1–3 %	4–6 %	7–9 Boys %	7–9 Girls %	10–12 Boys %	10–12 Girls %
Fundamental skills and games of low organization (including lead-up games to organized sports)	30	40				
Team games (including modified forms)			40	30	30	20
Individual and dual sports (including modified forms)			10	10	20	20
Gymnastics (including conditioning exercises, stunts, tumbling, apparatus, combatives, track and field, body mechanics, and self-testing activities)	35	35	25	25	25	25
Rhythmic activities (including singing games, rhythmic locomotor and gymnastic activities, and all types of dance)	35	25	10	20	10	20
Aquatics	*	*	15	15	15	15

* Aquatics are strongly recommended for all grades but are not included in the chart because less than 1 per cent of the elementary schools in the United States currently have swimming pools. Elementary schools fortunate enough to have facilities for aquatics should allot 10 to 15 per cent of the total instructional time to this area, modifying other areas accordingly.

possible in interscholastics. Both the intramural and interscholastic programs should offer a wide variety of activities and should be conducted in accordance with established standards.

BASIC CORE OF PHYSICAL EDUCATION

Six standards for organizing curricula have been listed. They will stimulate very little controversy among professional physical educators. But far less consensus exists regarding the implementation of these standards. The key question that must be resolved concerns fundamental physical education content. What is the essential content of physical education? What is the integrating core? What movement education is genuinely fundamental?

The authors believe that physical education is movement education. Our primary responsibility is the development of key movement concepts, the clarification of basic generalizations concerning human movement, and guidance of individuals in achievement of personal skills for effective and satisfying movement. The fundamentals of physical education include efficient performance of everyday movements, skills for relaxation, knowledge of the basis of human movement, familiarity with individual movement potentials, and genuine understanding of key concepts. However, a surprising variety of answers have been proposed to the question: "What is the basic core of physical education?" Perhaps these different views should be identified.

There are those who hold that a well-balanced series of posture exercises and body mechanics activities provide the most essential physical education content. Following this approach, the daily lesson plan includes exercises selected for different body segments; emphasis on knowledge of correct sitting, standing, walking, and running postures; and attention to principles of balance and motion. At the secondary level, particularly for girls, the program usually includes analysis and practice of such activities as pushing, pulling, lifting, and carrying. Sometimes good grooming is heavily emphasized in combination with posture and body mechanics units. This approach has been supported by enthusiasts of European gymnastics systems, by emphasis on individual physical examinations, and by remedial specialists. Most physical educators, however, now consider this a limited view of movement fundamentals.

A second view of the basic content of physical education stresses locomotor fundamentals, or "natural" human activities. The proponents of this approach emphasize mechanical and kinesthetic analysis of the walk, run, hop, jump, skip, slide, gallop, hanging, climbing, throwing, kicking, and striking. These activities are considered the proper foundation for more advanced movement skills. Two major criticisms have been

CONTENT SELECTION AND ORGANIZATION 109

leveled at this type of program. One is that children do not need to be taught these activities, that they will learn these without direct instruction, and that physical education time is wasted in this way. The other major objection is that it is a "piecemeal" plan. Children will learn a number of isolated skills, but there are no provisions for integration of their physical education experiences. Furthermore, the foundation is not sufficiently broad for building a total physical education.

If we survey practices in order to determine the basic core of physical education, undoubtedly the most popular practice is emphasis on sports fundamentals. Physical education curricula stress fundamentals of softball in areas where softball is a major sport, basketball fundamentals in communities where basketball is of primary interest. Grade school programs stress elementary sports skills; beginning units in secondary schools repeat analysis of these "basic fundamentals." This practice in curriculum organization is challenged as a narrow concept of physical education. The critics observe that pupils in intermediate and advanced sports classes demonstrate inefficient running technique, inadequacy in receiving a ball, and many other gross errors in body mechanics. It is unlikely that sports skills alone can provide an adequate foundation for a total physical education experience leading to achievement of varied long-range goals.

Others would place major emphasis on rhythmic movement as the basis of physical education. Pupils move to music or other forms of rhythmic accompaniment. Locomotor skills are analyzed in terms of their rhythmic patterns. Axial movement is used, with emphasis on swinging, sustained, percussive, and vibratory variations. Creative interpretation and self-expression are stressed. Those who strongly support this view contend that the individual can experience a complete movement education through dance. Many physical educators disagree, pointing out that the body requires movement education for relating to objects as well as controlled movement in space, that ballistic movements are underemphasized with this approach. Many argue that it does not give sufficient recognition to the interests of many students.

At intervals in our history, and indeed at the present time, a physical fitness emphasis receives strong popular support. As this becomes dominant, the basic program in physical education tends to become an exercise program. Strength, flexibility, and endurance are the primary objectives. Conditioning- and gymnastic-type exercises constitute the core activities. Testing and measuring status and improvement assume considerable importance. Again, the criticism is that this is a limited approach. Strength, flexibility, and endurance are maintained only by continuous effort. It is difficult to motivate students to carry on exercise programs outside the formal class situation or to stimulate their interest over a prolonged period within the physical education classes. It can also be argued that strength, flexibility, and endurance do not necessarily provide an adequate foundation for learning complex sports skills and coordinations.

A sixth view has come into prominence in this decade. Certain educators contend that the basis of physical education should be movement exploration and movement experiences that stress anatomical, mechanical, and physiological analysis. At the elementary level, this approach is usually described as "movement exploration." In secondary schools, it is variously labeled "basic movement," "fundamentals of movement," or simply "movement education." Its advocates believe that it provides a solid foundation for sports, dance, and gymnastic activities of all kinds. The emphasis is upon guiding students through exploratory experiences that will result in familiarity with the range of joint action, the nature of movements possible for various body segments, and a wide variety of movement combinations. Activities are performed both with and without apparatus, and may or may not be related to popular sports skills. Usually, intellectualization of movement principles is stressed. This approach is sometimes criticized for overintellectualization. It is claimed that, "We are taking all the fun out of physical education." Others object that the development of specific sports skills will be delayed by this much emphasis on movement outside the usual sports context.

Each of these approaches clearly has some merit. Obviously, there is some overlap and various combinations of these different emphases are possible. Surely it is vital that the profession answer the basic question: "What constitutes the core of movement education?" What should be stressed? Where should teachers begin? What kinds of activities will truly provide a sound foundation for the best possible physical education?

The authors maintain that the core of the physical education curriculum in the elementary school should become movement exploration, leading to the development of flexibility, strength, endurance, and rhythmic accuracy. As a part of carefully planned experience in movement exploration, every child should receive expert instruction and ample guided practice in developing efficient movement patterns for all those basic activities that are characteristically human—walking, running, throwing, and the like. His physical education classes should make extensive use of games and gamelike activities; but the selection of content should be determined by his need to extend the movement possibilities of his own body, and to learn specific movement patterns repeatedly demanded by common human activities, rather than by a concept of learning games.

The secondary school student needs continuing experiences in movement exploration as the body develops and changes through the period of physiological adolescence. He or she should be stimulated and challenged through self-testing procedures and other motivating techniques to maintain flexibility, to develop specific muscular strength, to increase endurance, and to refine rhythmic responses. He should be able to understand and should be encouraged to learn the mechanical and physiological principles that govern human movement. He should have extensive and intensive opportunities for adapting basic movement patterns to the specific demands of successful performance of sports, gymnastics, aquatics, and dance. Jumping, for example, was experienced as a basic locomotor skill during early childhood. Physical education experiences in the secondary school will include instruction and practice in specific modifications of the jumping pattern for skillful execution of a basketball rebound, a football pass interception, a volleyball spike, a forward mount to the parallel bars, a backward somersault in a tumbling routine, a trampoline seat drop, a springboard approach for a swan dive, a take-off for a back jack-knife, a vigorous Hora jump, a modern dance technique, and a multitude of additional variations.

Curriculum planners should select activities in terms of their relative potential for being physically educative. Teachers should capitalize more fully upon the educative possibilities of stunts and tumbling, apparatus activities, gymnastics, track and field, skating, skiing, and aquatic activities. Constant emphasis should be given to the development of individual potentiality through carefully selected progressive movement education experiences. All instructional activities should be guided toward breadth of movement experience and depth of understanding of key movement concepts. The individual's entire physical education experience should be integrated through the common fundamental skills and basic movement principles of the various activities.

PATTERNS FOR ORGANIZING ELEMENTARY SCHOOL PHYSICAL EDUCATION CURRICULUM CONTENT

A wide variety of practices are accepted in organizing physical education experiences for elementary school children. Essentially, most schools use a variation of one of the three patterns described below.

Basic Weekly Schedule Plan

A definite pattern, based upon alternation of activities according to certain days of the week, is favored by many educators, particularly for the primary grades. The same basic pattern is repeated from one week to the next. An example of a physical education program planned in this pattern is presented in Table 6–2.

TABLE 6–2

Physical Education Program, Washington School,
River Forest, Illinois *

Grades 1–3	Grades 4–6
Fall	
M. Low-organized games	M. Speedaway
T. Ball activities	T. Football
W. Relays	W. Speedaway
T. Ball activities	T. Soccer-softball
F. Low-organized games	F. Testing (fitness-skill)
Pre-Christmas	
M. Rhythms	M. Rhythms
T. Low-organized games	T. Volleyball
W. Tumbling-gymnastics-trampoline	W. Tumbling-gymnastics-trampoline
T. Ball activities	T. Badminton-volleyball
F. Low-organized games	F. Badminton-volleyball
Post-Christmas	
M. Rhythms	M. Rhythms
T. Low-organized games	T. Basketball
W. Tumbling-gymnastics-trampoline	W. Tumbling-gymnastics-trampoline
T. Ball activities	T. Basketball
F. Tumbling-stunts	F. Testing (fitness-skill)
Spring	
M. Ball activities	M. Track and field
T. Low-organized games	T. Softball
W. Relays	W. Track and field
T. Ball activities	T. Softball
F. Low-organized games	F. Testing (fitness-skill)

* Material supplied through the courtesy of Mr. Gilbert Magida, Physical Education Instructor, Washington School, River Forest, Illinois.

This plan has the advantage of insuring a particular balance in the program. It simplifies the sharing of facilities and equipment in situations where this is required, since the teacher knows in advance which type of activity will be emphasized on a given day. It permits the children to anticipate their activities and to be prepared with special clothing or equipment, as well as appropriate attitudes. The planned weekly schedule facilitates coordination of specific activities with classroom projects. On the other hand, there is a tendency for such a program to become somewhat inflexible if the teacher is not alert to this danger. Furthermore, this pattern does not lend itself readily to a schedule that is not planned on a daily basis.

Seasonal Units Plan

Many programs are organized as a series of seasonal units. A unit might be as short as a one-week orientation and testing unit or as long as several weeks. Usually, relatively brief units will follow each other in succession. In a daily program, it is sometimes advisable to offer two units concurrently. For example, during the period between Thanksgiving and Christmas, a fifth grade might be learning folk dance two days per week and volleyball skills and game activities three days per week. An illustration of a seasonal unit curriculum plan appears in Table 6–3.

This plan is advantageous in the intermediate grades since the attention span of the children is longer and the complexity of the activities greater. It provides for more continuity in the presentation of activities and permits the teacher to capitalize effectively on the seasonal motivations of the children.

The chief disadvantage with programs planned on this basis is that too many do not maintain balance. Too often, sports and games units are overemphasized at the expense of rhythmic and gymnastic activities. This need not occur, however, if the teacher plans the entire program on a yearly basis and considers the over-all balance in selecting and scheduling units.

Informal Yearly Balance Plan

Elementary school physical education is frequently very informal in its organization. No definite sequence of units is set; no specific pattern for the weekly schedule is followed. It is assumed that in the course of the year essential learning experiences will be included, and balance will be achieved. Obviously, this does not happen unless the person responsible for the program evaluates frequently and adjusts his daily plans within a definite framework of yearly objectives. The physical education specialist, who uses such a plan, relies upon his experience to anticipate probable outcomes and to be continually conscious of his long-range goals.

The classroom teacher working within this framework can be assisted by the physical education consultant in several ways. The specialist can plan the program on a seasonal basis (e.g., fall-winter-spring, or by six-week marking periods, or by calendar months), listing learning activities to be included during a given period. The outline may provide only a single list of suggested activities, or may specify essential experiences and list supplementary activities for use if time permits. Table 6–4 exemplifies this type of planning.

TABLE 6–3

Seasonal Units Plan

Month	Grades 1-3	Grades 4-5	Grades 6-8
September	Ball handling skills and low-organized games	Soccer skills	Touch football (soccer for girls)
October		Lead-up games to soccer	
November	Rhythms and folk dancing	Dancing (folk, square, circle, social)	Tumbling and apparatus
December			
January	Stunts and tumbling	Gymnastic exercise and apparatus	Basketball
February			
March		Newcomb	Volleyball
April	Ball handling skills and low-organized games	Track and field	Dancing
May		Softball	Softball

TABLE 6-4

Physical Education Program for Grade Three

Sept. 1 to Nov. 15	Nov. 15 to Mar. 1	Mar. 1 to Apr. 15	Apr. 15 to May 29
I. Fundamental skills	I. Fundamental skills	I. Fundamental skills	I. Fundamental skills
II. Selected games	II. Self-testing activities	II. Self-testing activities	II. Selected games
III. Softball-type games	III. Selected games	III. Selected games	III. Ball-type games
IV. Rhythmic activities	IV. Rhythmic activities		
V. Relays			

The program for each period is outlined in further detail, as illustrated by the following guide.

PHYSICAL EDUCATION PROGRAM
GRADE THREE
Phase III: March 1 to April 15

I. Fundamental skills
  A. Jumping
    1. Jump an individual rope with partner
    2. Jump a long rope, repeating rhymes or verses
    3. Jump a long rope that is turning:
      a. Toward jumper
      b. Away from jumper
  B. Kicking
    1. Kick a soccer ball, meeting the ball with inside of foot
  C. Bowling
    1. Bowl a soccer ball at a single Indian Club at least 15 feet away

II. Self-testing activities—stunts and tumbling
  A. Cock fight
  B. Free standing
  C. Full squat
  D. Scooter
  E. Handstand
  F. Corkscrew
  G. Forward roll
  H. Backward roll
  I. Cartwheel

III. Selected games
  A. Line soccer
  B. Ball pass
  C. Hill dill
  D. Pom pom pullaway
  E. Red light
  F. Wood tag

Another way of structuring the program in this informal pattern is to schedule special events at selected intervals during the year. Interclass tournaments, schoolwide holiday programs, annual physical education demonstrations, dance festivals, field days, and similar events will motivate both the pupils and the classroom teachers to place emphasis on certain types of activities during the appropriate preparatory season. An additional means of stimulating work in specific program areas is the use of a testing program that measures individual, class, and/or school achievement in those areas. The desire to achieve recognition increases interest in developing those skills that will be tested and thus influences local curriculum emphases.

The informal plan has the advantages of flexibility and ease of integration with classroom work. Its weakness is that it may lead to no plan at all, and the program will become aimless and of relatively little value. Because of this crucial limitation, the authors do not recommend this pattern, although it is admitted that expert teachers who conscientiously avoid the pitfalls of the informal plan can work effectively with a minimum of pattern.

PATTERNS FOR ORGANIZING SECONDARY SCHOOL PHYSICAL EDUCATION CONTENT

The secondary school physical education program is typically organized on some variation of the unit plan. The major alternatives are described in the following paragraphs.

Prescribed Single Block Plan

The most common pattern for secondary school physical education is the block plan that sets up a basic sequence to be followed by all students. Usually, the students are classified according to grade level; and the curriculum is planned on a three-, four-, or six-year basis, depending upon local secondary school organization. Special classes can be offered for handicapped or restricted students, for the physically underdeveloped, for talented students, for students with special interests in physical education, for leadership training, and for other groups of pupils who have some unique common need. It is also possible to offer alternative sequences based on ability or interest groupings. But the majority of the students follow a standard curriculum. Units may vary in length. This pattern encourages definite progression in the curriculum and provides for balance, planned sequence, and student motivation. Its chief limitations arise from the wide ability ranges typical of any one grade level and the difficulties of meeting individual differences within any stand-

TABLE 6-5

Prescribed Single Block Plan
Girls' Physical Education Curriculum at Elmwood Park High School,
Elmwood Park, Illinois *

Class	First 6 Weeks: Sept. 9 to Oct. 16	Second 6 Weeks: Oct. 19 to Nov. 25	Third 6 Weeks: Nov. 30 to Jan. 22		Fourth 6 Weeks: Jan. 25 to Mar. 4		Fifth 6 Weeks: Mar. 7 to Apr. 22		Sixth 6 Weeks: Apr. 25 to June 8	
Freshman	Orientation – 1 wk. Speedaway – 4 wks. Fitness tests – 1 wk.	Basketball	Modern dance		Tumbling – 3 wks.	Alcohol, narcotics, and tobacco – 3 wks.	Apparatus – 3 wks.	Volleyball – 3 wks.	Swimming	
Sophomore	Orientation Field Hockey Fitness tests	Health	Basketball – 3 wks.	Volleyball – 3 wks.	Circle and round dance 3 wks.	Apparatus – 3 wks.	Swimming		Softball	
Junior	Orientation Tennis Fitness tests	Modern dance	Driver education		Badminton		Swimming		Archery	
Senior	Orientation Field hockey Fitness tests	First aid	Rhythmic exercise		Swimming		Volleyball – 3 wks.	Golf – 3 wks.	Badminton – 3 wks.	Softball – 3 wks.

*Material supplied through the courtesy of Miss Shirley Jameson, Chairman, Girls' Physical Education, Elmwood Park Community High School, Elmwood Park, Illinois.

ardized program. These can be offset with careful planning and expert teaching, however.

The curriculum outline, which appears as Table 6–5, is based on the prescribed single block plan. It is a daily program for a four-year high school using a six-week marking period. All units run for three-week or six-week periods. Where three-week units have been included, they are offered in pairs to facilitate evaluation and reporting individual pupil achievement. It will be noted that health and driver education are scheduled as part of the physical education curriculum.

The prescribed single block plan lends itself especially well to the small secondary school in which enrollment is too small to schedule separate physical education classes for each grade level. In this case, the curriculum is planned on a cycle basis to avoid repetition in the learning activities offered. Table 6–6 serves to illustrate this possibility.

TABLE 6–6

Cycle Program

	Freshman-Sophomore A	Freshman-Sophomore B	Junior-Senior C	Junior-Senior D
First 6 weeks	Soccer	Field hockey	Speedaway	Tennis II
Second 6 weeks	Rhythmic gymnastics	Modern dance I	Folk and square dance	Modern dance II
Third 6 weeks	Basketball I	Volleyball I	Basketball II	Volleyball II
Fourth 6 weeks	Apparatus I	Tumbling	Badminton	Apparatus II
Fifth 6 weeks	Swimming*	Swimming*	Swimming*	Swimming*
Sixth 6 weeks	Softball I	Tennis I	Softball II	Archery

* Students are classified into swimming subgroups on the basis of individual swimming skill.

Let us assume that freshmen and sophomores are scheduled together for physical education, and juniors and seniors are mixed in other physical education classes. In odd years, the A and C curricula would be offered; and in even years, the B and D curricula would be used. This would mean that freshmen who entered high school in an odd year would follow an A-B-C-D sequence; students who were classified as freshmen in the even years would experience a B-A-D-C sequence. In some instances, sequence could not be ideal; but the problems of repeating beginning work for sophomores who had had introductory units as freshmen and are then scheduled with the new freshmen the following year are minimized. If the school can schedule separate classes for freshmen and for sophomores so that only junior-senior classes need be mixed, only the junior-senior curricula would need to alternate. The individual pupil would then follow either an A-B-C-D sequence or an A-B-D-C sequence, and much more flexibility would be possible within the A and B curricula.

Concurrent Unit Plan

Some physical educators believe that higher levels of interest and motivation in a daily physical education program can be maintained if more variety is offered to students through the scheduling of two units concurrently. Thus, a junior class might take volleyball Monday, Wednesday, and Thursday, and swimming on Tuesday and Friday, throughout one six-week period or quarter. It is possible to schedule more than two units concurrently, but this is not recommended because of the difficulty of providing continuity in any unit in less than two days weekly.

The concurrent unit plan is used in some schools that include classroom work in physical education in order to avoid long periods when a given class does not have regular vigorous activity. This plan is particularly adaptable to situations in which facilities are shared as, for example, a high school in which the girls use the pool two days per week while the boys use it three days per week. The weaknesses of the concurrent unit plan are the difficulty of maintaining continuity of instruction and the increased scheduling problems.

An example of a curriculum pattern organized on the concurrent unit plan appears in Table 6-7. The program has been scheduled to coincide with six-week marking periods, although some units are conducted through two or three grade periods. It will be noted that this curriculum includes a classroom unit and a swimming unit at each grade level. In operation, this program makes optimum use of available facilities and also allows for flexible pupil grouping and team teaching for appropriate units. Adapted classes are scheduled for those requiring modifications in their physical education activities. A superior leadership program and classes with special emphasis on swimming and dance for selected juniors and seniors are also included.

Elective Plan

If students have experienced a quality physical education curriculum through the elementary and junior high school grades, it is reasonable to expect a good foundation in physical education when they enter senior high school. When this can be demonstrated, pupil election of specific physical education courses is highly desirable. An elective program multiplies possibilities for meeting individual pupil differences and tends to increase student enthusiasm for participation in physical education

TABLE 6-7

Concurrent Unit Plan
Girls' Physical Education Program, 1962–1963
J. Sterling Morton High School West, Berwyn, Illinois *

Class	First Semester			Second Semester		
	First Grade Period	Second Grade Period	Third Grade Period	Fourth Grade Period	Fifth Grade Period	Sixth Grade Period
Freshman	Health, $2x$ Track, $3x$	Health, $2x$ Rhythms, $3x$	Health, $2x$ Ball gymnastics, $3x$	Swim, $2x$ Volleyball, $3x$	Swim, $2x$ Tumbling, $3x$	Social dance, $2x$ Softball, $3x$
Sophomore	Health and driving, $2x$ Soccer, $3x$	Driving, $2x$ Rhythms, $3x$	Driving, $2x$ Apparatus, $3x$	Swim, $2x$ Basketball, $3x$	Swim, $2x$ Badminton, $3x$	Swim, $2x$ Softball, $3x$
Junior	Swim, $2x$ Speedball, $3x$	Swim, $2x$ Health, $1x$ Modern dance, $2x$	Swim, $2x$ Health, $1x$ Modern dance, $2x$	First aid, $2x$ Volleyball, $3x$	First aid, $2x$ Apparatus and trampoline, $3x$	First aid, $2x$ Tennis, $3x$
Senior	Swim, $2x$ Field hockey, $3x$	Swim, $2x$ Health, $1x$ Modern dance, $2x$	Swim, $2x$ Health, $1x$ Modern dance, $2x$	Home nursing, $2x$ Basketball, $3x$	Home nursing, $2x$ Volleyball, $3x$	Mother and baby care, $2x$ Golf, $3x$
Leadership	All fall sports	Dance Conditioning exercises	Basketball Dance	First aid Swim Apparatus Home nursing	First aid Volleyball Badminton Home nursing	Softball Tennis Golf
Two classes of life saving	Junior life saving, $2x$; soccer – dance – driving, $3x$			Jr. life saving, $2x$; first aid – volleyball – softball, $3x$		
	Senior life saving, $2x$; speedball – apparatus – dance, $3x$			Sr. life saving, $2x$; home nursing – bsktball – sftball, $3x$		
Three classes of modern dance	Classroom theory Dance			First aid and home nursing – Swim Dance		
Restricted physical education	Individual exercises Health and driving		Shuffleboard	Table tennis Balloon volleyball	Ball gymnastics Quoits	Quiet games Croquet Putting golf
				First aid – Home nursing		

x = number of times per week.
*Material supplied through the courtesy of Miss Ruth Berman, Chairman, Girls' Physical Education, J. Sterlin Morton High School West, Berwyn, Illinois.

classes. Unfortunately, it is practical to offer such a curriculum only in the larger high schools with good instructional facilities. When planning an elective curriculum, it is important that educators insure for every youth a total physical education experience that will permit and encourage him to reach all essential physical education goals.

The illustrative curriculum pattern in Table 6–8 has been used in a suburban school that has an enrollment of approximately 2,500 pupils in

TABLE 6–8

Elective Plan
Girls' Physical Education Curriculum, Oak Park-River Forest High School, Oak Park, Illinois *

First Semester	
Sept. 5 to Nov. 10	Nov. 13 to Jan. 26
Field hockey Beginning tennis Apparatus Archery Life saving Driver education	Volleyball Badminton Posture Folk dance and square dance Beginning swimming Driver education

Second Semester		
Jan. 29 to Mar. 9	Mar. 12 to Apr. 27	Apr. 30 to June 12
Basketball Posture Modern dance Synchronized swimming Health	Badminton Speedaway Modern dance Intermediate swimming Health	Tennis Softball Apparatus Archery and golf Makeup swimming

* Material supplied through the courtesy of Miss Jane Axtell, Chairman, Girls' Physical Education, Oak Park-River Forest High School, Oak Park, Illinois.

grades nine through twelve. Physical education facilities are excellent (dance studio, pool, classroom, and three gymnasiums), and highly competent teaching staffs are employed to implement the program. Students are scheduled for physical education five days per week for four years but are not classified by grade level. Course offerings are the same during each period of the school day; classification comes within the physical education department on the basis of individual student need, ability, and interest. Every student must complete certain requirements, including health, driver education, posture, swimming, dance, tennis, and team sports, during her four years in high school. Approximately 60 per cent of her physical education curriculum is truly elective.

Elective programs are possible with many pattern variations. The basic program can be carried through the ninth, tenth, or eleventh grade, allowing for student election in the final year or in the last two or three years. Thornton High School, in Harvey, Illinois, uses a unique plan, requiring a balanced basic program for the freshmen and offering a common program for all seniors, which stresses individual and dual sports and preparation for adult recreational activities. For her sophomore and junior program, each student selects two of the three alternatives (sports, dance, and aquatics).

It is recommended that secondary schools, desiring to improve provisions for meeting individual needs, plan for some student election in the physical education curriculum. Since few districts succeed in establishing a sufficiently strong foundation in eight years, it is suggested that the necessary additional requirements be included in the freshman and sophomore program, placing emphasis on elective activities for all pupils in the eleventh and twelfth grades. Elective courses should include some new activities, intermediate level work in activities that have already been introduced in the basic courses, and advanced courses for those with special interests who can meet prescribed skill requirements.

A four-year curriculum that would incorporate these recommendations is outlined in Table 6-9. In this pattern, freshmen and sophomores would follow a standard daily program, consisting of six-week units of instruction geared to elementary and intermediate skill levels. Juniors and seniors would elect courses planned on a semester basis. Each student would choose four courses during her last two years; no student would be permitted to repeat any course.

Sample Plans for Boys' Programs

The general principles of the (1) prescribed single block plan, (2) the concurrent unit plan, and the (3) elective plan have been illustrated by charts from actual girls' physical education programs in secondary schools. It is obvious that the same principles apply to boys' programs.

Tables 6-10 through 6-13 illustrate these principles further, using ongoing programs for boys in schools in various parts of the country. Each of these programs has been developed to suit local circumstances. It will be noted that not all programs include all the activities recommended earlier in this section. Of course, geographical, seasonal, weather, and facilities differences will have strong implications for local program schedule variations.

TABLE 6–9

Elective Curriculum (Junior-Senior Levels)

Class	First Semester			Second Semester		
	First 6 weeks	Second 6 weeks	Third 6 weeks	Fourth 6 weeks	Fifth 6 weeks	Sixth 6 weeks
Freshmen	Movement fundamentals	Modern dance I	Basketball I	Swimming I	Tumbling	Softball I
Sophomores	Soccer	Apparatus	Swimming II	Volleyball I	Folk dance	Tennis I
Open to all juniors and seniors*	Tennis II	Basketball II	Modern dance II	Gymnastics II	Swimming III	Softball II
	Speedaway	Swimming III	Bowling	Modern dance II	Volleyball II	Campcraft
	Archery	Recreational games	Badminton	Bowling	Fencing	Golf
Open to qualified juniors and seniors	Life saving and synchronized swimming			Life saving and synchronized swimming		
	Advanced dance (folk, square, and modern)			Advanced dance (folk, square, and modern)		
	Advanced gymnastics, tumbling, and apparatus			Advanced gymnastics, tumbling, and apparatus		
	Hockey, speedaway, and advanced volleyball			Advanced basketball, lacrosse, and advanced softball		
	Leaders class (open to selected juniors only)					
	Adapted class (for students of all grade levels according to medical examinations)					

*Each student chooses a semester sequence of three activities.

TABLE 6-10
Physical Education Program for Boys in Junior High School *

Fall Program

Seventh Grade	Weeks	Eighth Grade	Weeks	Ninth Grade	Weeks
Organization, orientation	1	Organization, orientation	1	Organization, orientation	1
Touch football	4	Touch football	4	Touch football	4
Basketball	4	Basketball	4	Basketball	4
Soccer	3	Speedball	3	Speedball	3
Gymnastics	2	Gymnastics	2	Gymnastics	2
First aid	1	First aid	1	First aid	1
Individual and dual sports	2	Individual and dual sports	2	Individual and dual sports	1
Co-ed games and/or low organized games and relays	1	Co-ed rhythms and social dance	1	Co-ed rhythms and social dance	1
				Coed games	1
Health instruction	—	Health instruction	—	Health instruction	—
Total	18	Total	18	Total	18

Spring Program

Volleyball	3	Volleyball	3	Volleyball	3
Track and field	4	Track and field	4	Track and field	4
Gymnastics	2	Gymnastics	2	Gymnastics	2
Softball	4	Softball	4	Softball	4
Swimming	2	Swimming	2	Swimming	2
Individual and dual sports	2	Individual and dual sports	2	Individual and dual sports	1
Co-ed games and/or low organized games and relays	1	Co-ed rhythms and social dance	1	Co-ed rhythms and social dance	1
				Co-ed games	1
Health instruction	—	Health instruction	—	Health instruction	—
Total	18	Total	18	Total	18

Exercises: 3–7 minutes daily. Outside apparatus: used several times per week during part of period.

* *Boys' Physical Education Teaching Guide—Junior and Senior High Schools* (Los Angeles: Los Angeles City Schools, 1960), p. 7. Lawrence E. Houston, Administrator of Physical Education, Safety, Youth Services; and Jerrod R. Russom, Supervisor, Physical Education.

TABLE 6–11

A Suggested Cycle Program of Physical Education for Junior High School Boys for One Semester

Week	Administration	Athletic Sports	Remedial and Formalized	Hygiene	Rhythmic	Testing
1	Organization, attendance, excuses, lockers		Assignments to special classes, posture, etc.	Medical excuses		
2	Records	Fundamentals, soccer, touch football, etc.	Conditioning exercises: 10–20 minutes	Showers, suit inspection	Movement to music	
3	Same	Same	Same	Same	Same	
4	Same	Same	Same	Same	Same	
5	Same	Same	Same	Same	Same	
6	Same	Same	Same	Check for daily disability	Same	Tests on sports skills
7	Same	Same	Apparatus, tumbling			Same
8	Same	Fundamentals, basketball, etc.		Same	Same	Tests on rules, strategy, etc.
9	Same	Same			Same	Same
10	Organization, attendance, etc.	Basketball, leadup games, etc.	Apparatus, tumbling, pyramids	Inspect for mental and physical changes	Same	
11	Record keeping, locker room	Same	Same	Same	Same	
12	Same	Same	Same	Same	Same	
13	Same	Boxing	Same	Same	Same	
14	Same	Obstacle course	Same	Inspection	Same	Skill tests
15	Same	Same	Same	Same	Social dance	
16	Same	Volleyball fundamentals	Same	Same	Same	
17	Same	Same	Same	Same	Same	
18	Same	Leadup games	Same	Same	Same	
19	Same	Same	Same	Same	Same	Achievement tests

TABLE 6–12

Boys' Physical Education Program, River Forest Junior High School, River Forest, Illinois *

Fall Program

Team Games—Seasonal Activities	Self-Testing
Touch football	Punt for distance and accuracy
Punt	Pass for distance and accuracy
Pass	Test on rules
Place kick	Timed stops and starts
Center snap	AAHPER fitness tests
Defensive positions	
Offensive positions	
Team play-in	
Kick-off positions	
Receiving positions	

Early Winter Program

Team Games—Seasonal Activities	Gymnastics	Rhythms	Self-Testing
Regulation volleyball	Tumbling	Square dance	Volleyball serve
Team play in increased detail	Forward roll	Social dance	Continuous volley
	Backward roll	(co-educational)	Volleyball set-up
	Headstand		Volleyball spike
	Cartwheel		
	Individual stunts		Strength tests
			Agility tests
	Trampoline		Flexibility tests
	Knee drop		AAHPER tests
	Seat drop		
	Combinations		
	Pirouette		
	Tuck bounce		
	Swivel hips		
	Turntable		
	Flips		
	Stall bars		
	Horizontal bar		
	Rope climb		

Late Winter Program

Team Games—Seasonal Activities	Gymnastics	Wrestling	Self-Testing
Regulation basketball	Tumbling	Standing holds	Two-minute shooting tests (basketball)
Team play in increased detail	Forward roll	Mat holds	
	Backward roll	Wrestling rules	
Offensive position and play	Headstand	Legal holds	Lay-up shot
	Cartwheel	Illegal holds	Set shot
	Individual stunts		Continuous dribble

* Material supplied through the courtesy of Mr. Robert Skinner, Jr., Physical Education Instructor, River Forest Junior High School, River Forest, Illinois.

TABLE 6–12—Continued

Team Games—Seasonal Activities	Gymnastics	Wrestling	Self-Testing
	Late Winter Program (continued)		
Defensive position and play Basketball games	Isometrics Trampoline Knee drop Seat drop Combinations Pirouette Tuck bounce Swivel hips Turntable Flips Stall bars Horizontal bar Rope climb		Free throw shooting Basketball rules AAHPER tests Strength tests Agility tests Flexibility tests

Team Games—Seasonal Activities	Track and Field	Self-Testing
	Spring Program	
Softball Advanced fundamentals Team play and strategy Defensive positions Offensive positions Batting stance Bunting Selective field hitting	Relays Dashes Running broad jump High jump 12″ ball throw	Softball throw for distance and accuracy Timed base-running High jump for height Broad jump for distance AAHPER tests

TABLE 6–13

1961–1962 Boys' Physical Education Program, New Trier Township High School, Winnetka, Illinois

Class	First Quarter (44 days)	Second Quarter (43 days)	Third Quarter (43 days)	Fourth Quarter (46 days)
Freshman	Orientation Swimming I (20) Conditioning and posture (19) Basketball and testing (5)	Basketball I (26) Wrestling I (17)	Gymnastics I (18) Indoor track I (25)	Badminton and Tennis I (24) Soccer I (12) Softball I (10)
Sophomore	Orientation (5) Touch football I (15) Badminton and tennis II (24)	Gymnastics II (26) Volleyball I (9) Indoor track II (8)	Wrestling II (18) Basketball II and testing (25)	Swimming II (24) Softball II (12) Soccer II (10)
Junior	Orientation (5) Soccer III and weight training (15) Swimming III (24)	Wrestling III (13) Track relays I (13) Basketball III and handball (17)	Volleyball II (9) Weight training and testing (9) Gymnastics III (25)	Outdoor track I (10) Speedball I (14) Badminton and tennis III (22)
Senior	Orientation (5) Badminton and tennis IV (15) Touch football II (24)	Track relays II (13) Wrestling IV (13) Gymnastics IV (17)	Basketball IV and handball (18) Volleyball III (12) Weight training and testing (13)	Softball III (24) Swimming IV (19)

The Adapted Physical Education program is not included in the above chart.

CONTENT SELECTION AND ORGANIZATION

A high school in another part of the country lists its yearly progression in activities for boys as follows:

Tenth Grade	Eleventh Grade	Twelfth Grade
Team sports	Team sports	Team sports
Tumbling and gymnastics	Trampoline	Trampoline
Decathlon	Tumbling	Badminton
Co-educational:	Badminton	Ping-pong
dancing	Ping-pong	Tennis
softball	Decathlon	Archery
volleyball	Co-educational:	Decathlon
	advanced dancing	Co-educational:
	softball	advanced dancing
	volleyball	tennis
		archery

Another high school developed a program that features a "Sports Core," as shown in Table 6–14. This program obviously does not include experiences in the various physical education activity areas other than sports. Neither does it indicate an evaluation phase nor co-educational opportunities. It fails to show progression from beginning and elemen-

TABLE 6–14
Sports-Core Curriculum

Month	Tenth Grade	Eleventh Grade	Twelfth Grade
September	Health	Health	Health
October	Touch football	Touch football	Touch football
November	Touch football Soccer– Speedball	Touch football Soccer– Speedball	Touch football Soccer– Speedball
December	Games and relays	Games and relays	Games and relays
January	Basketball	Basketball	Basketball
February	Volleyball Basketball	Volleyball Basketball	Volleyball Basketball
March	Wrestling Boxing Tumbling	Wrestling Boxing Tumbling	Wrestling Boxing Tumbling
April	Track and field	Track and field	Track and field
May	Softball	Softball	Softball
June	Softball	Softball	Softball

tary levels of skill to intermediate and advanced performance.

Many schools now have a physical fitness emphasis in their programs. An example follows:

Week	Program
1st	Preschool teacher workshop and institute.
2d	Issue lockers. WHITES: Basic swimming strokes. REDS AND BLUES: Age, height, grade recording. Games.
3d	WHITES: Swimming instruction. Fitness swim tests. REDS: Military drills. Conditioning exercises. Ranger drills. BLUES: Conditioning exercises. Ranger exercises. Flagball.
4th	WHITES: Military drill. Conditioning and ranger exercises. REDS: Exercises. League flagball. BLUES: Exercises. League flagball.
5th	WHITES: Exercises. League flagball. Basketball. REDS: Water safety. BLUES: Fitness tests. League games.
6th	WHITES: Fitness tests. League games, flagball, basketball. REDS: Fitness tests. League games. BLUES: Fitness tests. League games.
7th	WHITES: Fitness tests. League games. REDS: Fitness tests. League games. BLUES: Fitness swim tests. League games.

End of first quarter grading period.

8th	WHITES: League games in flagball, basketball, volleyball. REDS: Fitness tests. League games. BLUES: League games.
9th	WHITES: League games. REDS: League games. BLUES: Football decathlon.
10th	WHITES: League games. REDS: Basketball decathlon. BLUES: Football decathlon.
11th	WHITES: Football decathlon. REDS: Basketball decathlon. BLUES: League games.
12th	WHITES: Football decathlon. REDS: League games. BLUES: Basketball decathlon.
13th	WHITES: League games. REDS: Football decathlon. BLUES: Basketball decathlon.
14th	WHITES: League games. REDS: Football decathlon. BLUES: League games.

End of second quarter grading period and end of the first semester.

The program for the second semester is planned in a similar manner. This program is heavily weighted with physical fitness exercises and tests and is supplemented with league games in a variety of sports. Testing also includes decathlon events in certain sports. The program devotes very little attention to skills instruction other than in the physical fitness testing events and exercises. It does not include co-educational activities.

CONTENT SELECTION AND ORGANIZATION

It is quite limited in the individual and dual sports activities that have carryover value for future years. It does produce excellent results in physical fitness tests and provides a differentiated program for three groups of pupils whose assignments to the various color groups depend primarily upon physical fitness test results.

Thus, the preceding examples show how individual schools build their physical education curriculum with differing emphases on objectives, which clearly are reflected in the types of activities planned in the yearly program.

The authors believe that the program should seek to attain a balance in progress toward the achievement of all physical education objectives, that it should be planned as an articulated program with built-in progression, and that it should emphasize instruction and evaluation. This book presents many suggestions for planning and conducting physical education programs in such a manner.

CO-EDUCATIONAL PROGRAMS IN PHYSICAL EDUCATION

Co-educational activities should be included in the physical education program for all boys and girls in elementary, junior and senior high school years. One of the important objectives of physical education is the social one. The development of social relationships and desirable social habits and attitudes is an area in which physical education can make a significant contribution. Boys and girls can learn to understand each other better and to gain greater respect for members of the opposite sex. Boys and girls are participating together in most of life's activities and soon will be starting homes of their own after leaving school. Sports, dance, and other recreational activities provide an excellent medium for such development and understanding. In addition, there will be many opportunities for social and recreational participation as family members and members of mixed groups throughout life. The case for co-educational activities in physical education seems clear. Exactly how such programs should be organized and conducted is a more controversial subject.

Activities should be selected in which boys and girls most naturally engage together during leisure time. Social, square, and folk dances are typically a part of such programs. Several sports can be enjoyed on a co-educational basis, such as golf, tennis, bowling, softball, volleyball, badminton, and archery. Swimming, diving, and other forms of aquatics are desirable co-educational activities. Tumbling, stunts, and trampoline, when properly selected and taught, are activities that interest many boys and girls.

The rules of some of the above activities may have to be adapted for co-educational use. The selection of team members must be carefully managed, and the caliber of performance must be considered so that some pupils are not placed in a position of ridicule for inept performance.

Some schools provide the co-educational opportunity on an elective basis. Only pupils who desire to participate in such activities are in the program. Teachers attempt to encourage recalcitrant students to "try it." The personal interest and the enthusiasm of the teachers are important factors in attaining a large voluntary attendance in such a program. It is highly desirable for members of the men's and women's physical education departments to share equally in the leadership and teaching of such programs.

Other schools have a compulsory requirement in co-educational activities but provide a number of options among which the pupil may make a choice. For example, perhaps each Friday will be designated as co-educational day and the following activities will be made available: swimming, volleyball, social dance, and tennis. Each student makes his selection of one activity, and he or she must remain in this activity for the duration of that co-educational block, which might be for a quarter (eight weeks), or even for a semester. In this way, a student who objects to being required to dance, or whose religious belief prohibits dancing, has the alternative of participating in another activity. The authors believe in this type of flexibility rather than a strict requirement with no alternatives open to the individual student.

It is believed that co-educational experiences are extremely desirable and should be included in the physical education program of all students. It may not be essential to require co-educational classes of each student each year; but some policy of regular, periodic co-educational activities should be followed. Opportunity for additional participation on an elective basis should be possible for students so desiring.

Space prohibits detailed discussion of the planning and administration of co-educational programs at every grade level. Dexter provides an excellent source of suggestions for this program.[2] The preceding charts of junior and senior high school programs indicate several ways in which co-educational activities can be scheduled, and they also indicate the types of activities these schools believe to be most appropriate.

The authors believe that the co-educational program is an essential phase of the total physical education program at each educational level. It is a phase that all too frequently is omitted from the physical education curriculum of American junior and senior high schools.

[2] Genevie Dexter (ed.), *Teachers Guide to Physical Education for Girls in High School* (Sacramento: California State Department of Education, 1957), pp. 273–83.

INTRAMURAL, EXTRAMURAL, INTERSCHOLASTIC, AND SCHOOL RECREATION PROGRAMS

The complete physical education program includes a voluntary intramural sports program available to any boy or girl. This program should include many of the activities of the required physical education program. It may include additional activities that are popular with the participants. Teams of comparable ability are organized into leagues as a basis for competition and to heighten interest. Details of organization, schedules, officiating, awards, eligibility, and essential elements in the program are described at length in the physical education literature and are readily available to personnel responsible for such programs.

Many schools provide an extension of the intramural program through extramural competition, wherein the winning intramural teams compete against similar intramural winners from neighboring schools. Other forms of extramural competition are possible in the way of sports days, play days, invitational meets, telegraphic tournaments, postal tournaments, aquatic arts competition, and so forth.

Interscholastic athletic competition for the talented and gifted students in physical education is a well-known program to all. It does not need further elaboration here as to organization and conduct. However, it is the apex of the total physical education curriculum, broadly conceived, and should be regarded as one of the several essential elements in the total school physical education curriculum.

The school recreation program is closely related to the physical education curriculum and its objectives, and hence should be mentioned in any consideration of the total physical education curriculum. More accurately, the physical recreation program of the school, which is one phase of the total school recreation program, has the closest relationship to the physical education curriculum. This program should provide widespread opportunity for all students to participate regularly and enjoyably on a voluntary basis in a variety of sports, games, rhythmics, exercises, aquatics, and similar activities. The school program should be closely integrated with the total community recreation program. In these programs, students have opportunity to practice skills and activities learned in the physical education classes. They have opportunity to participate more extensively in activities of their choice than is possible in the daily class. Students can organize their own groups and can determine the amount and extent of practice and participation they desire. There are many direct and concomitant social, physical, and emotional outcomes possible from this physical recreation program.

CONTINUITY IN PHYSICAL EDUCATION PROGRAMS

Suggestions have been made throughout this chapter for organizing curriculum experiences in physical education. In attempting to focus upon several specific aspects of the problem, one can easily lose sight of the vital importance of maintaining continuity in the total physical education program. Physical education should be skillfully guided toward the achievement of varied educational goals, but the differing learning activities and teaching methods used must result in a unified over-all experience for the pupils. A program organized as a series of sport, gymnastic, aquatic, and rhythmic activities units must be planned and conducted so as to provide students with continuous physical education learnings. Practices designed to adapt instruction to the divergent needs of many individual students must be interwoven with threads of continuity. Co-educational learning experiences must be well integrated into the over-all educational plan. Interrelationships among instructional classes, intramural activities, and interscholastic programs must support continuity of learning experience. Physical education curricula in secondary schools must be more effectively articulated with local elementary school physical education programs.

Continuity of learning experience or effective articulation of learning activities is of vital importance to all school children and youth. Carefully selected lesson content and high quality instruction will fail to achieve optimum results if problems of articulation exist. Children who face unnecessary and undesirable barriers to learning cannot achieve their own objectives or the school's objectives in the most efficient manner possible. The school "has a responsibility to provide conditions and experiences that nurture the continuity of individual growth within a framework that also fosters continuity for groups."[3]

How is continuity of learning experience achieved? Continuity may be achieved through consistent application of the fundamental principles of child development and learning. Individual readiness for learning must be recognized as an important factor. The necessity for relating new materials to familiar experiences and situations should guide planning of transitions between daily lessons and from each learning unit to the succeeding unit. Review activities to reinforce learning play an important role. Essential orientation must be included in beginning the program on a new grade level. Considerations of individual pupil needs for personal security may result in a wide variety of thoughtfully struc-

---

[3] Association for Supervision and Curriculum Development, *A Look at Continuity in the School Program* (Washington, D.C.: National Education Association, 1958), p. 177.

tured orientation activities. Appropriate procedures for grouping pupils may have a significant bearing on learning continuity.

Continuity may also result from wise selection of educational objectives. Ultimate objectives are the same at all levels; genuine and persistent effort to progress toward these goals will strengthen the continuity of learning experience. Physical education activities directed toward the development of individual fitness should be selected to reach specific strength, flexibility, and endurance objectives at any given point in the pupil's experience. At the same time, the relationship of daily objectives to over-all fitness goals will enhance learning continuity. Ultimate objectives in the mental, social-emotional, and recreational spheres can similarly be used to provide continuity for the group as well as the individual pupil.

A third approach to developing continuity is through curriculum content. A continuing concern of everyday living, throughout the school years and beyond, is the need to understand one's potential for movement, to learn to control one's body in movement through space and in relation to other objects, to acquire the skills of balancing relaxation and activity, and to develop individual ability for self-expression through movement. The physical education curriculum that consists of appropriately sequential experiences in movement education will improve continuity for individual learners. Content should be organized in terms of key concepts and basic movement skills. These can be developed through an extensive variety of physical education activities. It is essential, however, that key movement concepts guide the selection of specific experiences in the different areas of sports, gymnastics, aquatics, and dance. Teachers must stress the common movement fundamentals used in building skills in these specialized activities. The end result should be a total physical education in which continuity of learning is experienced through emphasis on key movement concepts.

The responsibility of the individual teacher for improvements in learning continuity cannot be overemphasized. This challenge is well stated in the 1958 Yearbook of the Association for Supervision and Curriculum Development:

A large proportion of children's barriers to learning progress appears within the framework of the individual teacher's study of the situation, study of the child or children, study of his own teaching objectives, study of his own teaching methods, study of his own concepts of the curriculum to be developed with children. . . . Whoever you are, wherever you work in the education of boys and girls, begin where you are to do your share in helping them to make steadier, more continuous progress toward educational goals which you and they recognize as good for them and good for the society in which they live.[4]

[4] *Ibid.*, pp. 267–70.

7

Teaching Values

Curriculum workers have studied a wide variety of educational problems in recent decades. Educational research specialists have designed and conducted many projects. Administrators have supported many experimental plans. Teachers have taken many approaches in their efforts to improve the learning experiences of children and youth. But few have given much serious study to the problem of more effective methods of teaching values. There has been a tendency to bypass this vitally important area because of the difficulties that compound scientific investigation of personality and character development. The authors contend that the teaching of values is among the most crucial of current curriculum problems and that it is therefore important to delineate the nature of the problem and to focus attention on possible approaches open to teachers for guiding the development of desired student values.

SIGNIFICANCE OF THE PROBLEM

It has been amply demonstrated that adaptations in our social institutions and advances in the field of human relations have been unable to keep pace with advances in the physical sciences and technology. The value crisis in our culture has been discussed extensively. Studies of American prisoners of war in Korea have provided evidence that inability to sustain traditional values was common. Increasing rates of crime, juvenile delinquency, illegitimacy, alcoholism, and drug addiction suggest serious breakdowns in individual value systems under peacetime conditions as well. Flagrant violations of public confidence in almost unbelievable instances of corruption, graft, and improper influence by those in high office have been widely publicized. Widespread public acceptance of deceptive advertising practices, dishonesty in television programs, academic irregularities, and governmental irresponsibility reflect serious challenges to our basic values.

Maslow asserts that "the value-illnesses which result from valuelessness . . . are far more important for the fate of the world than the classical neuroses or even the psychoses."[1] A study of history and of the power struggles among leading states teaches us that civilizations fall because of lack of moral vitality. Disintegration of moral and ethical values saps the internal strength that makes nations great. The preservation and improvement of our democratic society depend upon the participation of individual citizens committed to our traditional basic democratic values. Leaders at all levels have expressed concern for stabilizing and strengthening individual values. Early in his administration, President Kennedy called for re-examination of our national goals. He repeatedly asked Americans to consider what each, as an individual citizen, can do for his country.

Sports constitute a significant aspect of American culture. Sports reflect the values of individual participants and of the spectators whose participation is less active, but nonetheless real. The conduct of sports may also shape the values of individual participants and spectators. Not surprisingly, the current national value crisis is evident in the realm of sports, in recruiting abuses, "fixing" game outcomes, unethical coaching techniques, and questionable training procedures. Physical educators who hope to play a role in the development of individual value systems must understand how values are learned. Although there are many unresolved questions in this area, including some of vital importance, it behooves us to take cognizance of the best current knowledge.

Peck, Havighurst, and associates have described "basic character" in five developmental stages in the attainment of psychological and moral maturity.[2] These categories can serve as a basis for identifying major developmental tasks faced by the individual in achieving an appropriate adult pattern of moral behavior. Although individual variations are numerous, these types correspond generally to the successive developmental periods of infancy, early childhood, middle childhood, later childhood, and adolescence and adulthood. In actuality, a given individual is apt to demonstrate characteristics of more than one type. In many instances, development is arrested at one of the lower levels; we recognize these individuals as persons who have never succeeded in reaching moral

---

[1] Abraham H. Maslow, *Toward a Psychology of Being* (Princeton, N.J.: D. Van Nostrand Co., Inc., 1962), p. 192.
[2] Robert F. Peck, Robert J. Havighurst, *et al.*, *The Psychology of Character Development* (New York: John Wiley & Sons, Inc., 1960).

maturity. The five categories as conceptualized by Peck, Havighurst, and associates are:

Amoral . . . He has no internalized moral principles, no conscience or superego. He feels no need to control his personal impulses, and exhibits no control. His impulses may or may not be actively *immoral*, antisocial, or destructive in intent; but in any case he disregards the moral connotations and consequences of his behavior. . . .

Expedient A person of this type is primarily self-centered, and considers other people's welfare and reactions only in order to gain his personal ends. . . . He behaves in ways his society defines as moral, only so long as it suits his purpose. . . .

Conforming This kind of person has one general, internalized principle: to do what others do, and what they say one "should" do. He wants to and does conform to all the rules of his group. He wants to do what others do, and his only anxiety is for possible disapproval. . . . It differs from the expedient approach in that social conformity is accepted as good for its own sake. . . .

Irrational-Conscientious This is the person who judges a given act according to his own internal standard of right and wrong. . . . An act is "good" or "bad" to him because he defines it as such, not necessarily because it has positive or negative effects on others. . . .

Rational-Altruistic . . . Such a person not only has a stable set of moral principles by which he judges and directs his own action; he objectively assesses the results of an act in a given situation, and approves it on the grounds of whether or not it serves others as well as himself. . . .[3]

It is generally agreed that the first decade of life is crucial in the formulation of basic values. Within his own family circle, the child's values are significantly influenced by his relationships with each parent and by the values held by others in the family group. According to Jacob, "The conscience of the growing child is largely introjected from the disciplinarian of the family, and this conscience becomes consolidated as an 'institution' of the mind at a fairly late stage of development." [4]

While recognizing that the first decade of life is the period of fastest growth in the development of values, as in other aspects of growth, many authorities hold that the value system of the individual is not in any final sense determined at any given age. Arsenian states:

Values and value systems of individuals grow and change with the full operation of the principle of individual differences: the value systems in some individuals cease their development early, and others continue for a life time; in some the value systems engage but few parochial or provincial loyalties; in some the value system is rigid and rule bound, in others it is flexible and bound only by broad humanitarian principles.[5]

[3] *Ibid.*, pp. 5–8.
[4] Joseph S. Jacob, "Psychiatric Views on the Development and Utilization of Value Systems," in *Values in Sports* (Washington, D.C.: AAHPER, 1963), p. 18.
[5] Seth Arsenian, unpublished portion of a paper read at the Joint National Conference of the DGWS and the DMA at Interlochen, Michigan, June 19, 1963.

Recent studies of American college students, summarized and reported by Webster, Freedman, and Heist,[6] lend support to the position that important changes in personal values *do* occur beyond early childhood. Among the changes that take place in students during college are "changes in interests, which are often accompanied by changed attitudes toward the self and the world. And in some cases there are more fundamental personality changes, accompanied by the emergence of new values."[7]

Although the weight of evidence indicates that basic character is shaped to a significant degree by interpersonal relationships and experiences within the family circle, the research in this field offers hope for educating persons to undergo value changes at all age levels. Certain key factors in influencing values have been identified. Above all, such education must be personalized. Learning experiences must be meaningful in terms of the student's own self-concept and must be guided by instructors who demonstrate warmth toward individual students and consistent, clearly expressed values. The educational environment must be stimulating as well as supportive. The individual must be confronted with value issues and encouraged in the process of re-examining his values by adults who communicate faith in his ability to grow toward moral maturity.

What is the school's responsibility for teaching values? This question is frequently raised and is seldom answered with unanimity of opinion. The public school is only one of several social institutions concerned with the growth and development of American citizens. Yet it provides the living and learning environment for American children and youth during a large segment of their lives. Thus, it influences the value systems of individuals. Teachers and administrators have a clear-cut responsibility to assure that the school's impact upon individual values will be in a positive direction. Furthermore, as society's designated agent for maintaining, transmitting, and improving our culture, the public school has a responsibility to maximize its influence and to strengthen its contribution toward the development of democratic value systems.

Every phase of the school curriculum must accept a share of this responsibility. Physical education has unique potentialities for personalizing education in order to affect individual values. Because students typically interrelate with each other in active game situations, opportunities for structuring value orientations are extensive. Since physical education experiences tend to focus the student's attention upon the conditioning

---

[6] Harold Webster, Marvin B. Freedman, and Paul Heist, "Personality Changes in College Students," Chapter 24 in N. Sanford *et al.*, *The American College* (New York: John Wiley & Sons, Inc., 1962).

[7] *Ibid.*, p. 811.

and effective use of his body, they may have a significant impact upon his body image and his self-concept. Competitive sports engage the student's whole being, his emotions as well as his body and mind. For these reasons, physical education has tremendous possibilities for facilitating self-actualization and for teaching personal values. It is of vital consequence that we capitalize fully upon these opportunities to contribute to the development of individual values.

Many difficulties confront educators in their attempts to guide students in building sound and stable value systems. One of our most basic limitations is that most of our work as teachers is done under conditions that do not emphasize one-to-one relationships. We are working with individuals but they are in groups. We must use approaches that are effective with groups.

Furthermore, many of us have yet to clarify our own values. The coach whose own value system is confused and inconsistent cannot favorably influence individual player values. Have we as physical educators accepted the responsibility for guiding individuals in achieving a satisfactory body image? Do we understand the difference between working for excellence in performance and striving to defeat opponents? Have we established a hierarchy of values to provide guidelines for resolving value conflicts? Do we really know which values are of the greatest consequence?

In addition, we are beset by measurement problems. The complex nature of human behavior has discouraged many investigators who have sought to describe the underlying orientation in an individual's personality and to identify the generalized tendencies that integrate his particular attitudes and values. Acceptable techniques for assessing personal values are limited. Instruments validated on representative "normal" populations are scarce. Clinical data and behavior sampling data are much more useful than paper-and-pencil-type test results but much harder to secure. The collection of longitudinal data is crucial in measuring changes in values but is tedious, time-consuming, expensive, and difficult.

Equally important, we must still resolve questions regarding approaches to the teaching of values. It is the authors' view that we should stop debating and get on with research that will lead us toward more effective teaching in this important field. Let us not argue the relative potential for teaching values in school as compared to other areas of living or at other age levels; let each of us do what he can at the point at which he is working. We should use both direct and indirect methods wherever each is appropriate. Let us explore various approaches and use them in whatever combinations bring best results.

UNIQUE RESPONSIBILITIES OF PHYSICAL EDUCATION

The emphasis in this chapter is upon physical education's place in the curriculum in relation to the educational goal of building a sound moral and ethical code of behavior. Before turning to a discussion of several approaches to teaching values, it seems wise to call attention to certain values that are of unique concern to the physical educator. It is assumed that educators with professional training in this area will make specific contributions in teaching these values.

Physical education fulfills a significant role in teaching youth to respect the complex and marvelous physiological functioning of the healthy human body, to value its optimum fitness, and to strive to gain and maintain positive dynamic health. Through participation in physical education classes and in intramural and extramural sports, the individual should establish the habit of regular exercise and active recreation. He should learn to appreciate the value of exercise in "the development of greater efficiency and reserve capacity in the cardiovascular and pulmonary systems; the preservation of ideal body weight and contours; the prevention of degenerative disease states; the provision of muscular strength and coordination adequate for normal work loads; and the prolongation of life."[8] He should also learn to protect himself from sports injuries and other accidental effects of exercise.

Physical education should also teach the place of physical performance activities in self-actualization. Physical recreation should be healthful, joyful, and integrative. A physical performance that represents genuine achievement to the individual participant can be a "peak experience" that helps him toward self-actualization. This implies an elementary school physical education program that develops a sense of body mastery and that provides a solid foundation in fundamental movement, permitting recognition of many types of individual achievement at this level, as well as providing the basis for greater achievement at more advanced levels. It demands a secondary school program with enough variety of activities for selection of a medium for successful participation and self-expression, and sufficient depth. It includes concern for the developing self-image, stimulation to achieve a satisfying level of performance, and guidance in appreciating appropriate masculine and feminine roles in sports participation. It requires emphasis upon maximum effort, not to win at any cost, but to achieve excellence of performance.

A third area in which physical educators should assume a major re-

[8] Allan J. Ryan, "Contributions of Sports and Athletics to Physical Well-Being," in *Values in Sports* (Washington, D.C.: AAHPER, 1963), p. 41.

sponsibility is in teaching values associated with competitive sports and games. This point has been effectively summarized by Malpass:

> The values of competition are significant. Competition can be used to further allegiance to group ideals and thus to strengthen the existing group as well as the individual. Competition can be a means of teaching cooperation, responsibility, respect for property and person, and other social virtues the group wishes to perpetuate. Competition can also be used to teach the pursuit of excellence in performance. . . . We have said that competition is a desirable social value when its chief aim is excellence in performance; . . . conflict typically occurs when rules for competition are disregarded and opponent degradation supersedes striving for excellence; . . . intra-group cooperation encourages more effective effort in inter-group competition.[9]

The physical education teacher and coach is in the key position to guide students in learning these values.

LEARNING VALUES BY IMITATION

Values are learned by experience and by imitation. It has long been recognized that an individual's values reflect those of the persons who have played significant roles during the formative stages of his life. As a child matures, he seeks to define his own identity through a process of viewing himself as like others in his environment, trying out behaviors that they demonstrate, and incorporating his perceptions and understandings of their behaviors into his own image. Parents, teachers, and other adult leaders impart values to young people through personal example. What teachers are as persons is frequently more important to their pupils than the subject matter of their courses. Youth identify with adults whom they admire and absorb their attitudes. The coach and physical educator may well be influential in the development and modification of values because of the enthusiasm of students for sports, gymnastics, and dance activities, and their keen desire to be successful participants. Thus, the importance of being a model worth emulating can scarcely be overestimated. The physical education teacher must set a fine personal example, while expressing spontaneous human qualities and warmth in his relationships with others. He needs to treat all of his pupils as individuals and to communicate interest, concern, and faith in them in his non-verbal responses as well as in his spoken instructions and conversations.

The teacher who seeks to influence values can increase his effectiveness through insight and skill in empathizing with students. He puts himself into the pupil's own world and sees the situation through his eyes, in order to understand him better. He is able to accept the pupil as he is.

---

[9] Leslie F. Malpass, "Competition, Conflict, and Cooperation as Social Values," in *Values in Sports* (Washington, D.C.: AAHPER, 1963), pp. 61–65.

With more accurate knowledge of the other person, he is able to utilize his instructional and guidance skills to the student's greater benefit. In order to develop empathy, the teacher must learn to know himself. The adult who understands his own needs, values, weaknesses, and prejudices will be more successful in understanding the needs and aspirations of individual boys and girls and in teaching them desired values. He is more likely to be emulated by his pupils. The broader his own interests and experiences, the better will be his opportunity for empathizing with students of varying backgrounds, abilities, and personalities.

Much is required of the effective teacher. To *know* himself is not enough. He must also *be* himself. The child or youth in search of his own identity incorporates the behaviors of significant adults with whom he lives, works, and plays. The teacher or adult leader must behave consistently and without artificiality; he must "be himself" in order to minimize communication barriers and to establish a foundation of trust so vital for the understanding and sympathetic guidance of youth.

Many teachers who express the conviction that their responsibilities include teaching values fall back upon "incidental teaching" as the chief method. Incidental teaching depends upon learning by imitation. The pupil learns values incidental to the instructional goals toward which the teacher is aiming. But this method relegates values to a secondary position and does not guarantee instruction in all areas essential to the development of adequate value systems. For this reason, the authors underscore the importance of the teacher's personal example for learning values but insist that other avenues for teaching values should be explored.

STUDYING VALUES AS SUBJECT CONTENT

All thinking persons agree that values are not acquired simply by talking about them. An individual cannot be said to be committed to a given value unless he acts in accordance with it. Personal values have significance only in terms of the behavior patterns through which they are expressed.

But does this mean that it is foolish to define specific values, to intellectualize value concepts, and to discuss value questions with students? Certainly not. If teachers hope to influence student values, to effect changes in behavior based on modifications of existing value systems, an essential first step is to define the desired values in behavioral terms with the students. The teacher is not limited to the lecture method in presenting information about culturally sanctioned values. He is free to select from his entire repertory of teaching techniques. But the students must acquire certain knowledges and understandings. They cannot learn efficiently ways of behaving that have not been made clear to them. In discussing education for values and feelings, Taba makes the following statement:

> In view of what has been said about the inconsistencies and pluralities of value orientations in our culture, a special task of education regarding values might also be that of integration and conceptualization. This conceptualization may very well become the basis for the new ethics based on scientific knowledge of man and of society which was referred to earlier as a current need. In a culture such as ours, with many contradictions and ambiguities, individuals need systematic aid in clarifying the contradictions and in making conscious the many emotional habits which the culture implants on an irrational and unconscious level.[10]

In concluding presentation of this topic, however, she cautions the reader as follows:

> . . . changes in the content of curriculum need to be accompanied by alterations in the conditions under which learning occurs. These include the character of discipline, the quality of interpersonal relations, the degree of attention to individual needs, and the nature of motivational devices used.[11]

The public schools do not list courses in moral and spiritual values in their curriculum guides. And yet there is practically unanimous agreement that the schools have a responsibility for teaching democratic values. Is there a place for direct instruction in this field? The authors maintain that the school curriculum should be organized to include a minimum of direct teaching in this area and that the knowledges that students acquire through direct instruction should be continuously reinforced by commitment to these values in administration of the informal curriculum as well as the formal curriculum and by personal examples set by faculty members.

Direct instruction in the values that enrich democratic living can be offered to physical education students in a variety of ways. In some instances, classroom discussions may be scheduled to deal with topics of this nature. It seems appropriate to provide orientation to a new group of elementary school students to physical education class regulations, for example. The teacher may list and explain the procedures to be followed and then guide pupil discussion of the specific underlying reasons. Why should you follow these procedures for sharing equipment? Why should everyone listen carefully to directions? Why should each person accept the position assigned by his squad leader?

In introducing a unit in the secondary school program, it might be appropriate to discuss the importance of putting maximum effort into the

[10] Hilda Taba, *Curriculum Development: Theory and Practice* (New York: Harcourt, Brace & World, Inc., 1962), p. 69.
[11] *Ibid.*, p. 70.

execution of conditioning exercises, the value of striving for excellence of performance in apparatus stunts, and the need for learning to appreciate the creative contributions of other class members. Most well-planned units of instruction in physical education do include some topics that are value oriented. Sports etiquette, responsibilities of officials, spectator behavior, and defensive strategy are examples. Consideration of these topics affords opportunity for direct instruction and class study of the appropriate values.

Frequently, specific instances of questionable behavior occurring in the class situation give rise to instruction directed toward the learning of certain values. Arguments as to which of two opponents fouled, taunting of children who are unsuccessful in meeting a given skill challenge, sulky or vengeful losers, failures to admit being tagged, starting before the signal to begin, and unacknowledged line violations are familiar to all physical educators. Direct instruction in these situations may be considered "incidental teaching," but it should not be purely accidental or unplanned. Any experienced teacher will anticipate common problem situations in which individual values will be tested. If his objectives for a given class group include specific attitude and behavior goals, he will plan instruction to maximize the probability of certain experiences and plan appropriate techniques for utilizing these learning situations most effectively when they arise.

Illustrative subject content that might be stressed in physical education classes includes the concept of society as "we" rather than "they"; the relationship of cooperation to competition; appropriate competitive behavior in different activity situations; concepts of success and failure and the values to be gained from experiencing each; the meanings of true "maleness" and "femaleness"; and specific sports and games behaviors manifesting the general values of courage, perseverance, integrity, friendliness, responsibility, and cooperativeness. Many teaching techniques can be utilized. The following examples may suggest varied possibilities. Most of them can be adapted for students of different age levels and abilities. They can utilize the unique possibilities of almost any sports, gymnastics, or rhythmic learning activity. They should give rise to other creative approaches to direct instruction in the teaching of values.

1. Prior to election of new squad leaders, the teacher guides a class discussion of the responsibilities of a squad leader, the responsibilities of squad members in working with their leader, and how to identify in individual class members the qualities of a good squad leader.

2. A school sportsmanship code is formulated through suggestions drawn from each of the physical education classes. Class representatives

are elected to a committee to draft a proposal for submission to the student council.

3. The physical education teacher presents to his classes an outline of qualifications for selection of pupils for the school playground patrol. These are discussed with the class, and students are encouraged to make written application for consideration by the student council.

4. Students are invited to play roles in a dramatic incident in which a member of the visiting football team charges that the referee failed to call several personal fouls committed by members of the winning home team and a fight ensues. The behavior of the play characters is analyzed with the class, with emphasis on the underlying values expressed through specific behaviors observed.

5. A fifth-grade group sets up standards for behavior in its physical education class. Five class members are selected to serve on a class committee charged with the responsibility of enforcing these regulations.

6. A national scandal involving the acceptance of bribes by college basketball players is made the subject of discussion in a high school physical education class.

7. Fourth-grade pupils are asked to set behavioral goals that they will work toward in the physical education class, e.g., "winning a game without bragging or making unkind remarks," "beginning warmup work without being reminded," and "keeping hands off other pupils and their property." At six-week intervals, each student is asked to score himself on how he usually acts as regards each of these goals.

8. In a high school girls' field hockey class, during game play for which class members have been assigned as student officials, a wing receives a pass after the ball has crossed the side boundary line. Realizing that the umpire is too far away to see the play well, she continues to dribble toward the goal. Her opponent stops pursuit when she realizes the ball is out-of-bounds and objects to a subsequent call of a foul on one of her teammates, arguing that the ball was already out of bounds. The teacher stops play and guides the entire class in analyzing appropriate behavior for each class member in this situation.

9. A sixth-grade class plans and conducts a track meet for all boys and girls in grades four, five, and six, including selection of events, rules governing entries, procedures for individual qualification, and duties of student officials.

10. A junior high school group plans for a districtwide basketball tournament, setting up a round-robin tournament schedule, local ground rules, regulations governing substitution of players, conditions governing participation, and guidelines for serving as good hosts as well as appropriate conduct for guests visiting in neighboring schools.

11. An elementary school teacher particularly interested in developing cooperative behavior sets up a progression of experiences for his students. From teacher-directed activities requiring cooperation with the teacher only, the children progress to partner activities that demand cooperation with a single classmate; to informal small group activities involving cooperation with several other children and an appointed pupil leader; to more complex team activities requiring specialization of roles and teamwork for successful cooperation with teammates, opponents, and larger class and school groups.

TEACHING VALUES THROUGH INDIVIDUAL COUNSELING

Teachers are seldom qualified psychologists or therapists. Yet the teacher does play an important role in the personal guidance of individual students. Fulfillment of this role provides particular opportunities to influence the development of his pupils' values. Through his personal contacts with each individual student, he attempts to assist him in the process of self-knowledge. Maslow has asserted that self-knowledge seems to be the major path of self-improvement.[12] "The human being is so constructed that he presses toward fuller and fuller being and this means pressing toward what most people would call good values, toward serenity, kindness, courage, honesty, love, unselfishness, and goodness." [13] "A teacher or a culture doesn't create a human being. It doesn't implant within him the ability to love, or to be curious, or to philosophize, or to symbolize, or to be creative. Rather it permits, or fosters, or encourages or helps what exists in embryo to become real and actual." [14] The good teacher encourages his pupils to achieve fuller self-actualization.

Much of the guidance that the teacher lends to the young person in the clarification and stabilization of his personal values is of an informal nature. He may direct an appropriate observation to the pupil in the course of class activity. He may offer suggestions to the athlete sitting on the bench during an interscholastic contest. He may make a personal comment to the student in the locker room following the class period or practice session. He may raise a personal question when he meets the pupil in the corridor. He may discuss a matter of concern with the student who seeks him out in his office or in the gymnasium. He may ask a student to come to his office to talk over a particular problem. In each of these ways, he is offering individual counsel.

[12] Maslow, *op. cit.*, p. 156.
[13] *Ibid.*, p. 147.
[14] *Ibid.*, p. 152.

In addition to this informal guidance, the teacher may use other approaches to lend more specific direction to his efforts to assist students in building behavior patterns securely based on democratic values. One possibility is critical incident reporting through which the teacher keeps accurate, objective records of specific behavior incidents. The following material indicates how one physical education teacher has used this approach over a period of several years with considerable satisfaction.[15]

In order to give emphasis to the development of responsibility by fourth-grade pupils, this teacher selected four categories of responsible behavior for continuous observation. For each child in the class, he kept a record of specific behavior incidents, which could logically be classified in any one of these four categories. Brief factual descriptions of the incidents were classified, dated, and entered in chronological order. Entries that indicated positive manifestations of the behavior classification identified were made in blue ink; those indicating negative aspects of the behavior categorized appeared in red ink. The teacher held a personal conference with each child during which his record for a period of approximately six weeks was shared and discussed with him. Follow-up conferences were held at intervals of two to three months.

Children having particular difficulties in developing satisfactory patterns of responsible behavior were quickly identified by the accumulation of "red" incidents on their records. The teacher conferred with these individuals much more frequently. Specific possibilities for helping the four children whose records were considered "unsatisfactory" at the end of the third week were discussed with the classroom teacher, the principal, and the parents. The school psychologist was asked to work with the two whose difficulties persisted. Three additional children were later singled out for special assistance, but none of these was judged to need the specialized professional help of the psychologist.

Response to these procedures was quite favorable. The children evidenced interest in improving their records, and the proportion of "red" incidents decreased during the year. Most of the parents who were invited to discuss the records seemed to appreciate the specific information that they provided and were reasonably cooperative in helping to deal with the problems identified. Parents who were not requested to make specific appointments to discuss pupil records, but who learned of the study through their children, expressed interest and general approval of this approach to teaching responsible behavior. The classroom teachers sought the help of the physical education teacher more frequently in analyzing individual behavior difficulties.

[15] For this material, the authors are indebted to Mr. Gilbert Magida, Washington School, River Forest, Illiniois.

The limitations of critical incident recording should not be overlooked. Its effective use depends upon the skill of the teacher as an observer and recorder, as well as his ability in individual counseling and in interpretation of the records to parents and appropriate colleagues. It is extremely time-consuming; from a practical standpoint, a full-time teacher cannot keep adequate records of all his pupils at once, nor can he expect to make accurate observations in more than a selected few categories of behavior while carrying on his usual daily responsibilities. In addition to these factors, it must be added that the teacher whose successful efforts have been cited works with the same pupils in daily physical education classes from grades one through six in a relatively stable community in which the schools have enjoyed a high degree of parental cooperation and lay support. In spite of its limitations, however, the method seems to have promise.

Role-playing is another technique that is sometimes used by teachers concerned with the teaching of values. It has many variations. The teacher can set up several typical problem situations, assign roles to individual class members, and guide the analysis of the behavior of each of the players that follows. A form of group guidance is involved in the discussion of specific behaviors demonstrated, in evaluating actions observed and in encouraging critical thinking about alternative behaviors that might have been employed in the situation. Sometimes it is desirable to replay the situation with the same or a different cast of characters, after the class has agreed upon the preferred behaviors.

Personal guidance can be furnished to the individual through role-playing techniques by giving him the opportunity to hear his classmates evaluate his manner of playing an assigned role, by selecting a situation that will result in thoughtful analysis of a behavior pattern that he characteristically displays, and by assigning him to a role that forces him to consider the situation from "the other person's viewpoint." Often, a follow-up of one or two individual conferences may be suggested by specific aspects of the actual role-playing or of the class discussion. The ultimate purpose, of course, is to give guidance to individuals, even though the group setting is utilized.

Many variations of role-playing are possible. Paper-and-pencil techniques have been used by some teachers to gain insight for individual guidance. One example is the playcasting device in which the teacher presents the possibility of planning a class play. Each child is given a list of roles or characters in the play with instructions to mention one or more class members, including himself as appropriate, who best fit the descriptions. The children's responses give the teacher information concerning individual self-concepts as well as peer evaluation of individual members of the class. Hopefully, such information will serve as a basis for more understanding teacher guidance.

Role-playing techniques probably have a place in education. The dramatization and personalizing of situations involving value concepts helps to involve the feelings and emotions of the individual, an essential condition for influencing personal values. Such techniques lend themselves to use with groups of typical class size. It is usually important to provide for other types of follow-up with individuals, however. And the obvious limitation of the method is the potentiality for misuse by the inexperienced or inept teacher. A situation that is charged with emotion requires skillful guidance if it is to be utilized for the benefit of those participating. Misinterpretation of observed behaviors, misleading analyses of suggested actions, emotional involvement of the leader, and exposure of confidential information are other possible dangers.

The physical education teacher's efforts to teach values through individual counseling must always be carried forward within the total school framework. Working with colleagues is even more important in this area than in the teaching of subject matter. In situations in which he is fortunate enough to have the assistance of qualified counselors, psychologists, and psychiatrists, he will work closely with these specialists in guiding individual children. He must not assume counseling responsibilities beyond his training and skill. Furthermore, he must not lose sight of the impact of the child's total environment. Working with the home and with appropriate community agencies is essential.

TEACHING VALUES THROUGH ENVIRONMENTAL MODIFICATION

The achievement of moral maturity depends in large measure upon the development of an acceptable, heathful self-concept. The young person whose self-esteem is low, who has little regard for himself, experiences difficulty in respecting and appreciating others. The child or adolescent who is unhappy with his self-image does not relate effectively to others. Values become distorted for the individual who fights what he believes to be a losing battle for acceptance, affection, and recognition. The person who is reasonably secure with a satisfactory self-concept is free to express the values that define true humanity and that people in his culture consider "good." If teachers can control or manage the educational environment in ways that multiply satisfying experiences, that strengthen positive self-concepts, that encourage behaviors consistent with culturally approved values, pupils will develop values in a climate that fosters sound psychological and moral learnings.

Physical educators can modify the educational environment in several ways. A common procedure is to plan instruction to permit selection by the individual student from among two or more parallel class activities. In essence, this offers the student an opportunity to choose the environment in which he feels most comfortable and most likely to succeed. This procedure also insures a variety of activities in the program to facilitate success experiences for all students.

The instructor can also control the individual's learning environment and thus set the stage for the acquisition of desired values, through methods of pupil grouping. Assignment of pupils to physical education classes in relatively homogeneous groups puts most individuals in situations in which they can compare themselves satisfactorily to their classmates. In arranging groups for competitive play, the teacher attempts to provide for equal competition. For individual contests, students are matched according to weight, or some type of age-height-weight classification, or by some plan of handicaps or seeding based on previous experience in competition. Teams are balanced so as to give each team "a fair chance to win." Equal competition enhances the individual's self-concept through the knowledge that he can meet the challenge with an adequate performance.

All students should experience both winning and losing. Different values are learned in winning and in losing. Every individual needs to lose and to win under varying conditions if he is to learn the important values associated with competition. He needs to win and lose in situations that pit his personal strength and skill against the abilities of other individuals. He also needs to win and lose when his personal contribution may be stronger or weaker than that made by the majority of his teammates, both as a player on winning teams and as a member of losing teams. The teacher can control the environment to assure all students these different experiences.

Pupil groups may also be arranged for instructional purposes primarily in terms of individual personalities. Most people participate more effectively in groups in which they feel accepted as persons. Numerous sociometric techniques are available for studying patterns of acceptance within groups. Particular care should be given to place isolates and fringers in subgroups that will give them the best chance for gaining acceptance. The simple device of asking each class member to list three classmates with whom he would like to play supplies information for arranging teams of individuals who desire to play together and should be able to develop effective team relationships. It also identifies those who need special help and guidance in building satisfying personal relationships. Studies of group structure can be used by the teacher to suggest ways of modifying the personal environment of students to improve self-images, to increase readiness for learning, and to teach positive values.

Controlling the educational environment to strengthen self-concepts through greater opportunity for success and increasing acceptance by classmates is an indirect approach to teaching values. It is assumed that individual behavior will improve because these efforts have contributed to the development of healthier, happier, integrated personalities. On the other hand, it is possible to approach the problem more directly, placing pupils who need value reorientation in situations in which other students who consistently express the appropriate values in their class behavior can be expected to influence them in desired directions. The limitations of this technique are obvious, the most serious being the possibility of negative identification. Yet it can be useful, provided adequate consideration is given to other relevant factors.

Values may also be learned through participation in a class environment of carefully selected organizational procedures. The pupil learns the value of physical protection of himself and others in a class in which proper protective equipment is used, skillful "spotting" is provided, and essential safety precautions are enforced. The use of squads and rotation of groups and positions aids him in learning cooperation. Sound procedures for taking partners, organizing teams, assigning positions, and sharing equipment assist him in understanding that all members of the group are entitled to equal consideration. Group participation in decision-making and reliance upon student leadership increase his ability to demonstrate responsible behavior.

The physical educator should give special attention to control of the environment for intramural and interscholastic activities. Because of the relatively high level of motivation and the deeper emotional involvement that usually characterize these facets of the educational program, the potential for influencing values is especially great. Competitive sports should be conducted in an environment that includes competent officiating, adequate protection of the physical health of players, and observance of the basic principles of sportsmanship and courtesy. Attainment of an atmosphere conducive to learning desired values will also require changes in the morality of many local adult communities: the elimination of gambling on athletic contests for unethical profit, the control of advertising that negates the positive values of sound training practices, the avoidance of pressures on athletes and coaches that conflict with educational goals, and the building of good spectator sportsmanship.

USE OF REWARD AND PUNISHMENT IN TEACHING VALUES

The learning process is complex, involves many different kinds of learnings, is engaged in by varying categories of learners, and includes certain controversial aspects explained by conflicting analyses. Any behavioristic model used for purposes of brief discussion necessarily results in oversimplification. The authors have chosen to use this device, however, for clarification in considering the role of reward and punishment in learning values. Continuing support of a field theory of learning that emphasizes the "wholeness" of the learning situation and the nature of learning as a cognitive and social process may be assumed.

The development of habitual behavior patterns involves a good deal of trial-and-error learning. As a young person growing up in our culture experiments with various behavioral responses, the consequences of specific behaviors, to him as an individual, determine which responses will become established in his pattern of behavior. Those types of behaviors that bring pleasant consequences tend to be repeated and reinforced. Those whose consequences are unpleasant are repeated less frequently, possibly completely eliminated.

Reward and punishment enter into the teaching of values in terms of controlling these consequences. The sixth-grader who helps two third-graders amicably resolve an argument over turns at the jungle gym, and finds this behavior rewarded by appointment to the school playground patrol, will tend to repeat such behavior. The basketball player who is benched as a result of losing his temper and swearing at his opponent is apt to avoid repeating such action. On the other hand, desired behavior may be discouraged or undesirable action reinforced when behavior is followed by inappropriate consequences or lack of consequences. If an eight-year-old shares his new bat and this leads, not to approval and acceptance, but to highlighting the fact that others are more skillful batters than he, he will be loath to share the next time. If the coach smiles indulgently or overlooks the incident when a football star takes a towel or an ashtray or some other item belonging to a hotel or a restaurant, this type of behavior is apt to be repeated and imitated by other members of the team. Generally speaking, the reinforcement of desired behavior is preferable to punishing undesired behavior. But, in the teaching of values, both reinforcement and punishment are usually necessary.

In the process of establishing behavior patterns, what happens following a given action is often more important than what the teacher does in advance to stimulate desired behavior, since the consequences serve as stimuli for subsequent behavior. Stimuli may be primarily verbal, emphasizing praise, statements of recognition, enthusiastic comments on the desired results, or criticism, disapproving comments, explanations of why such behavior is undesirable. Verbal stimuli should be accompanied by appropriate gestures that serve as additional stimuli: facial expressions, hand-shaking, a pat on the back, a steadying hand on the shoulder, and similar gestures. Action consequences are often important as well, such actions as designating a boy as captain, assigning a child to a coveted position as teacher assistant in distributing equipment, promoting a student to a more advanced group, asking a troublemaker to withdraw from the class activity, suspending a cheerleader from her position on the squad, and reporting misbehavior to the student council.

It is important to recognize that what we as teachers conceive of as rewarding and punishing may not always be similarly regarded by our students. For example, verbal approval by the teacher may sometimes embarrass the pupil or subject him to the ridicule of his classmates rather than serving to reward him. In some situations, punishment is a mark of status and prestige and actually reinforces instead of discouraging undesired behavior. Individual differences may play an important role in this regard too. A given child may feel rewarded by being directed to sit on the sidelines, although most of the children consider exclusion from class activities punishment. One child may consider an expression of approval from the teacher a higher reward than permission to jump on the trampoline, while the reverse may be true of another child in the same class. Teachers need to learn to discriminate in using reward and punishment and to individualize instruction in this respect as in so many other ways. It should also be noted that the pupil's response to the use of reward and punishment will reflect his over-all relationship with the specific teacher. An expression of praise or an indication of disapproval will vary in its meaningfulness according to his feeling toward the responsible teacher.

One elementary school physical educator has recently made an interesting study of this phase of his work in teaching values.[16] He began by analyzing his own methods of class discipline and systematizing his procedures for dealing with violations of class regulations.

A series of ten class regulations were listed, posted, and explained to the fourth-grade physical education class. These included such items as: "Never push, strike, slap, pull, or punch a classmate." "Accept positions and take turns." "Never scold or ridicule a classmate." "Use the equipment in the manner demonstrated and explained by the teacher." Procedures for treating violations were classified. After some modification, the categories were as follows:

    A. Group Procedures.
        1. Explanation of what is expected.
        2. Stopping and restricting activity.
        3. Waiting for complete attention after blowing whistle.
    B. Individual Procedures.
        1. Talk with the child; explain what is expected.

[16] For this material, the authors are indebted to Mr. Frank C. Brown, Lincoln School, River Forest, Illinois.

2. Take away privileges.
3. Refer to the child by name while talking to the group.
4. Ask the child to sit on the sidelines until he is sure he can behave.
5. Exclude the child from an entire class period or from the before-school playtime.

For a period of approximately six months, he recorded daily all violations of the class regulations by individual fourth-graders. In each instance, he also recorded which procedure or procedures he used in dealing with the incident.

In the context of this discussion, this was a study of an individual teacher's use of punishment in attempting to teach responsible behavior to fourth-grade pupils. His procedures resulted in consistent treatment of violations of class regulations, a decrease in the number of violations, and a strong positive-type class discipline. On the whole, pupils were reasonably self-disciplined; serious violations were rare. (This situation reflected the group's previous three years' experience with this same physical educator as well as teaching procedures during the period of the study.) It will be noted that the approach is limited in flexibility. Thus, individualization of instruction must be achieved through selection of the appropriate technique for treating violations, through the use of rewards that were not systematized to the same degree, and through aspects of instruction beyond the basic methods of establishing constructive discipline. It is also relevant to point out that this method is highly personal. It could not be demonstrated that the class response was entirely consistent when a student teacher tried to use the same procedures in the physical education class period or when the children were working with classroom teachers in other fields of learning. Yet there was evidence of considerable success in teaching certain values specific to the situation.

HOW SHALL WE TEACH VALUES?

In this chapter, value education has been considered successively from several specific angles. It is important to keep in mind, however, that values are learned within the larger framework of dynamic personality development. Human growth is a process of change, a series of anatomic, physiological, and psychological changes through which the individual blends everything that is happening to him with his genetic inheritance. The result is a distinct and unique individual who, at any given moment, is a product of all his heredity and all his environment. The individual is always active; he is constantly "becoming." In attempting to achieve maximum personal organization and integration, he chooses, in a particular situation, that behavior that appears to preserve and increase orderly arrangements within his world. Maturational and interpersonal forces interact constantly within him to develop a unique organization. As he orders his experience, both internal and external, a unique and personal self-concept emerges. As he develops his individual personality, he behaves so as to maintain this self-concept. Consequently, his values are significantly related to his concept of self.

Our efforts in the area of teaching values are admittedly exploratory. Yet physical educators are agreed that our contribution to this important field of learning should be significant. The potential of physical education for teaching values can be realized only through constant study and intensive work. We need research on the learning of values. We need experimentation in controlled laboratory situations to the extent that such experimentation is possible. We also need action research in situations where children and youth are studying, working, and playing, and at the same time learning values. We need teachers who set excellent personal examples in their own lives. We need educators who will seek new and better methods for teaching values as they work with students. We must test those approaches currently available to us: teaching values as subject content, teaching values through individual counseling, teaching values through environmental modification, and teaching values through utilization of reward and punishment. We must discover other approaches. We must combine different approaches for the most effective teaching of values. But let us not neglect this vital responsibility simply because we have so many unanswered questions.

8

Individualizing Instruction

The problem of adapting instruction to the needs of individuals has challenged and discouraged generations of educators. With the advent of the space age and increasing general concern for the relative effectiveness of American public education, lay interest has mounted rapidly. Citizens have focused much attention on the school's role in stimulating the gifted toward higher achievement levels. Public agencies and private foundations have encouraged the study of new organizational patterns and new techniques for effective guidance of individual learning. The problems of individualizing instruction in physical education have varied historically with shifting emphases in philosophy but have remained essentially the same through the current flurry of public interest in educational outcomes. These problems have been left to our own professional group for solution, and we have yet to devise satisfactory means for individualizing physical education.

SIGNIFICANCE OF THE PROBLEM

Every teacher is faced with the problem of individualizing instruction. One of the most common difficulties of inexperienced physical educators is learning to analyze individual performance errors and to offer appropriate individual corrections. Experienced teachers experiment with a variety of class activities and procedures to stimulate maximum individual learning and growth. The coach constantly seeks new methods for developing the individual abilities of athletes to the fullest. Administrators search for more effective grouping policies and scheduling techniques in order to facilitate more successful individualization of instruction. We may well ask why this consensus of concern for individualizing physical education.

Individual Differences in a Democracy

Democracy is built upon a belief in individual worth. We are committed to respect for and concern with each member of our society as an individual human being. Human dignity is our highest value. We believe that each individual's differences should be identified, appreciated, and developed toward optimum self-realization and maximum contribution to social welfare.

The tremendous range of individual differences in a nation of almost 190,000,000 people is impossible for any one of us to fully appreciate. Statistical means tend to obscure the wide variation in such physical characteristics as height, weight, body type, pulse rate, blood pressure, metabolic rate, joint flexibility, and muscular strength. Test scores, while useful, cannot reflect accurately all the specific differences in verbal reasoning ability, spatial orientation, clerical accuracy, numerical ability, or perceptual speed within our total population. We vary extensively in such special aptitudes as sensory acuity, finger dexterity, artistic talents, and mechanical aptitude. The breadth and variation of individual differences in emotional stability, social intelligence, character traits, and relations with other persons defy adequate measurement. Differences in individual interests and motivation are of great significance in determining a person's role in a democratic culture.

Democracy values individual differences. Many differing personalities with widely varying specific interests and abilities are needed to sustain our highly specialized economy; to increase our intellectual, aesthetic, and spiritual satisfactions; and to fulfill our increasingly complex role in international affairs. As our culture advances, individual differences do not decrease; on the contrary, the range grows wider and the differences with which we must be concerned multiply. Medical science increases physiological variability among individuals by preserving the lives of those with deviations that in earlier times would have been critical. The Darwinian principle of selection is not allowed to operate; the extremes in a "normal curve of distribution" are not eliminated; the range in individual differences increases. In a similar manner, a truly democratic environment will increase the range of psychological, intellectual, and personality differences by accepting, encouraging, and perpetuating these differences among individuals. As American democracy progresses, individual differences will grow *more* important, never less crucial.

Instructional Difficulties Resulting from Individual Differences

The schools deal with children in groups. If each child in a given class were to receive instruction appropriate to his individual differences, the class would require as many different programs of instruction as there were children in the group. Since we cannot provide individual tutors for each of our children, we must find ways of individualizing group instruction. Class size becomes an important factor in solving this problem. The larger the group, the more individual differences it includes and the more adaptations the teacher must devise for individualizing physical education.

Class size is not the only obstacle to individualizing instruction. Many other aspects of school organization may impede efforts toward the goal of meeting individual needs. Inflexible time schedules that do not allow sufficiently long blocks of time for effective individual skills practice may minimize the efficiency of individual learning. Some children need longer periods of time to achieve a given daily instructional goal than others; school schedules seldom permit such variation. Facilities that are inadequate for utilization of a variety of learning activities may prevent the selection of those methods that would be most successful for certain individual class members. It should also be remembered that the teacher's own limitations may be an important obstacle to individualization of instruction.

Many schools have introduced grouping schemes designed to minimize these difficulties. A number of these will be discussed in succeeding sections. In spite of the relative successes of certain grouping plans, we must recognize that groups are always heterogeneous. Certain types of individual differences within a group can be minimized by narrowing the range through ability grouping, but individual differences cannot be eliminated. If there are twenty-five boys in a swimming class, there will still be twenty-five levels of performance in the front crawl, even though the gaps between these levels may not be as great in an "advanced" swimming class as in a group of ninth-grade swimmers not otherwise classified. The teacher will never be free to overlook individual differences.

Intraindividual variability leads to other difficulties. Each pupil's profile of individual traits shows a pattern of amazing variability in comparison with group means. Even a single characteristic within the individual pupil is subject to much variability at different times and under changing conditions. Thus, a group of "gifted" pupils, so classified in terms of verbal reasoning and numerical ability, are not likely to be an equally "gifted" group from the standpoint of motor performance. The pupil who qualifies for the "high ability" group in physical education, on the basis of physical fitness tests, may be at the very bottom of the distribution in a swimming ability classification test. The high school girl who scores high on a motor ability test battery may lack the motivation to perform well in an intermediate level apparatus unit.

Variations within individuals must be recognized in any plan aimed toward ability grouping. Teachers must resist the tendency to assume homogeneity and the temptation to give less thought and energy to individualizing instruction. They must also accept responsibility for helping the student to become aware of his own individual differences; to assess realistically his own pattern of abilities, interests, and needs; and to utilize his individual assets most effectively.

Uniformity and Diversity

Analysts of our national culture, philosophers, social psychologists, authors, educators, and civic leaders have all called attention to the trend toward conformity in the United States. Sociologists point toward the increasing emphasis in selecting occupations upon establishing security, as contrasted with meaningful social service. Critics decry the sameness and the mediocrity of our tastes in entertainment, so effectively supported by the mass media. Manufacturers capitalize upon our desire to possess an article of clothing, a household appliance, or a car that conforms to a certain popular image. Parents and educators express concern over the difficulties of guiding youth toward responsible self-direction. Editorialists berate the lack of public interest in local, national, and international political issues. Many believe that we are indeed becoming a nation of conformists.

As we demand conformity to certain cultural expectations, are we suppressing creativity? Does our emphasis upon verbal communication discourage potential artists and dancers? Have our educational methods and our system of credits and grades hindered rather than stimulated the development of creative thinking? Have our highly structured youth groups, overorganized recreation programs, and adult-dominated athletic teams minimized opportunities for the discovery and enjoyment of creative hobbies and recreational pursuits? Can we afford to lose even a portion of the creativity of our citizens? Is it not possible to educate our children and youth for competent participation in the grim business of America's survival and at the same time to develop the creative potential needed to enrich her future?

We must have both uniformity and diversity. The important question is: What uniformity and what diversity do we want? We want uniformity in the possession of certain basic competencies such as minimum skills in speaking, reading, and writing the English language; essential human relations skills for living and working with others; an understanding of the individual's role in local, state, and national government; and physical fitness adequate for the demands of daily living and for reserve resources for emergencies. But we want to maintain and encourage diversity in family customs and home environments, in ethnic and religious traditions, in occupational choices, in recreational and social interests, and in aesthetic preferences. The schools must educate for the uniformity required for successful group living in our federal democracy and for the diversity essential to performance of its many specialized roles and the creating of new and improved cultural patterns.

The public schools have usually attempted to provide for the desired uniformity through required courses, core curricula, and common experiences in heterogeneous groups. Efforts to diversify educational experiences have centered in differentiated curricula, elective courses, and ability groupings. The current trend toward ability grouping has been reflected to some extent in physical education; but this is less common than in such areas as mathematics, science, and language. Some schools have embraced ability grouping enthusiastically in most subject fields, pointing to the opportunities for democratic group experiences remaining in the heterogeneous physical education classes. It behooves physical educators to examine this philosophy carefully. Can we accept the total responsibility for providing the "broadening group experiences," the core of shared group learnings needed by all students? Can certain educational goals of the individuals in our classes be achieved more effectively in groups of more nearly similar abilities? What is the proper role of physical education in educating for both uniformity and diversity?

It seems reasonable to suggest that no one subject field could provide children and youth with all the knowledges, skills, and attitudes that constitute our common core of learnings. Physical education shares with other subject fields concern and responsibility for achieving these objectives of the total educational endeavor. But physical education, like every other subject field that rightfully claims a place in the curriculum, has certain unique objectives to achieve as well. In order to accomplish its goals, physical education instruction must be individualized so that each student's characteristics will be effectively modified to develop an adult capable of the minimum uniformity our group life requires and so that his specific pattern of abilities can contribute maximum diversity toward advancement of our complex culture. The major function of this chapter is to consider means for effectively individualizing physical education.

INDIVIDUALIZATION THROUGH RATE OF PROGRESS

Early plans for education were completely individualized. The student learned in a one-to-one relationship directly from his teacher. As schools were organized to educate children in groups, a graded structure was devised to standardize curriculum content and to facilitate the teacher's role in giving instruction. The first clamor for individualizing public school instruction resulted from the obvious fact that all children of a given age assigned to a particular grade did not progress equally well.

In attempting to solve this problem, educators experimented with several plans that were designed to permit each child to progress at his own rate of speed. The Winnetka Plan and the Dalton Plan were perhaps the most famous of these, but there were many variations. The curriculum content was organized in relatively small units to be completed in sequence. Each child worked through the basic series of assignments as rapidly as he was able; the brighter children completed additional, more advanced lessons in the time remaining to be devoted to the subject, or turned their attention to other major subjects. It should be noted that instruction is individualized only to a very limited extent within this framework. All children learn essentially the same subject content. There is nothing individual about what each child learns except how fast he learns it and how much of it he learns—and the attitudes he develops toward his learning experiences.

Individualization through permitting differences in the rate of progress is used in today's schools with contemporary variations. Examples can be cited from current physical education practice. Physical education classes are sometimes organized on the basis of minimum cutting scores in physical fitness tests. Certain exercises must be performed achieving a minimum passing score in each. After a general testing period and certain group instructions, the student works on his own until he completes these basic requirements. Then he is deemed ready to progress to other, more advanced learning activities.

The individual scorecard or squad checkoff method is frequently used in stunts, apparatus, aquatics, and other similar activities. Specific stunts or activities are listed in order of degree of difficulty on a chart or scorecard. When the individual student can perform the stunt correctly, it is checked off on his card and he moves to another mat, another piece of apparatus, or another part of the gymnasium or pool to join the group working to perfect the next stunt or series of activities. Each student thus progresses at his own rate.

Such techniques have a place in learning specific skills. As a procedure for individualizing instruction, however, value is limited. No individual adaptation is actually made in the curriculum content or in the method of guiding learning. Individual learning is facilitated only by flexibility in the time allotted to learning a given activity. Other approaches to individualizing physical education instruction should certainly be considered.

INDIVIDUALIZATION THROUGH METHODOLOGY

In discussions of individualizing instruction, physical educators have tended to assume that a professionally trained teacher will provide adequately for individual differences if only class size is limited to a certain approved maximum. While it is true that individual correction and assistance with individual learning problems are facilitated in small classes, observation discloses that many teachers seldom give significant individual guidance whatever the size of their classes. Furthermore, this is a very limited concept of adapting methodology to individual differences. It would be wise for every teacher to examine and experiment with several methods for individualizing instruction.

Variety in Teaching Techniques

No two individuals learn in exactly the same way. Some students will grasp the basic elements of a new skill most quickly by observing a well-executed demonstration. Certain individuals focus more effectively on verbal description and analysis. Others prefer to concentrate on kinesthetic awareness of the correct movement patterns. The teacher who recognizes these differences will vary his class presentations and use several techniques in combination in order to reach more individuals within the group.

The experienced physical educator should strive continually to expand his repertory of teaching techniques. While increasing his skill in demonstration, explanation, organization of practice drills, coaching of game play, group and individual correction, testing, guidance of pupil participation in educational planning, supervision of student leaders, and other familiar instructional procedures, he should also be alert to possibilities of techniques less frequently used. What worthwhile field experiences could be made available to his students? Are there individuals in the local community who could serve as resources to enrich learning? What teaching techniques observed at professional meetings or reported in journals might enliven and improve his instruction? What modifications of rules and class procedures might make popular activities more adaptable to the individual needs of his pupils? Are some of the newest teaching aids required for more effective instruction in his classes?

Utilization of varied teaching techniques is desirable for broadening learning experiences and increasing individual motivation. But this too is a limited approach to individualizing instruction. It must be recognized that all pupils will still be exposed to the same curriculum content and the same methods of guiding learning. Its value in serving individual differences lies in the possibilities for meeting a wider variety of individual needs. Its effectiveness depends upon the ability of the pupil, with skillful teacher guidance, to profit from those aspects of the learning environment most appropriate to his needs.

Variations in Class Activities

Although physical education classes are normally organized for group instruction, it is possible within this framework to vary the activities of individual pupils. One relatively simple procedure is to prescribe different individual warmup activities, allowing the students to work independently during the first minutes of the class period. Each class member can be assigned a series of calisthenic or gymnastic exercises selected according to his specific body mechanics problems or muscular weaknesses. Or he may be assigned specific skills practice activities appropriate to his personal needs as well as to the learning unit in which the entire class is engaged.

Another way of varying class activities to provide for individual differences is to plan for several different learning experiences for a single class period. For example, the lesson might be devoted to basket shooting, a dribbling drill, rope-skipping, a vertical jump self-test, and a gymnastic exercise routine designed to increase cardiovascular endurance. A learning area would be designated for each activity. Each student would be assigned to an activity or a combination of activities in accordance with his specific needs, or he would select his activity with appropriate teacher guidance. Such a plan for alternative activities could easily extend beyond one class period. In a particular situation, it might be desirable to provide concurrent units in such activities as tennis, golf, and bowling, steering each individual into a sport in which he had had no previous opportunity to participate. Another possibility would be to encourage each student to plan his own physical conditioning unit, following a good testing procedure and a group orientation to facilities and safety limitations, available supplies and equipment, and potential outcomes of various activities. Teacher guidance and approval of student plans would be essential.

It should be noted that the above suggestions go beyond a mere rotation of groups from one teaching station to the next. Rotation plans facilitate class organization and are particularly useful when space and equipment are limited. But all students perform the same activities; only the sequence varies. The examples cited above provide for individualizing instruction through actual differences in curriculum content.

More extensive use of problem-solving activities is another method for stimulating individualization in physical education. A child can find his own way to get through a small space. A junior high school girl can be allowed to seek her own way of changing direction without losing her balance on the beam. A basketball enthusiast could be encouraged to determine through individual experimentation his most effective technique for shooting a free throw. Individuals, singly or in groups, can be challenged by creative problems such as composing a sequence of aquatic stunts, developing a ball gymnastics routine, selecting movements to fit a rhythmic pattern, working out a new out-of-bounds play, or planning a tumbling performance. Individuals within a class may seek personal solutions to the same or similar problems, or they may work on completely different problems during the instructional period.

Individual Study Procedures

Traditionally, very little attention has been given to the use of individual study methods in physical education. The authors contend that physical education, like other content fields in the curriculum, needs to give more emphasis to encouraging and facilitating individual study. Individual study is not limited to reading books and other printed materials, although many publications in the physical education literature could be recommended for student reading. The school library should include a physical education collection for student use; if arrangements can be made for adequate supervision and services, it is desirable to house this collection in the physical education area.

Physical education references should include books designed for student study such as the textbook prepared by the American Association for Health, Physical Education and Recreation [1] and various commercial publications providing orientation to a variety of physical education activities. The latter are usually designed for basic instruction classes at the college level, but most are of interest to the typical high school pupil and adapted to his understanding. Books dealing with physiology of exercise; history of sports, dance, aquatics, and physical education; and analysis of the various physical activities employed in the curriculum should be procured. Rule guides for popular sports and games should be kept up-to-date. Current periodicals devoted to sports, gymnastics, dance, and physical education, as well as references detailing careers in physical education and related fields, should be available to the student reader.

Other study materials can be provided in quantity for independent work. The Athletic Institute and several individual sporting goods firms supply free and low-cost pamphlets, charts, and pocket-size handbooks that are excellent for pupil study. The individual teacher can prepare

[1] AAHPER, *Physical Education for High School Students* (Washington, D.C.: National Education Association, 1955).

simplified rules digests, study guides, and similar materials for duplication, posting, and distribution to students.

Individual study opportunities in physical education should certainly stress movement activities and skills practice, although reading and study directed toward the achievement of specific knowledge objectives can be included. Crowded facilities, limited equipment, scheduling problems, and lack of administrative and instructional imagination and skill have combined to minimize the use of active independent study procedures. It is suggested that this situation need not necessarily continue.

Where facilities can be made accessible, individuals can practice badminton, fencing, wrestling, apparatus activities, and any other individual or dual activities outside of the large-group instruction periods. Practice areas can be designed to accommodate individual practice in golf techniques, batting, serving, isometric exercise, weight training, and throwing. Work areas can be supplied with record players and tape recorders for practice of folk and square dance patterns, for learning rhythmic routines of all kinds, and for choreographing dance studies. A visual aids facility could be equipped for physical education use.

Self-testing activities should play an important role in independent study. The physical education student would profit from the provision of testing stations set up for easy administration of wall volley, basket shooting, target throws, service placement, and backboard tests. Teaching machines could be programed for testing physical education knowledge; relatively inexpensive types could be developed locally.

The reader will raise many questions concerning the administrative feasibility of scheduling such independent study activities. Local programs must certainly be adapted to facilities available. But most of the activities suggested in the above paragraphs do not require full-size gymnasium areas. A few individuals can engage in worthwhile vigorous activities in foyer, stage, balcony, corridor, or classroom spaces; in some plants, limited use can be made even of locker room and extra storage areas. Several activities requiring gymnasium space or fixed equipment can usually be scheduled at the same time if thoughtfully planned.

Supervision is another difficulty that must be met. Basic control must result from the assumption of responsibility by the individual pupil. He must have a carefully developed plan for independent practice activities. He should be required to identify his goals, outline his plan, and give evidence that he understands and is prepared to follow minimum regulations and safety precautions. Clearly worded, easily read, concise, specific safety regulations and directions for using equipment should be conspicuously posted in all practice and independent work areas. Carefully trained student leaders and subprofessional assistants can be assigned to provide minimum supervision and help in activities in which safety standards can be met satisfactorily by these procedures. Activities that involve inherent safety hazards requiring the supervision of a fully trained professional physical educator can sometimes be scheduled in a gymnasium or other large area permitting adequate supervision of several activities at once. When this is not possible, those activities that cannot be safely supervised should be eliminated from the independent study program and restricted to group teaching situations in which close professional supervision will be provided.

Any program designed to encourage independent study activities must free student schedules from the traditional secondary school organization. Minor schedule modifications in a daily program will permit use of one or two periods weekly for individual activities. But maximum value from independent study procedures can probably be gained in a flexible scheduling pattern based on a shorter time module. Flexible scheduling, including specific illustrations, will be discussed in Chapter 10.

Guidance and Special Services

Guidance and other special services have become important aspects of the curriculum because of the difficulties of meeting individual needs within the group framework. They were brought into the curriculum in order to individualize instruction. These services to individual pupils and to the teachers and parents who guide them are vital to the success of the formal instructional program.

Guidance is an integral part of the teaching-learning process; many educators would be willing to defend the statement that "teaching *is* guidance." Certainly, guidance occurs in every classroom, including the physical education laboratories. The teacher provides individual guidance to the learner when he analyzes the learner's performance errors and makes specific suggestions to him for correcting and improving his performance. The competent physical educator is constantly offering this type of guidance as his students participate in the various learning tasks that he selects and conducts for the class group. The bulk of individual instruction in physical education is of this nature. The skill of the teacher in individual analysis and correction is likely to be the crucial factor in determining individual pupil achievement. It is a skill based on both knowledge and experience; it is not easily acquired. Increasing his skill in guidance of individual performance is a continuing challenge for every professional physical educator.

Every teacher is also concerned with the personal guidance of individual pupils. He attempts to instruct students in appropriate behavior responses to situations that occur in class and extraclass activities and to offer adult counsel to individuals who discuss their personal problems with him in informal out-of-class circumstances. It is essential, however, that he learn to recognize his own professional limitations and to identify student problems that should be referred to trained counselors and guidance specialists. It is especially important that he develop skills for guiding students to the experts who are best qualified to help them.

School guidance and other special services can achieve maximum effectiveness only if the facts and insights gained are used for optimum individual instruction and if the basic services rendered are followed up well by the teachers. School health services, in particular, should play a vital role in providing a sound foundation for individualizing physical education. The physical education department that offers a complete curriculum based on a concern for meeting individual needs will also provide special services to the physically handicapped and temporarily disabled pupils.

INDIVIDUALIZATION THROUGH GROUPING

Educational experimentation over the years has included many attempts to solve the problems of individualizing instruction through different plans for pupil grouping. Shane asserts that, "Most of the historically significant plans for dealing directly with human individuality within the organization of the school have been related to grouping for instruction."[2] He lists *thirty-five* specific approaches to grouping and comments as follows:

The foregoing list of thirty-five plans and proposals, while by no means comprehensive, serves to emphasize the fact that during the last century or longer many ideas have been expressed with a view to personalizing teaching and recognizing individual differences. Patently, the challenge of human individuality has engaged the attention and stimulated the imagination of scores of educational leaders.[3]

New approaches to grouping pupils are among the most promising techniques for more effectively individualizing instruction in physical education.

Course Selection

Individualization can be facilitated to some degree by the provision of alternative courses within the curriculum. The graded program in physical education is a first step in this direction. The instructor has a

---

[2] Harold G. Shane, "The School and Individual Differences," in Nelson B. Henry (ed.), *Individualizing Instruction*, Sixty-first Yearbook of the National Society for the Study of Education, Part I (Chicago: University of Chicago Press, 1962), p. 48.

[3] *Ibid.*, pp. 49–50.

better opportunity to guide children in meeting individual needs if the nine-year-olds follow the fourth-grade course of study while the ten-year-olds enroll in fifth-grade physical education and the eleven-year-olds take the sixth-year program than if fourth-, fifth-, and sixth-graders are all scheduled for physical education together. In the upper grades, separate classes for boys and girls permit better adaptation of instruction to physiological and culturally determined sex differences.

In secondary schools, it is sometimes possible to provide for varying individual interests by permitting students to elect specific physical education courses of their choice from among several offered. Some schools are able to offer special classes for certain groups within the student population. Such classes include remedial classes for individuals needing corrective work for posture weaknesses and orthopedic difficulties, developmental classes for those needing particular emphasis on physical fitness, and classes in modified physical education for pupils with physical disabilities that limit their participation in regular class activities. With the cooperation of qualified medical personnel, some schools nave scheduled obese students in special programs, including appropriate physical education experiences as well as nutrition education and carefully conducted individual and group guidance. Special classes also include those provided for advanced work in specialized areas, courses designed for the highly skilled in aquatics, modern dance, gymnastics, or specific sports. Special classes for leadership training may be particularly effective in individualizing instruction.

Class Size

Too often, educators make the mistake of overemphasizing the significance of a given class size as a criterion of excellence in curriculum evaluation. There is no magic number for ideal physical education class size. Optimum class size varies with the specific learning objective and the nature of selected learning activities.

Flexibility in the size of instructional groups is an important aspect of individualizing instruction. Theoretically, the more teachers who can be assigned to work with a given number of pupils, the more time the instructor can give to each pupil, and the more guidance of individual learning is possible. But, in practice, the number of qualified teachers and the number of adequate teaching stations are limited. If pupils can be grouped in large sections for those activities in which class size is of minor importance, staff time can be saved for meeting with smaller groups and providing more individual help in those activities in which direct professional assistance is more crucial. Flexibility in the composition of student groups will further enhance potential opportunities for individualization, permitting pupils to be regrouped in accordance with specific instructional purposes. Flexible scheduling is discussed in greater detail in Chapter 10.

Ability Grouping

The most frequent recommendation with regard to classification of pupils for physical education advocates assignment to classes according to grade level. This policy combines administrative convenience with some degree of homogeneity in age and physical education experience. Many attempts to improve instruction have incorporated other bases for grouping pupils, however. Age-height-weight classifications and somatotype scores have been used to plan physical education instruction in terms of physical development rather than simple chronological age. Different strength indices have been used as criteria or as factors in combination with other measures of physical fitness. A medical examination is considered essential for identifying those unable to participate in a normal vigorous program. When sufficient qualified medical personnel are available, a thorough physical examination can be used as the basis for classifying students into several groups requiring different types of activity programs. Interest and previous participation in physical education activities are additional criteria for grouping students.

At various periods in the history of public education, homogeneous grouping of pupils has been advocated as a means of improving instruction. Recommendations for ability grouping are based on the assumption that the teacher can help individual students to meet their needs more effectively if the range of ability within the class group is restricted. It is contended that students who have similar abilities will require similar lesson content, similar learning experiences, and similar teaching procedures in order to achieve desired instructional objectives. For the gifted learner, the teacher can plan a program with more scope and depth, including more individual learning activities, and providing greater intellectual challenge. It is also argued that separating the gifted from the less-able learners encourages the less-talented students and offers them more recognition and motivation.

On the other hand, there are cogent arguments against ability grouping. The gifted students may develop snobbery and undemocratic attitudes, while average students lose the stimulation toward learning provided by the gifted. Probably, the outstanding problem is the difficulty of identifying the gifted. This problem is further complicated by the fact that an individual's ability in one factor measured often does not correlate with his other individual abilities.

One of the difficulties that has beset all schemes for ability grouping is the problem of intraindividual variability, which poses serious obstacles to the selection of satisfactory methods for classifying ability. Physical education has relied chiefly upon two approaches to this problem. One is the classification of pupils according to specific sports abilities. Pupils can be classified for swimming instruction according to the American Red Cross achievement standards or some comparable battery of aquatic skills. They can be grouped for tennis classes according to standardized tests of selected tennis skills or by means of teacher ratings of tennis playing ability. They can be classified for tumbling or apparatus instruction on the basis of a performance test that requires the successful execution of a number of stunts selected from a prepared list.

The second approach to ability grouping for physical education attempts to classify students on the basis of a general motor ability score. Specific components of motor ability are identified, and a battery of tests selected to measure each of these. Through this approach, the instructor hopes to assign students to groups that will be more homogeneous for instruction in a variety of physical education activities, while avoiding the difficulties of retesting and reclassifying for each different activity included in the curriculum.

Bush and Allen have proposed a classification based on both ability and interest for grouping high school students for physical education. Teachers assign all pupils to one of the following groups, on the basis of objective test data and subjective, professional judgment.

Group I   — Comprehensive, Low Interest
Group II   — Comprehensive, High Interest
Group III   — Talented, Low Interest
Group IV   — Talented, High Interest
Group V   — Gifted
Group VI   — Adapted [4]

Students of average ability are assigned to the two comprehensive groups (I and II) and take an all-inclusive physical education program. The talented groups are made up of students with substantial ability in physical education. Gifted students are those endowed with some unusual talent or potential, the ablest 5 to 10 per cent in physical education activities. In the adapted group are those students with permanent physical disabilities and pupils with temporary defects, limitations, or illness, for whom special physical education programs are necessary.

Interest in physical education is judged by teacher observation and through the use of pupil interviews and inventories. It is anticipated that students in the high-interest groups (II, IV, and V) would not need

[4] Robert N. Bush and Dwight W. Allen, "A New Design for High School Education: Assuming a Flexible Schedule" (unpublished material, Secondary Education Project, School of Education, Stanford University, July, 1961), pp. 13–17.

to be scheduled for maximum concentrations of time because they would voluntarily participate in intramural and interscholastic sports, dance, exercise, and recreational programs. It would be essential to schedule Groups I and III for sufficient time periods to achieve a complete basic program. The handicapped students in Group VI will need all the specialized attention and instruction the school can provide at each grade level.

Extraclass Activities

Many physical educators find teaching experiences in the extraclass curriculum among the most satisfying. This is often attributed to the advantageous pupil grouping procedures and the opportunities for individualizing instruction that are characteristic. Since participation in the extraclass program is voluntary, a common interest among group members can be assumed. Because these activities are usually scheduled when classes are not in session, the teacher, intramural director, coach, or athletic director is free to group participants on the basis he considers most relevant for immediate and long-range purposes.

In practice, intramural groups are usually interest groups. Ability grouping is frequently used in popular activities for subdividing players into flights or leagues or scheduling smaller club or instructional group meetings. Most extramural programs are designed primarily for high-performance ability groups. Homogeneity is enhanced by clear-cut common purpose, strong motivation, and pride in belonging to a high-prestige group. Individualized instruction is also furthered by a favorable teacher-pupil ratio and by continuous experimentation and effort to apply the most effective modern teaching methods.

INDIVIDUAL DIFFERENCES AMONG TEACHERS

The discussion in this chapter has focused upon individual differences among pupils. But we must not overlook the fact that individual differences among teachers are also important in determining educational outcomes. Teachers differ in their interests in various curriculum activities. They vary widely in their abilities to guide learning experiences in fundamental movement, sports, dance, and gymnastics. Their experiences have led to different teaching specializations. They use specific teaching techniques with widely ranging degrees of skill. Their procedures for individualizing instruction differ. Their patterns of teaching effectiveness vary considerably.

Meeting the individual needs of pupils in physical education classes depends upon recognition and effective utilization of individual differences among teachers. Class assignments should consider the abilities, interests, and preferences of individual teachers. Schedules should be built with a concern for using each staff member in the activity areas in which his preparation and experience are strongest. Some teachers are most effective with the younger pupils; others contribute more if assigned to work with the upper classes. Certain teachers are most successful in guiding beginners in a given sport; other individuals achieve superior results with highly skilled pupils. Some teachers excel in making large-group presentations and motivating students in large-class situations; others find that their primary strength lies in guiding small groups or directing independent projects. All of these individual differences among teachers are highly relevant. Effective staff utilization is a crucial educational problem and will be the focus of Chapter 9.

PRACTICES IN INDIVIDUALIZING INSTRUCTION

The suggestions for individualizing physical education that have been made in the preceding sections have been presented as illustrative of several approaches to dealing with the problems of individualizing instruction. Within any one curriculum, it is hoped that these approaches can be combined to find effective local solutions. The descriptive materials that follow provide examples of current practice in specific school physical education curricula.

The River Forest, Illinois, Public Schools offer a daily physical education program in grades one through six. Superior teachers, facilities, and equipment, and an education philosophy stressing personal self-realization make it possible to individualize physical education more effectively than in the average school situation. Each teacher uses his own approaches to individualizing instruction. Willard School has been selected for the following description of practices: [5]

Self-testing is used extensively, with the emphasis upon maximum activity in enjoyable exploration. Physical fitness items and basic sports skills tests are established for grades one through six. Arranged progressively in degree of difficulty, these skill checks serve as a motivation in earning additional time for self-selected activity, as prerequisites for advanced trampoline work, and as one factor in the determination of the grade in physical education. (Pupils also rate themselves on behavior items related to physical education class goals and on their own report card grade.) Individual score cards are kept from year to year, for pupils in the upper three grades, showing their achievement on standardized tests and indicating their progress in terms of class averages and national norms. These cards are available to parents, at regular intervals, and aid in helping pupils set up their individual goals and in planning group activities.

[5] For this material, the authors are indebted to Mr. Donald P. Slutz, Physical Education Instructor, Willard School, River Forest, Illinois.

Station teaching is frequently employed. Several learning stations are available during a given class period. In a 30 or 40 minute period, each student will rotate to three or four out of a possible five or six activities. In a gymnastic unit, he is expected to work at those stations which will give him the best opportunity to improve his areas of weakness. During a softball skills day, the pupils who are having difficulty with the overhand throw are encouraged to take advantage of the opportunity for additional practice, in skill checks, partner practice, or small group games stressing the isolated skill. If the lesson combines a volleyball game with badminton practice for eight couples, self-directed activity guides the volleyball play while the instructor is free to give individual assistance as players rotate to the badminton courts.

Pupil choice days are popular, especially with the lower grade groups. The instructor selects three pupils as game leaders (being careful to see that all pupils get an equal opportunity to serve) and each leader announces the activity of his choice. Pupils cast their votes by lining up behind the leader of the activity they wish to take, and play begins and continues until either the leader, or the followers, fail to assume their respective duties. This practice offers opportunities for developing leadership and followership, as well as serving as an accurate evaluation of pupil interest and the effectiveness of "carry-over" values in teaching.

In addition to the regular after-school sessions offered to boys and girls of grades four through six, four days each week, pupils are encouraged to pursue individual activity programs before school, during the indoor season, and at the supervised playground period at noon, during the outdoor season. The indoor pre-school sessions are devoted exclusively to developmental type activities, such as weight training, rope climbing, trampoline and tumbling, and fitness activities. The outdoor, noon-time sessions stress ball control and running games.

To stimulate self-direction, the pupils also participate in evaluating their own achievements, the investment of time to be spent in the various types of individual and group activity, and their grades on the report cards sent home. This establishes a sound basis for pupil responsibility in future class work and a foundation for further individualization of instruction. With the exception of the standardized achievement tests, most of the tests are self-administered, offering opportunity for pupils to practice honesty, decision-making, and critical thinking, in activities which directly influence their habits of, and attitudes toward, regular physical activity.

All competition, individual or group, is on the basis of classification by age, height, and weight. Emphasis is placed on evaluating progress in terms of comparing the improvement of skill against a pupil's best previous record, as well as with the norms for his particular classification group. Track events, ball control, strength and speed are scored on the basis of body type. In an informal track meet, for example, each event is run by classification groups, and a single pupil, in group F, gets credit for his first place plus one point for participation.

Oak Park, Illinois, is another school district in which physical education is viewed as an important tool for meeting individual pupil needs. Highly qualified physical education specialists work directly with elementary and junior high school classes on a three-day-per-week basis.

INDIVIDUALIZING INSTRUCTION

They maintain a close association with the classroom teachers in order to achieve a high level of integration in the child's total school experience. The following procedures for individualizing instruction in the junior high school girls' physical education classes at Hatch and Mann Schools are illustrative:[6]

During the posture screening program conducted in September, girls needing special help are identified by the physical therapist, working with a team of physical education teachers and nurses, and consulting with local physicians as required. Individual exercise programs are planned and conducted with parent cooperation.

Warm-up activities are individualized as a usual procedure. When exercises are used, each student works independently, varying the number of times the exercise is performed, and in some cases varying the exercise itself, according to her individual needs. If sports skills are practiced, each girl follows a progression of basket shooting, or target throwing, or wall volleying appropriate to her level of skill in the unit in which the class is engaged.

Ability groupings are sometimes used for skills practice. Those students with more ability in throwing and catching a softball practice together in order to improve through practicing with increased distance, harder and faster throws, or more complex combination skill drills. Practice activities for the poorer performers are modified to provide realistic goals and adequate opportunities to experience success.

Physical education classes are small (15 to 25 girls). Games are frequently modified to fit the needs of the given class group. Many original game variations have been created to solve unique local instruction problems.

Opportunities for individual personal guidance abound. It is felt that the teacher's informal guidance of students in the locker room before and after class is especially needed with the junior high school age group. Students are given complete responsibility for administering their own locker room procedures in order that the teacher may be free to talk with students during this time. Additional counseling time is provided by use of the individual warm-up procedure. Each student knows in advance which activities constitute her daily warm-up. She assumes the responsibility for completing her warm-up at her own pace prior to the time when the class is called to order. The teacher uses this eight to ten minute period for guidance of individual class members.

Individualizing instruction may be a particularly difficult challenge in a large high school. Steps taken to solve this problem at the Niles Township High Schools, Skokie, Illinois, are described below.[7] The Niles Township High Schools enroll approximately 3,000 girls in daily physical education programs in two four-year high school buildings. The community has provided excellent financial support for the physical education program and has endorsed a forward-looking educational philos-

---

[6] For this material, the authors are indebted to Miss Margaret K. Polerecky, Physical Education Instructor, Hatch and Mann Schools, Oak Park, Illinois.

[7] For this material, the authors are indebted to Miss Helen Heitmann, Chairman, Girls' Physical Education Department, Niles Township High School West, Skokie, Illinois.

ophy. Administrative leadership has been a key factor in building an outstanding physical education curriculum. These favorable circumstances do not eliminate the problems of individualizing instruction, however.

In an attempt to provide for individual differences, classes are divided on the basis of AAHPER fitness tests, administered to all freshman girls. Girls with composite scores at the 50th percentile or above are grouped together, and those below this level make up the other class.

This method of class division is helpful in individualizing instruction if teaching can be adjusted to accommodate the differences in learning rate and ability between the two groups. Generally, the upper group responds well to the usual demonstration-practice procedures, and is quick to learn given skills reasonably well. If top performance is desired, specific individual guidance is necessary on the basis of body build and efficient movement patterns.

On the other hand, the lower percentile students have to be helped through the mechanics of a skill more carefully. Lesson plans, even though they are for the same sport, do not reflect the same specific aims, objectives, and goals for both classes. Certain problems in mechanics, weight, muscular weakness and the lack of desire to move are general in the lower group, and can be treated collectively.

The activity curriculum is the same for both ability groups, with the exception of the elimination of certain apparatus activities for the lower group. This is due to their usual lack of success in this sort of activity, and the safety factor created by little strength or skill. Instead, this group is given a course in fundamental movement. In this course, the student identifies her major areas of muscular weakness, appraises her ability to balance, and determines her degree of flexibility. Work is individually assigned on the basis of these factors. Rhythmic exercise, ball gymnastics, balance beam, Indian clubs, and hoop activities are incorporated.

For those who, for medical reasons, cannot participate in regular physical education classes, an adaptive program is offered. Each student is given activities designed to meet her own needs relative to her temporary or permanent handicap. These include strength, flexibility, and balance exercises, recreational skills within the range of individual physical ability, and sports and physical activity appreciation. Specific work is assigned daily, and progress toward a preset goal is recorded on special charts.

There are three phases to the adaptive program. The first is for students returning to school after serious illness. If the doctor advises, these students are assigned to bed rest. During the second phase, when rest is no longer necessary, the student is given mild physical activity. When the doctor indicates, the student enters the third phase of the program, adaptive physical activity, under the direction of a teacher who is an adaptive specialist. A plan for movement rehabilitation is designed by the teacher and doctor. If the ailment is corrected the student may return to the regular program, or certain phases of it. Certain activities might be excluded from the student's program, but she would not remain in the adaptive classes. In some instances, it might be psychologically advantageous for an individual to remain in regular activity with restrictions on full participation. For instance, one might play fullback in soccer, rather than halfback or forward.

Adjustments are also made for religious convictions concerning dancing and health instruction. Accommodations to individual differences in the Niles Township High School Girls' Physical Education program range from occasional modifications within the classroom, to administrative assignments of students to classes, to complete individualized programs to meet specific physical limitations of students.

Ridgewood High School, Norridge, Illinois, is a relatively new high school, built to offer an educational program organized in accordance with the recommendations of the Trump report.[8] Facilities have been constructed to permit flexible scheduling, varying class size, and opportunities for individual study. The staff members employed are creative and experimental in outlook and sympathetic toward the development of new patterns in secondary education. Provisions for individualizing physical education at Ridgewood High School are described in the following paragraphs: [9]

I. *The general plan*

The first two years of physical education at Ridgewood High School are designed to give the student a broad general background in basic physical education activities. Emphasis is primarily on physical fitness, team sports, and activities which are most fitting to this age group.

In the junior and seniors years, the student experiences a curriculum which is geared toward individual activities and individual sports. Physical fitness is integrated within the program and presented with the hope that it will be important enough to the student to carry over into adult life.

In order to facilitate the program, students are scheduled for four one hour class periods per week. We have found the one hour class period far more satisfactory than a shorter class period meeting each day of the week.

We believe that it is quite apparent that our basic program is not unlike other excellent physical education curriculums. Our aim is to develop a superior physical education course of study for the students of Ridgewood High School.

II. *How is the physical education program of Ridgewood High School different from the conventional physical education program?*

A. Physical education individual study

This phase of the program allows any student to come into the gymnasium during a resource period (study period). At this time, the student meets with the teacher and plans a continuous course of study. For example: the student may wish to practice volleyball skills, or work on the trampoline, or practice tennis skills. With the teacher, he or she plans a program to undertake during subsequent physical education individual study periods.

B. Seminar size groups (fifteen or less)

These groups plan their courses for each nine week period. It is easily recognized that a group of this size has a marvelous advantage in activi-

[8] J. Lloyd Trump, *Images of the Future*, National Association of Secondary-School Principals (Washington, D.C.: National Education Association, 1959).

[9] For this material, the authors are indebted to Mr. James Smith, Director of Physical Education, Ridgewood High School, Norridge, Illinois.

ties such as tennis, badminton, archery, etc. Individual attention and instruction is readily given to a group of this number.

C. Science enrichment

Through science enrichment, which consists of one large group lecture and one seminar class per week, we present our health program. The health program is integrated with biology and science classes. Consequently, teachers in the science area and the teachers in physical education work cooperatively. For example: When the biology classes were studying a unit on the human body, a lecture on bones and muscles was given in one enrichment, and in another, a lecture on the effects of exercise on circulation. This arrangement allows for superior instruction by providing the most capable teacher available for the lecture.

Numerous other health lectures have been given during enrichment. Some of these are as follows:

Lectures on—
  Alcohol
  Narcotics
  Mental health
  Dental health
  Physical fitness
  Nutrition
  Heredity and environment
  Skin care

D. General aides:

With the use of general aides (adults from the community who do not have a degree, but who do have the ability to work with youngsters), we are able to eliminate time consuming tasks which are not of a teaching nature. General aides assist in preparation for class, take attendance, grade papers, supervise physical education individual study areas, supervise the locker room, repair equipment, etc.

Individualizing instruction is an extremely complex task facing all educators. No format exists for dealing with individual differences. No standard plan of operations can be routinized; no perfect pattern is apt to emerge. Although it is not possible to prescribe solutions to the many difficulties involved, progress is being made in this important area. Clymer and Kearney have listed ten needs that must be taken into account as teachers attempt to adjust to individual differences in working with instructional groups: [10]

1. The need to know the students
2. The need to recognize that not all teachers will adjust to individual differences in the same way
3. The need to provide generous time allotments
4. The need to plan carefully whatever is to be done in the classroom
5. The need to work effectively with the group as a whole

[10] Theodore Clymer and Nolan C. Kearney, "Curricular and Instructional Provisions for Individual Differences," *Individualizing Instruction*, p. 276.

INDIVIDUALIZING INSTRUCTION

6. The need to move slowly into any type of adjustment to individual differences
7. The need to accept more noise and more confusion
8. The need to recognize failure and begin again
9. The need to accept less than 100 percent adjustment to individual differences
10. The need to recognize that adjusting to individual differences calls for plain, hard work.

Recognition of the importance of individual differences is the first step. Perception of those needs listed above should lead to more effective teaching. And, with better individualization of instruction, physical education will become more meaningful in the lives of students.

9

Staff Utilization

Basically, the quality of the educational experiences of pupils in American public schools and the degree to which students attain worthwhile educational objectives depend upon the quality and competence of the teachers. The shortage of capable teachers is one of the greatest problems facing the teaching profession today. In many schools throughout the country, it is not unusual to find a teacher replacement factor of 30 per cent or more each year, even in districts that pay relatively high salaries. Each year larger numbers of children enter school, and more pupils remain in school. These two forces combine to require a larger and larger teaching staff in our schools, but the supply of new teachers of sufficient competence to maintain the quality of education desired is not keeping up with faculty needs in many states and districts.

Another problem, with particular relevance to male teachers, is that industry, business, and other professions offer financial rewards that are more attractive than teacher salaries so that competition for the type of person best qualified for teaching drains away many persons who would become superior teachers.

Still another problem lies in salary schedules, which vary greatly from state to state, and even from district to district. The net effect is that many of our better teachers are recruited to, or voluntarily apply for, positions in districts with higher salaries and better working conditions, which in turn tends to lower the quality of the teaching staff of the schools these persons leave.

All in all, there are several basic reasons for the present-day concern regarding how best to provide quality teaching in America's schools and how best to utilize the talents our qualified teachers do possess. This situation has led to the widespread concern expressed throughout the country about this serious problem. Several significant projects have been developed in recent years to alleviate this crucial situation. One outstanding example of leadership in this area is the Commission on the Experimental Study of the Utilization of the Staff in the Secondary School, appointed by the National Association of Secondary School Principals of the National Education Association, supported by the Fund for the Advancement of Education, established by the Ford Foundation. This commission has stimulated thought and experimental programs of action throughout the country.

BASIC ASSUMPTIONS

Underlying the problem of shortage of qualified teachers and the development of new ideas for the most effective utilization of the existing staff are several basic assumptions expressed by the Commission on the Experimental Study of the Utilization of the Staff in the Secondary School: [1]

1. The quality of education depends largely upon the quality of teaching.
2. The results of instruction depend largely upon the ways in which teachers function in a school.
3. Methods of teaching should be related to the purposes of instruction.
4. Teaching is a complex art; different levels of competence and training are needed for the various functions teachers now perform and which they are likely to do in the future.
5. Teachers differ in their interests and abilities to perform the various functions of teaching; the quality of teaching may be improved by recognizing these differences.
6. Education must compete with other professions and industry for the services of the most able young people.
7. Unless changes are made in the use of the teachers we now have and are likely to obtain in the next few years, the present trend to increase class sizes, eliminate courses, and employ more and more teachers with inadequate preparation will become accepted policy; such developments will cause deterioration in the quality of education.
8. Educators must continuously explore designs for the improvement of instruction.

THE EVOLVING ROLES OF TEACHERS

There are many factors operating that contribute to make the present-day teacher's duties and responsibilities more complex and different than they were in the earliest days of American public education. The effec-

[1] J. Lloyd Trump, *New Horizons for Secondary School Teachers,* Commission on the Experimental Study of the Utilization of the Staff in Secondary Schools, National Association of Secondary-School Principals (Washington, D.C.: National Education Association, 1958), pp. 31, 32.

tive utilization of teachers must be considered in light of these conditions. The vast "explosion of knowledge" and the ever increasing rate at which new knowledge is being produced has tremendous implications concerning the role of the teacher. The steady increase in the population in the United States, resulting in a large increase in the school-age population, along with our concept of free public education for all persons through high school, plus extensive opportunities for higher education combine to provide new challenges for today's teachers. Worldwide developments in the areas of government and politics as exemplified by the rapid formation of new, independent countries, and ideological struggles and the economic complexities as indicated by the development of the European Common Market plan, are examples of other significant forces that affect the role of the schoolteacher. Three characteristics might be applied to sum up the above and many other factors that affect the teacher's role; namely, that we are now living in a world of rapid change, that staggering amounts of new information are accumulating daily, and that the world is smaller now and its peoples are more interrelated and interdependent. The teacher's traditional role of passing along his personal knowledge and stimulating students to gain more information from standard sources such as textbooks and encyclopedias has now changed most significantly.

TRADITIONAL TEACHER UTILIZATION

A brief analysis of the ways in which teachers traditionally have used their time may assist in proposing suggestions for the more effective utilization of these teachers in the future.

In general, most teachers have been assigned the same load in terms of the number of classes they teach per day and per week. Some provision has been made for modifying class load because of administrative duties and extracurricular assignments. Beginning teachers are assigned the same class load as experienced teachers. In fact, in many instances, beginning teachers or teachers new to a school are assigned not only the same number of classes as other teachers, but are given classes containing more unruly and disinterested students, or students of low ability. Compared with other professions, the teaching profession is remiss in its policies and procedures for the proper gradual induction of beginning practitioners into full professional duties. New teachers sometimes have larger classes and more classes with students of low ability than do experienced teachers, when probably the policy should be just the reverse.

Teachers usually are assigned classes that conform in size to some predetermined teacher-pupil ratio, which is constant for most of the subjects in the school, particularly in the so-called "academic" subjects. Exceptions to this policy are more likely to be found in physical education, music, and typing.

Teachers perform many tasks that can be classified as "non-professional," such as monitoring, clerical work, housekeeping, record keeping, and similar subprofessional work. Some studies have estimated that as much as two-thirds of a high school teacher's time is devoted to such non-professional tasks, leaving only one-third of his time to the performance of his central professional purpose.

Teachers receive salaries that are based on years of teaching service and number of graduate credits earned, rather than upon the individualization of duties performed and a recognition of the quality of that performance.

Authorized teachers receive credentials that are general in nature and that make untenable assumptions about background and training for a broad spectrum of professional duties and teaching assignments, if high quality instruction is the chief goal to be attained.

Teachers must organize their subject matter and teaching procedures in many instances to conform to a pattern dictated by the standards of the Carnegie Unit, which is a prerequisite for admission to college by the college-oriented high school students. This obligation upon the teacher stifles creative ability and innovation that might improve the quality of instruction.

Teachers must teach in restrictive and inflexible classrooms and laboratories that frequently have not been constructed on the basis of the educational specifications that should be the central core of school planning.

Many teachers lack the proper supplies, equipment, and the mechanical aids to teaching that would make their services much more efficient and would contribute to higher quality in teaching.

Thoughtful, perceptive teachers and administrators; school-board members; professional educational authorities; and subject-matter scholars have viewed the above practices with increasing concern in recent years. It is imperative that the quality of the schools be improved continuously. Much progress now is being made in the problem areas listed above. The following chapters will discuss these topics as they are relevant to the teaching of physical education in the public schools. A more detailed analysis of each problem in the context of the physical education curriculum will be made, followed by examples of experiments and innovations that schools throughout the country are undertaking. Each chapter will conclude with suggestions by the authors for consideration, trial, and evaluation by interested physical educators and administrators who believe that the profession of education has the obligation of evaluating continuously its policies and procedures, rather than relying on tradition, common practice, and opinion as a basis for effective teacher utilization.

IMPROVING TEACHER UTILIZATION

In order to make more effective use of teachers, Trump suggests the following: [2]

1. Reduce the number of hours a teacher teaches to not more than 15 hours per week so he may have more time to prepare materials for instruction, study his subject field, keep up to date professionally, and confer with colleagues.
2. The educational profession must show the importance of more public recognition for the professional role of the teacher and must interpret this role to the public.
3. Modify the criteria for grouping students, and change the organization of the curriculum and instruction.
4. Provide the teacher with competent clerical and instruction assistants.
5. Make optimum use of modern mechanical aids to teaching.
6. Teachers should be assigned on the basis of their individual abilities, interests and physical energies.
7. Teachers should have private offices and working areas properly equipped to facilitate professional productivity.
8. Emphasize the necessity for quality teaching in order to insure quality education for all pupils.

All of these comments apply to physical education teachers as well as to teachers in other subject fields. This chapter and the next two chapters discuss most of Trump's suggestions as they relate specifically to physical education teachers, indicating what some schools currently are doing to improve these situations and offering proposals for further innovation and experimentation that seek better solutions to these problems.

PROFESSIONAL AND NON-PROFESSIONAL DUTIES OF TEACHERS

All public school teachers are well aware of the considerable amount of time they devote daily to tasks that cannot be regarded as "professional" in nature. That is, these tasks could be performed by other personnel with less academic subject-matter preparation and less training in professional education. Relief from such tasks would enable teachers to spend most of their time in performing the tasks for which they are professionally trained. There are several advantages to such a plan. (1)

[2] J. Lloyd Trump, *New Directions to Quality Education,* Commission on the Experimental Study of the Utilization of the Staff in Secondary Schools, National Association of Secondary-School Principals (Washington, D.C.: National Education Association, 1960), p. 5.

The same number of teachers could perform a variety of professional services for a larger number of students. (2) The teachers themselves would be more highly challenged and motivated in their daily work and hence would receive greater pleasure and satisfaction. (3) Many potentially able persons who reject teaching as a career because of their objection to having to perform non-professional chores would be attracted to the profession. (4) When teachers are permitted to spend a majority of their time on professional duties and receive the assistance of subprofessional and non-professional personnel, it can be demonstrated that the total cost of the school staff is no greater than under the present typical organization. In fact, at least one plan has been suggested whereby a school could be staffed with professional and non-professional personnel for the same cost as previously and still permit a 15 per cent salary increase for the professional teachers.[3]

A review of the physical education literature on this topic fails to reveal published research that describes the duties typically performed by public school physical education teachers and that judges the extent to which each of these duties could be considered "professional." Neither does there appear to be any study that indicates the amount of time the physical educator spends on non-professional tasks. Estimates in general educational literature indicate that teachers spend as much as two-thirds of their time on non-professional duties. If this truly is the case, there is urgent cause for alarm, which should stimulate study and experimentation with a view to improving this situation as rapidly as possible.

The education profession should take a cue from the medical profession wherein a highly elaborate hierarchy has been established of clearly defined duties and the qualifications required to perform them. Salary scales are dovetailed into this personnel framework. The physician thus is freed to spend a great majority of his time in the performance of the highly skilled and professional work for which he is carefully selected and trained. Trump has summarized this area of concern in education by proposing that in the school of the future machines do the figuring, clerks do the clerking, teachers do the teaching, and students do the learning.

To study this problem, three major steps are necessary. (1) Criteria must be established and described in behavioral terms to identify each teaching task as being either professional or non-professional. (2) Procedures must be set up to observe and record accurately the actual duties that teachers do perform and the amount of time devoted to each task. Two suggestions for carrying out this phase of the study are (a) to

[3] J. Lloyd Trump, "New Directions in Scheduling and Use of Staff in the High School," *California Journal of Secondary Education*, XXXIII, No. 6 (October, 1958), 366.

develop a teacher diary report procedure and (*b*) to use qualified and trained observers. A combination of these methods would also be feasible. (3) The duties reported and described in step (2) would be evaluated in terms of the criteria established in step (1), and a determination would be rendered for each teacher task as to its classification in the professional or non-professional category.

Briefly, the following criteria have been proposed for identifying a task performed by a physical education teacher as a professional task. These criteria will be refined and improved with experience, and additional criteria will be developed in future studies. A professional task is one that (1) requires the special competence of a physical educator as a professionally trained person and (2) must be embodied in teacher roles.

This approach involves a careful analysis of teacher role and teacher competence. One such analysis is provided by a study that emphasizes the importance of developing criteria of teacher competence described in operational terms to indicate what a teacher should be able to do and the educational outcomes he seeks to accomplish.[4] Another step in the study is to define the major areas of responsibility that are common to successful teachers. Within each major area of responsibility, the degree of expertness required is described.

The Teacher Competence report lists six major roles of teachers:[5] (1) The teacher is a director of learning and also (2) is a counselor and guidance worker. These two roles make major contributions to the promotion of pupil growth. Additionally, the teacher has two liaison roles, namely, (3) as a mediator of the culture and (4) serving as a link with the community. Finally, two more roles are classified under the general heading of program-building roles, which include (5) the teacher as a participating member of the school staff and (6) the teacher as a responsible member of the profession. The report gives detailed examples of the competence required for the teacher to perform each of these essential roles at a minimum satisfactory level of success.

It would seem feasible to use this teacher competence study as a framework for the development of an analysis of teachers' duties and the classification of these duties into professional or non-professional categories. By using these six general areas of teacher responsibilities as an over-all framework, more specific descriptions of teacher duties and the degree and nature of expertness required to carry out each duty should be developed in the local school district or even in the department of physical education in each school. It would be folly for anyone to attempt to develop a statement of specific criteria of teacher competence and

[4] The Commission on Teacher Education, *Teacher Competence—Its Nature and Scope* (San Francisco: The California Teachers Association, 1957).
[5] *Ibid.*, pp. 12–21.

professional behavior that would be applicable to all teachers and to every learning situation. Rather, by using the six general areas of teacher responsibilities listed previously, a local subject-matter department could develop special standards of practice unique and most applicable to its own situation.

One final point, which is crucial to an understanding of the whole problem of distinguishing between professional and non-professional duties of teachers, concerns the use of theory. The mark of a professional person is that he determines the practices he will employ from reference to an existing body of theory. The technician or craftsman usually has a high degree of skill in carrying out his particular practice; but he does not necessarily understand, or even care to know about, the theories from which these practices are derived, or how such theories and their modifications can lead to improved practices. Furthermore, the professional person continually tests the theoretical assumptions that underly his practices, and he modifies the theory as new knowledge and discoveries become available in his area of special competence.

Many physical education teachers and curriculum leaders in the past were vulnerable to the charge that they failed to give sufficient attention to the above concept and did not follow it in practice. Physical educators today must base their practices upon current knowledge of teaching and learning theory, contribute to the testing of this theory in practice, and work for continued improvement both of the theory and the practice of physical education.

Another related approach to the identification of teacher duties as either professional or non-professional in nature is exemplified in the *Stanford Appraisal Guides, Evaluating Teaching and Learning*, Part I, "Competence in Teaching."[6] In effect, this work is an extension of the study[7] discussed on the previous pages. Twenty-five items of teacher behavior have been classified into the following categories of competence:

    Competence in Developing Goals for Teaching and Learning
    Competence in Planning for Teaching and Learning
    Competence in Fulfilling Plans for Teaching and Learning
    Competence in Evaluating Teaching and Learning
    Competence in Professional Responsibilities
    Competence in Community Responsibilities
    Over-all Appraisal

Physical education specialists on the project staff are preparing specific descriptions of physical education teacher behaviors that exemplify the

---

[6] "Competence in Teaching," Part I, in *Stanford Appraisal Guides, Evaluating Teaching and Learning*, Secondary Education Project, School of Education (Stanford, Calif.: Stanford University Press, September, 1962).

[7] The Commission on Teacher Education, *loc. cit.*

performance of the twenty-five general competences listed in the *Guide*. This detailed series of descriptions of specific physical education teacher behaviors could be used as a list of criteria against which to judge all teacher duties found in a job analysis and could serve as a useful method for categorizing each duty as being either professional or non-professional in nature.

Despite the logical desire to relieve the teacher of as many non-professional duties as possible, it is important to note that the professional teacher still must be prepared on occasion to direct, assist with, or actually perform non-professional tasks. There are times of emergency and pressures of expediency that will require such action by the teacher in the non-professional category of duties.

DIFFERENTIATION OF STAFF PERSONNEL

Recognizing the inefficiencies in uses of teachers indicated in the previous section, many schools now are embarked on teacher utilization plans and experiments. Various categories of professional and non-professional personnel have been established in different school systems; and, as a result, the nomenclature at times becomes confusing. However, much attention has been focused on the instructional staff classifications suggested by the Commission on the Experimental Study of the Utilization of the Staff in the Secondary School.[8] One report of the Commission lists the following types of personnel that should compose the instructional staff of the school of the future:

    Professional Teachers
        Teacher Specialists
        General Teachers
    Instruction Assistants
    Clerks
    General Aides
    Community Consultants
    Staff Specialists

Detailed descriptions of the responsibilities and qualifications of each category of personnel are included in the report.

Table 9–1, which is a chart devised by Trump, concisely summarizes the types of staff, basic training required, and an estimate of numbers of such staff required in a high school.

---

[8] J. Lloyd Trump, *Images of the Future, A New Approach to the Secondary School*, Commission on the Experimental Study of the Utilization of the Staff in the Secondary School, National Association of Secondary-School Principals (Washington, D.C.: National Education Association, 1959), pp. 15–18.

TABLE 9-1

Instructional Staff in a Secondary School *

Type of Staff	Functions	Training	Numbers
Professional teachers	Plan methods and materials of instruction; teach ideas, concepts, appreciations; direct learning activities; counsel and consult; supervise evaluation; assist with student activities; provide specialized services for which competent and interested; employed on year-round basis if able and interested	Master's degree and beyond with specialization as needed	About one for each forty students aggregate in school
Para-professional assistants	Perform specific aspects of teaching below professional level of teachers and above clerks; read and evaluate English themes, science reports, etc.; confer with students about their progress and provide teachers with reports; serve as laboratory assistants; supervise specific out-of-school projects; assist with student activities typically employed ten–twenty hours per week	Usually college graduates but always trained for specific duties assigned	About twenty hours' services per week per professional teacher
Clerks	Type; duplicate materials; check materials and prepare reports; grade objective tests; keep records; check and distribute supplies; take attendance and perform other routine services; other clerical duties; employed on forty-hour-per-week basis	High school graduate: business education	About ten hours' services per week per professional teacher
General aides	Control and supervise students on school grounds, in cafeteria, corridors, study halls, auditorium, etc., and at extraclass activity functions; work with students in developing maximum self-controls; assist in student activities when competent; typically employed ten–twenty hours per week	High school graduate: general courses; some college desirable	About eight hours' services per week per professional teacher
Community consultants	Lecture; consult; make tapes, records, kinescopes, slides, films, etc.; typically volunteers, although might be paid; used whenever needed or desirable to provide special information and services	Unusual competence; selected from file of available persons	Indefinite, depending on local circumstances
Staff specialists	Special services in such areas as guidance, research, health, reading, aid to exceptional children, audio-visual materials, and curriculum development; supplement work of professional teachers; full-time persons who might serve several schools as needed	Highly trained in area of specialty	Indefinite, depending on local circumstances

* From J. Lloyd Trump, "New Directions in Scheduling and Use of Staff in the High School," *California Journal of Secondary Education*, XXXIII, No. 6 (October, 1958), 367.

Trump illustrates how such personnel might be utilized effectively in a high school physical education department.[9]

Professional Teachers

These teachers would be responsible for planning, supervising, and evaluating the total program of the physical education department. In addition, they probably would become members of teaching teams.

Instruction Assistants

These assistants have sufficient professional preparation and competence to perform specified teaching duties, such as supervision and evaluation in laboratories; supervision of athletic fields, gymnasium rooms, and swimming pools; assisting in the teaching of specific skills; and similar duties.

General Aides

These persons, who do not have professional preparation in physical education, can be utilized for non-technical services, such as patrolling corridors and entrances, directing traffic and spectators at games, selling and taking tickets, and similar tasks.

Community Consultants

These are individuals who may be better qualified, or more prominent in reputation, in a specific area of ability within the physical education field, such as a major league baseball player or a physician with a strong interest in sports medicine. These consultants can be invited to the school at specific times for particular purposes relating to the attainment of an objective in the physical education program, where they can render a unique and highly expert service.

Professional Consultants

These are specialists who use a technology in instruction, pupil personnel services, health services, and similar specialized areas, and who serve on an invitational consultant basis to assist with the solution of special problems. A program of adapted physical education might utilize the periodic services of such a professional consultant. A curriculum consultant from a nearby university might be employed by the school district to carry out a physical education curriculum evaluation.

[9] J. Lloyd Trump, "An Image of a Future Secondary School Health, Physical Education, and Recreation Program," *Journal of Health, Physical Education and Recreation*, XXXII (January, 1961), 16–18.

Clerks

These persons are assigned to relieve the teachers of such duties as record keeping, care and issue of equipment and supplies, typing and filing of letters, reports and other necessary paper work, and similar duties.

Bush and Allen, in their proposal for a new design for high school education, list three major categories of staff personnel.[10] One of the authors of this book has had the privilege of working as a member of the Stanford University Secondary Education Project and participating in the development of the material cited in this study here and in other references throughout this book.

Professional Staff

This suggested staff consists of senior teachers, fully qualified teachers who do not have the lengthy experience and advanced professional preparation of the senior teachers, beginning teachers, and intern teachers who are in a teacher credential preparation program in a nearby college. The senior teacher is in charge of the course, including the curriculum design, the administration of the course, the major instructional responsibilities, and the assignment of staff to assist with instruction. Regular teachers and beginning teachers have more limited responsibility, such as assisting with the conceptual development of the course outline and content, and will assume considerable instructional responsibility for designated portions of the course. Interns will provide curriculum development assistance under direction and can also help with instructional and administrative details.

Supporting Staff

This title refers to teaching assistants and to clerks who give direct support and assistance to the professional staff members. A teaching assistant could have limited instructional duties, could correct papers and grade projects, and could assist with research and preparation of instructional lessons and laboratory experiences. Clerks would provide typical clerical assistance and, in addition, might be given certain proctoring duties. These aides should have a minimum of two years' community college or junior college education as a qualification for employment.

---

[10] Robert N. Bush and Dwight W. Allen, "A New Design for High School Education: Assuming a Flexible Schedule" (unpublished material, Secondary Education Project, School of Education, Stanford University, July, 1961), pp. 13–17.

Resource Personnel

This designation is for specialists from other fields whose primary employment generally is with an organization other than the school. Examples are physicians, attorneys, newspaper editors, engineers, psychologists, authors, artists, professional athletes, and so forth. These persons may be invited by the school to assist with the part of the instruction of a course involving their specialty.

The Trump and Bush-Allen plans seem similar in many respects. However, it is obvious that differentiation of staff categories, functions, and qualifications can be attained in many different ways. Local school districts will want to work out the classifications best suited for their local situation rather than to follow the plans of others without discriminating study. The Trump and Bush-Allen plans are presented here as examples of proposals that clearly indicate the recognition of the crucial problem of effective utilization and that attempt to improve this deficiency in secondary schools. Physical education teachers, supervisors, administrators, and professional education leaders are urged to study these proposals for the stimulation they can provide in the development of local plans for best solving the staff utilization problem in a given school district or even in one school.

TEAM TEACHING

The term "team teaching" has been given to the practice of using two or more members of the instructional staff in the teaching of a course. It is evident that the planning, teaching, and evaluation of a course involves the performance of a wide variety of both professional and nonprofessional duties. The reorganization of the staff into categories, such as those discussed in the previous section, permits the assignment of these duties to personnel with proper qualifications and competence and results in the most efficient use of personnel at all levels.

Anderson describes a teaching team as follows: "Specifically, a teaching team is a group of several teachers (usually between three and six) jointly responsible for planning, carrying out, and evaluating an educational program for a group of children." [11]

The administrative problems then arise concerning organization of the two or more members of the staff who will compose the "instructional team," and how to combine their talents and abilities in order to bring about the best combination of competences to result in an effective learn-

---

[11] Robert H. Anderson, "Team Teaching," *NEA Journal*, March, 1961, p. 52.

ing experience for all the pupils. Team teaching is now the subject of widespread experimentation and controversy and apparently is being carried on in most school subjects and at most grade levels, according to reports in the educational literature.

In considering the development of teaching teams, it must be realized that many kinds and varieties are possible. There is no one set pattern best for all schools or best for any particular subject area. The interests and qualifications of the personnel available, the administrative climate, and public acceptance are important factors to be considered in each local situation. In practice, a majority of teaching teams seem to be organized within subject-matter fields. However, there are many examples of such teams operating across subject-field lines, ranging from the combination of two fields to schools that have organized an entire staff representing several subject fields into "teams" serving a "house," or a school-within-a-school.

Trump indicates several ways in which a school can introduce the team teaching concept and develop it gradually.[12] One common way is for two teachers, who each formerly taught their own classes in a particular subject, to combine the students of the two classes into one large class and to divide the teaching duties so that each teacher teaches those phases of the course in which he is most interested and most qualified to instruct. Logically, the next step is for those teachers to do joint, advanced planning for the course the next time it is offered, followed later on by the possibility of adding teachers to the team from other subject fields where there is optimum opportunity for the correlation of subjects.

Another easy step is to make use of community consultants on special occasions and for a particular phase of a course. Increasing the availability of clerical assistance for teachers is another forward step to changing staff patterns. The employment of instruction assistants is another early step that can be taken. Many high schools have begun this program by the employment of assistants to grade themes and compositions for English teachers. Some states now authorize schools to employ playground supervisors for the noon-hour period to relieve teachers of that long-standing, traditional duty. Schools are making greater use of instructional aides or assistants in the form of candidates in professional education programs from nearby colleges and universities. Sometimes these students are paid, or sometimes they perform these public school duties as a part of a field experience requirement in their professional

[12] J. Lloyd Trump, and Dorsey Baynham, *Focus on Change: Guide to Better Schools,* Commission on the Experimental Study of the Utilization of the Staff in the Secondary School, National Association of Secondary-School Principals, National Education Association (Chicago: Rand McNally & Co., 1961), pp. 105-9.

education program. There are many individual possibilities for developing the team and for accomplishing more effective staff utilization.

In one evaluation report concerning team teaching projects, Trump and Baynham reported these conclusions:

Opportunities for improving classroom instruction were greater in the project classes than in customary classes;
Classes of varied sizes offered opportunity to use a variety of techniques, instructional materials, and sources of information;
The use of the specialized talents of available staff was extended in all cases.

When all the returns were in from team teaching projects, these reports stood out:

Team teaching provides the setting in which individual teachers can best use and further develop their individual talents.
Students can benefit from the best that teachers have to offer.[13]

Team teaching in physical education was involved in some of the projects, but the extent to which physical education was considered in the above conclusions is not precisely known. However, it seems reasonable to believe that these conclusions are tenable for the team-teaching opportunities available in physical education.

In general, it is believed that the following values of team teaching are likely to accrue: teachers will teach in their areas of greatest competence and interest; teachers may use special abilities more effectively; teacher morale and dedication to the task will materially improve; teachers will have more time for planning and study; and a greater recognition of individual differences will result.

Appraisals concerning the usefulness of team teaching for the pupils instructed in this manner are very tentative in nature at this time. Cunningham, apparently evaluating team teaching in elementary school projects, suggests that there is little evidence that team teaching increases pupil achievement.[14] Subjective reports by school administrators range from highly favorable with respect to pupil achievement and interest to various degrees of unfavorability. This last comment perhaps is indicative of the status of measurable evidence at this time. Varying degrees of success have been achieved in many schools using the team-teaching concept, but the data available in total do not lend themselves to broad generalizations of a statewide or national scope. Perhaps this innovation, like many others in education, is a highly individualized matter dependent upon many crucial variables existing in each local situation.

[13] *Ibid.*, pp. 86, 87.
[14] Luvern L. Cunningham, "Team Teaching: Where Do We Stand?" in *Administrator's Notebook* (Chicago: University of Chicago Press, April, 1960), Vol. VIII, No. 8.

STAFF UTILIZATION IN ELEMENTARY SCHOOL PHYSICAL EDUCATION

Several examples of innovations in the use of staff personnel in elementary school physical education are described in this section. It is hoped that the enterprising administrator or physical education supervisor will study these examples in order to discover possibilities for initiating a program of improved local staff utilization.

The Franklin Elementary School in Lexington, Massachusetts, is organized on the basis of three teams composed of varying combinations of experienced teacher (team leader), senior teachers, regular teachers, and clerical aides. Each team conducts instruction for part of the five hundred pupils in the school. There is one senior teacher who teaches music, art, and physical education. She serves all three groups of pupils. She receives occasional help from visiting specialists. One of her main educational objectives is to integrate art and music in several lessons and to include such physical education activities as singing games and folk dances in the art-music lessons.[15]

An example of team teaching in physical education at the elementary school level is reported in Ontario, California.[16] This team-teaching plan was started in one school; it was so successful that it was instituted in seventeen more schools in that district. The basic concept is that each classroom teacher becomes a specialist in one phase of the physical education program that this teacher applies to all pupils in grades four, five, and six in her school. Pupil groups are rotated so that they progress through the program and receive instruction from each teacher in her area of specialization. Each child takes physical education daily for a twenty-minute period. Table 9–2 illustrates a nine-week schedule.

Variations of staff utilization introduced into this plan in some schools include: (1) The above rotating schedule is used four days a week, while allotting one day per week for the elementary teacher to teach physical education to the pupils in her own room. (2) In one large school involving eleven teachers and rotating groups, a physical education specialist is assigned on a "roving" basis; he assists where needed and also helps with the planning of the program and some phases of its organization and administration in cooperation with the school principal and the district office.

---

[15] Arthur D. Morse, *Schools of Tomorrow-Today* (New York: Doubleday & Co., Inc., 1960), p. 15.
[16] Al Colebank, "Team Teaching Improves Elementary School Physical Education," *CAHPER Journal*, January–February, 1962, p. 10.

TABLE 9–2

Activity and Teacher	Weeks								
	1	2	3	4	5	6	7	8	9
Square dance (Miss Snead)	1	7	6	5	4	3	2	1	7
Relays, leadup activities (Miss Wilson)	2	1	7	6	5	4	3	2	1
Team games—boys (Mr. Arthur)	3–4	2–3	1–2	7–1	6–7	5–6	4–5	3–4	2–3
Team games—girls (Mrs. Cox)	3–4	2–3	1–2	7–1	6–7	5–6	4–5	3–4	2–3
Rhythms—folk dance (Mrs. Bon)	5	4	3	2	1	7	6	5	4
Stunts and Apparatus (Mrs. Gill)	6	5	4	3	2	1	7	6	5
Circle games (Mrs. Henry)	7	6	5	4	3	2	1	7	6

STAFF UTILIZATION IN HIGH SCHOOL PHYSICAL EDUCATION

In Beecher, Illinois, high school students were selected to be cadet teachers in physical education in order to lighten the teacher's load and at the same time to offer opportunities for experiences that will encourage students to enter the teaching profession. Also, extensive use of student clerical help was assigned to relieve teachers of clerical duties.[17] The staff of this school also kept a record of a complete week of teaching and related duties, including after-school tasks and night and week-end time that related to the teacher's work. From a review of the data found in this study, the teachers concluded that: (1) more time might be spent on preparation for classes, (2) time wasted in waiting for pupils to change gym shoes, etc., might be studied, (3) the time consumed on repairing equipment should be reviewed, (4) more time should be allotted for professional work, and (5) time taken from classwork for extracurricular activities should be examined.

Covina Valley High School at Covina, California, employed physical education aides to relieve teachers of some non-professional duties.[18] An attempt was made to assign one aide to each regular teacher each period. Most of the aides were physical education major students from a

[17] Bernice Bammann and John French, "A Variety of Improvements in Staff Utilization Are Tried in a Small High School at Beecher, Illinois," *The Bulletin of the National Association of Secondary School Principals,* XLII (January, 1958), 115–25.

[18] "How Aides Can Improve a Physical Education Program," *School Management,* VI (February, 1962), 57–58.

nearby college. Some qualified housewives were also employed. An aide had to agree to be present at the school for at least two consecutive periods daily. The salary averaged $2.00 per hour, depending upon length of service. This pay scale permitted the employment of three aides for the cost equivalent to the salary of a regular teacher. The aides' duties were to organize students for instruction; supervise or officiate physical education activities; supervise locker rooms; care for athletic equipment; check out equipment; keep records; assist teacher with planning, organizing, and conduct of the physical education program; assist in planning, administering, and scoring examinations; and to assist in appraising pupil performance for grading purposes.

During a two-year period, 1958–1960, the Crawford High School, San Diego, California, conducted an experimental program of team teaching in physical education. According to a report on the experiment, the purposes were to extend the use of regular teachers over a large group of students, to utilize non-credentialed personnel for certain instructional purposes to relieve regular teachers, and to improve the quality of instruction by the team-teaching method.[19] The team consisted of one team leader (a credentialed teacher), one team teacher (credentialed teacher), and two teaching aides (non-credentialed). This team was responsible for three classes of students from the same grade level. These students were grouped into one large group, or smaller groups, depending upon the nature and purposes of the instruction on a given day. The team leader was responsible for over-all planning. The credentialed teachers did the teaching; and the aides performed such duties as supervising group activity, locker-room supervision, equipment care and issue, and similar tasks. In evaluating the program, the report indicates that it was possible for teachers to capitalize on their special abilities in teaching, that teachers said they covered more material than they did in traditionally organized classes, and that they had a better opportunity to work individually with pupils.

One of the increasingly crucial problems in public school physical education is the lack of fully qualified women teachers. Many authorities have predicted that this situation will lead to more and more assignments of qualified men teachers to certain classes of physical education for girls and women in schools and colleges. In order to try out this type of staff utilization, one high school assigned the male chairman of the department of physical education to be instructor for a class of high-ability tenth- and eleventh-grade girls. After a period of initial adjustment to this new situation on the part of both the teacher and the girls, the class proceeded most satisfactorily for the remainder of the semester. The

[19] Letter from Ash Hayes, Assistant Supervisor of Physical Education, San Diego City Schools, San Diego, California, to John E. Nixon, March 26, 1962.

combined judgment of the girls in the class, the male teacher, and the two members of the women's physical education staff was favorable and clearly indicated that this method of staff utilization could be conducted in a satisfactory manner.

In concluding this section on examples of staff utilization in physical education, it might be pertinent to recall that the school athletic program has long used the principles emphasized here. Coaches should be credited with developing organizational plans that clearly are team-teaching models, just as the physical education program was the pioneer in providing a comprehensive program for the gifted students, namely the interscholastic athletic program. Team teaching in athletics is exemplified by Table 9–3.

PHYSICAL EDUCATION STAFF UTILIZATION IN THE FUTURE

The final section of this chapter presents ideas for the future concerning more efficient staff utilization in physical education. These suggestions are stated as hypotheses to be tested in practical school situations. It is hoped that interested schools will use and adapt these suggestions to their own situation and will conduct experimentation and evaluation of the outcomes so that the importance of these suggestions can be assessed. By continual efforts to conceive new, improved methods and practices and to test their consequences in action, education will truly advance as a scientific profession. Physical education should make its full contribution to this highly desirable goal.

Trump denotes how the school of the future appears to him with respect to staffing patterns in physical education.[20] He suggests that schools will make more effective use of the teacher's professional qualifications by the employment of six types of staff personnel; namely, professional teachers, instruction assistants, general aides, clerks, community consultants, and professional consultants. He indicates the nature of the duties each category of personnel would perform and emphasizes the professional roles of credentialed teachers in the areas of planning, supervising, and evaluating the entire program, and teaching in team situations so that each teacher makes his maximum contribution in his area of greatest teaching competence. Trump also specifies that this staffing pattern will make it possible for teachers to spend more time in physical education with small groups of fifteen pupils—a condition that rarely exists under today's organizational schemes and teacher assignment policies. There are many worthy suggestions for consideration in Trump's proposal.

[20] Trump, "An Image of a Future Secondary School Health, Physical Education, and Recreation Program," *op. cit.*, pp. 15–17.

TABLE 9-3

The Football Coaching Staff—A Teaching Team

Staff

Senior Teacher—Head Coach		
Teachers		
End Coach	Line Coach	Backfield Coach
Interns or Clerical Staff		
Trainer	Managers	Equipment Handlers

Students

Large Group—Team			
Small Group			
Line	Backfield	Offensive Formations	Defensive Formations
Individual			
Conditioning	Training Rules	Skills punting passing blocking tackling	Eligibility

As part of the Secondary Education Project at Stanford University, proposals have been developed for more effective utilization of physical education staff personnel.[21] Other phases of this proposal are discussed in the other chapters concerning flexible scheduling, grouping of pupils, and use of mechanical aids to teaching. Although reference to the entire proposal would make more clear the meaning of the symbols and details of Table 9–4, which follows, it seems useful to discuss briefly the nature of the suggestions made for the utilization of physical education staff.

Table 9–4 illustrates a flexible scheduling proposal for one group of high school girls. Although the chart includes all the dimensions of the study, a perusal of the column labeled "Staff" indicates the thinking involved in the utilization of staff, the specific concern of this chapter. Pupils in this study are grouped on the combined basis of interest and ability in physical education. The total proposal incorporates the categories of staff personnel listed previously in this chapter by Bush and Allen.

For example, referring to Table 9–4, the fifteen seventh-grade girls who are assigned to the Talented, High Interest Group will have one thirty-minute period per week of small group (SG) instruction and for this purpose will be combined with the fifteen seventh-grade boys, who also are classified in the Talented, High Interest Group. This class of thirty students (fifteen boys and fifteen girls) will meet once per week for thirty minutes. It will be taught by one professional teacher (T), probably a senior teacher. Moving to the eleventh grade, it will be noted that fifteen girls in the Talented, High Interest Group will have one period of thirty minutes for large group (LG) instruction per week. This large group will also be composed of tenth-grade boys and girls from the Talented, High Interest Groups, plus the eleventh-grade boys in the same classification. This will make a total of seventy-five boys and girls in this large group class. Looking at the staff assignments, there will be a senior teacher (T), one teacher aide (TA), and occasional use will be made of invited resource persons (R). During the six laboratory periods, the professional teacher (T) will be assisted by an intern (I), a teacher education candidate assigned by a nearby college for field experience. The staffing pattern for each grade level and for each type of instruction can be found in the column labeled "Staff." Similar charts exist for the other five types of groups of pupils involved in this total proposal.

In summary, it is clear that the need is urgent, the challenge is great, and the opportunities are unlimited for the improvement of staff utilization in physical education.

---

[21] Bush and Allen, *op. cit.*, section on Physical Education by John E. Nixon, pp. 97–110.

TABLE 9-4

Girls' Physical Education
Group IV-G: Talented, High Interest

Grade	Number of Students / Number of Student Modules	Total Periods	Periods Each Line	Type of Instruction	Staff	Other Groups Included	Student Modules from Other Groups	Total Student Modules	Student Modules per Section	Sections To Be Scheduled	Periods per Meeting	Meetings per Week
1	2/3	4	5	6	7	8	9	10	11	12	13	14
7	15 / 1	9	1	SG	T	7IV(B) (a) (g)	–	–	–	Dup	1	1
			4	Lab	T-I	7V(G) (b)	1	2	2	1	2	2
			3	Lab	T-I	7V(G) (b)	1	2	2	1	3	1
			1	Lab	T	(b)	–	1	1	1	1	1
8	15 / 1	9	1	LG	T-2TA-R	8IV(B), 9IV(B&G)	–	–	12	Dup	1	1
						8V(B&G), 9V(B&G)						
						8VI(B&G), 9VI(B&G)(a)						
			6	Lab	T	9IV(G) (b)	1	2	2	1	2	3
			2	Lab	I	(b)	–	1	1	1	2	1
9	15 / 1	8	1	LG	T-2TA-R	8IV(B&G), 9IV(B) (a)	–	–	12	Dup	1	1
						8V(B&G), 9V(B&G)						
						8VI(B&G), 9VI(B&G)						
			6	Lab	T	8IV(G) (b)	–	–	–	Dup	2	3
			1	Lab	I	(b)	1	1	1	1	1	1
10	15 / 1	8	1	LG	T-TA-R	10IV(B), 11IV(B&G) (a)	–	–	5	Dup	1	1
			6	Lab	T-I	11IV(G) (b)	1	2	2	1	2	3
			1	Lab	I	(b)	–	1	1	1	1	1
11	15 / 1	7	1	LG	T-TA-R	10IV(B&G), 11IV(B) (a)	–	–	5	Dup	1	1
			6	Lab	T-I	10IV(G) (b)	–	–	–	Dup	2	3
12	15 / 1	7	1	SG	T	(d) (g)	–	1	1	1	1	1
			6	T-TA	T-TA	12V(G) (b) (c) (d)	1	2	2	1	2	3

Note: The meanings of symbols (a), (b), (c), (d), (e), (f), and (g) are explained on pages 264–65.

10

Flexible Scheduling

It has been indicated previously in this book that one of the changes needed to improve the quality of public education lies in the organization of the school schedule. Over the years, most American schools have become deeply rooted in the traditional daily schedule wherein each day is divided into a set number of periods, each period being of equal length. All subjects offered in the total curriculum are scheduled for one of these periods daily for a semester, or sometimes for a year. The elementary school has shown more flexibility over the years than has the secondary school in its willingness to permit varying lengths of time to be allotted to different subjects and in not requiring that any given subject terminate immediately upon the sound of the school bell. Secondary schools, by and large, have bound themselves into a "straitjacket" by adopting the rigid schedule of five or six periods daily. Many schools now are breaking this pattern and are experimenting with so-called "flexible schedules," which will be discussed in detail later in this chapter. Also, the colleges in years past have shown more imagination and thoughtfulness than have secondary schools in scheduling some classes three times per week instead of daily, and in organizing laboratory periods of varying lengths up to three hours, rather than requiring all instruction to terminate at the end of a specified forty-five-, fifty-, or fifty-five minute period.

The major reason for reconsidering the organization of the schedule is to attempt to develop a framework that will result in the most effective learning by pupils undergoing a variety of educational experiences, and to utilize staff talents to the maximum. Essential also is the optimum utilization of available facilities, equipment, and supplies, and the assumption of responsibility to expend public funds for the support of schools as economically as possible and consistent with the achievement of the objectives of the educational program.

One good example of concern about economy of use of facilities is apparent in many physical education programs. Facilities often are not scheduled for maximum use throughout the school day. Tennis courts, swimming pools, and sports fields can be found unused for many hours during a week due to improper scheduling. The organization of the schedule should be guided by the desire to serve the purposes and programs of the school. Unfortunately, in many cases, the schedule is made to serve as an administrative convenience, and the educational program is forced to fit into the prearranged schedule.

Another problem that makes flexible scheduling more of a concern than ever before is the so-called "curriculum squeeze," which has been intensifying its pressure upon local school boards and school faculties. Many special-interest groups, both from within and outside the educational profession itself, have pleaded strongly in recent years for the addition of subjects and requirements in our schools. State legislatures, particularly in the years since the first "sputnik," have passed an increasing number of laws requiring the teaching of more subjects at specified grade levels for designated periods of time. Examples of such subjects recently added to the curriculum in many schools and many states are foreign language instruction in elementary schools, driver education, narcotics and alcohol education, economic education, safety, and first aid. At the same time, state laws and local school-board regulations are requiring longer study in several of the subjects that already are a basic part of the curriculum. Additional requirements have been added in science, English, and mathematics, as well as foreign language in many schools. In reflecting on the implications of these added requirements for the school schedule, the relevance of the term "curriculum squeeze" becomes apparent. How does a school find time in its schedule to include all these required subjects? And how does an individual pupil schedule his program so that he meets all these requirements, plus additional ones that may confront him if he aspires to attend a particular college, and at the same time add valuable elective courses to his total class load?

It seems quite apparent that the traditional five- or six-period day of the American high school no longer meets the challenge indicated above. The need for revision of the schedule seems obvious. Also, there are crucial assumptions about learning that in themselves constitute a valid argument for consideration of schedule improvements. These assumptions are discussed in the next section. "Flexible scheduling" is the term assigned to the efforts of schools to find more effective ways of organizing school time in order to provide more desirable learning conditions.

BASIC ASSUMPTIONS CONCERNING FLEXIBLE SCHEDULING

The basic assumption underlying traditional high school schedules, namely, that all students should study each subject in their programs for an equal length of time daily for a semester, seems untenable in the face of logical analysis. Rather, a much more rational assumption by Bush and Allen states that "Class size, length of class meeting, number and spacing of classes ought to vary according to the nature of the subject, the type of instruction, and the level of ability and interest of the pupils." [1] The nature of each subject varies widely and learning outcomes differ. The abilities and interests of pupils vary tremendously as any experienced teacher knows. Pupils' vocational and educational goals in future years differ. Administrative arrangements for time necessary to conduct a particular class cover a wide range. The laboratory science class requires long periods for the setting up of equipment, the conduct of experiments, and the cleaning up at the end of the lesson. Other types of classes can be conducted in a short concentrated space of time. Physical education requires time for dressing and showering. To impose an artificial time length to be required daily for all pupils in each subject, without attempting to relate it to an evaluation of student achievement of specific objectives, is inadequate for today's educational requirements.

One of the fundamental assumptions underlying new proposals for flexible scheduling is that teacher specialists in each subject field should be able to develop and state a reasonable hypothesis concerning the optimum time required for each class in order to assure that the pupils in the class will achieve the specific course objectives at a satisfactory level of competence. There are several important implications in this statement that will be elaborated upon in the remainder of this chapter. Flexible scheduling does not occur in a vacuum. There are considerations of pupil grouping criteria, class size, teacher competence and interest, administrative feasibility, and similar factors that must enter into the deliberations. These factors are discussed elsewhere in this book. It is not feasible to repeat these discussions at this point where flexible scheduling is the topic of immediate discussion, but the reader must bear them in mind at all times.

The plea here is for teachers within a subject field to analyze the types of pupils who will come to each of their classes in accordance with the grouping policy used in their schools and the class size criteria imposed, and to relate these elements in the teaching situation to the proposed

[1] Robert N. Bush and Dwight W. Allen, "A New Design for High School Education: Assuming a Flexible Schedule" (unpublished material, Secondary Education Project, School of Education, Stanford University, July, 1961), p. 4.

course objectives for those particular students. In this process, the teacher or teachers must use their best professional judgment and previous experience as the guides to determining the optimum length of the class period and the composition of the class time cycle, which will be explained later. In fact, the class may meet for varying lengths of time and for different instructional purposes within the time cycle. The teacher may decide that there should be one short period for small group discussion, two longer periods for large group instruction, and some other length of time for individual study. These time allotment decisions by teachers represent their best thinking. It may be wise to use consultants, who are specialists in the subject-matter field from colleges, universities, and the State Department of Education, to assist in making these time schedule decisions. These decisions rightfully deserve the label "hypotheses."

There are several authorities in the physical education literature who recommend that the high school teacher of physical education determine the time allotment for his subject by insisting that his classes be offered as frequently and for the same length of time as the other subjects in the school. The criterion of determining the physical education time allotment on the basis of time accorded other subjects seems to be the most persistently advocated and followed by writers and teachers. It is disappointing to note that, in general, physical educators have not deemed it essential to examine their own subject and its objectives for all types of pupils as a basis for recommending desirable time allotments. The rationale for making an important decision on such an irrelevant basis as time allotted to other subjects is difficult to understand. It is our responsibility to determine as scientifically as we can the appropriate time allotment needed to meet the objectives we state for the various pupils we serve. Then, we must make this time allotment recommendation known to the decision-making authorities in education, accompanied by supporting evidence. It may well be that the time allotment standards thus developed will have little or no relation to those developed similarly by specialists in other subject fields. When all fields have developed proposals, then the administrative authorities must arrange the over-all school schedule that best accommodates these recommendations within the realistic and administratively feasible limitations existing, such as total length of the school day, number of school days per year, maximum class load permitted a student, and similar considerations.

The next assumption in flexible scheduling is that the teacher, after having been assigned his classes on the basis of a hypothesized "desirable time allotment," will organize his instruction and its evaluation in such a manner as to permit examination and comparison of pupil learning results with results obtained in the previously used schedule or with results from still another hypothesized time allotment for the same subject with the same grouping of children. Again, specialized consultant service may be required to assure the proper design of the action research study, which, in reality, is what is required in this situation.

At this point, it should be emphasized that it is indefensible to adopt a flexible schedule just to be in tune with the times, or because it is popular at the moment. The staff must be convinced that it can develop a more effective time schedule for classes, and that it can and will undertake the necessary work to test the efficacy of the new program in action.

SCHEDULE MODIFICATIONS

There are a variety of ways to modify the school schedule of which several examples are cited below.

1. The "back-to-back" method introduces some flexibility into the traditional school schedule by arranging two regular classes of students, totaling perhaps sixty to seventy pupils, into one large group that is kept together for two or three consecutive periods. Table 10–1 indicates how this plan would work.

Either teacher A or B may instruct the large combined class, thus saving the time of the other teacher. This plan can be expanded to even

TABLE 10–1

Back-to-Back Schedule

Traditional Schedule		Modified Schedule
Social Studies	English	
Teacher A	Teacher B	Teachers A or B
Period 1, Section 1	Section 2	Sections 1, 2
Period 2, Section 2	Section 1	Sections 1, 2

larger combinations of classes in a subject field; for example, it might be particularly adaptable to certain phases of physical education instruction where the same material is to be presented to all freshman boys.

2. Some schools have increased the schedule flexibility and have found a way to provide all subjects with a longer time for classes at least once per week by adapting the traditional daily schedule. In this plan, each pupil attends each of his classes three times weekly for the regular length of the daily school period; and on one of the remaining two days, the pupil attends the class for two consecutive periods. Thus, every subject has three classes one period long three days per week, and one class two periods long one day per week. Although this plan at least attempts

FLEXIBLE SCHEDULING 207

to break the rigid traditional schedule by providing each class with one longer period per week, it does not seem to move very far in the desired direction of setting up a schedule that will more nearly facilitate the scheduling of classes for the length of time judged to be best for each particular group of pupils involved. Every subject has to fit its program into two prescribed lengths of class time without apparent consideration of the desirability of such a "fit." Physical education for two consecutive periods, or a total of perhaps one hundred minutes, probably would be excessive for several types of students and would not seem to be a good hypothesis of desirable time allotment for such pupils.

3. Some critics of public education have advocated seriously that the school week be extended to six days. Such a proposal came very recently from the chairman of the state board of education in one of our most populous states. It is doubtful that this suggestion was motivated by the desire to introduce more flexibility into the school schedule as much as it was a proposal to bring about more study and more rigor. It is interesting to note that many countries in Europe schedule school six days a week, so there is sufficient precedent for such a practice. We know that many critics of public education in America are anxious to introduce features of educational systems in Europe into our schools. These critics must remember that European educational authorities are studying American education, too, and are using and adapting many of our more successful practices to improve their own schools. The authors doubt that the six day per week suggestion will be approved by a majority of parents; however, such a plan would permit more flexibility in scheduling. In the first place, it would help to alleviate the "curriculum squeeze," because immediately it would provide 20 per cent more time for the scheduling of additional courses or the extension of existing ones. Also, it would make it easier to schedule classes three times per week on alternate days at the same hour, such as is typically done at the college level. This proposal seems to be a "trial balloon"; it will be interesting to observe its reception over the coming years and to see who backs this notion and how it is promoted. At the present time, the authors know of no school operating on such a basis for all of its students. There are many schools that have so-called enrichment programs operating on a voluntary basis on Saturdays, both on campus and, in some instances, in industry and scientific laboratories. Driver training also is offered on an optional basis on Saturdays in many schools. Perhaps these are "straws in the wind," and we will see a continual encroachment on the Saturday time for school courses.

4. A similar suggestion concerns the scheduling of some classes at night during the week, particularly for senior high school students. This is typical practice in many junior colleges and two-year community col-

leges, as well as in colleges and universities. Some high schools offer voluntary classes at night for high school pupils, as well as for adults. The additional flexibility involved here is apparent.

5. Variations in the length of the school year are being proposed throughout the country, also. There seems to be a growing number of people who would like to see the number of school days per year extended from the typical 175 (or in some cases 180) days now required in many states. These proposals range from merely extending the 175 days to an arbitrary larger number, to the idea of establishing so-called *four-quarter schools*. Summer school programs are increasing in number and scope at a rapid rate each year throughout all parts of the United States. Although most of these programs are voluntary at the present time, they have served to indicate the tremendous interest of parents and pupils in such programs and the unrealized potential the summer session provides for extending or speeding up the education of many children. Flexibility thus provided permits the scheduling of classes smaller in size than typically is the case for special-interest groups or for groups with remedial needs. In addition, it permits the offering of enrichment classes; makes possible the teaching of certain subjects in a short, concentrated period of time; and has other advantages. However, precautions also are necessary. Some schools have attempted to offer a complete semester course in world history in a four-week summer session, in a daily class meeting three hours consecutively. Evaluations of this work were quite negative. In any subject, extreme care must be taken to select wisely the scope and depth of the course content and the daily time allotment assigned to it, in order to achieve maximum learning results. A concentrated youth fitness program offered in the summer session of one school district is reported in detail later in this chapter.

The four-quarter plan is receiving serious consideration in many parts of the country and has its strong advocates. The argument most frequently used to support it is based on the assertion that (*a*) only three-quarters of the total school age population would be in school at any one time—therefore classes could be smaller—and (*b*) that expensive public facilities would be more efficiently utilized because they would be in use throughout the school year, thus requiring the construction of fewer schools. Bullock, expressing his viewpoint as an anthropologist, makes several pertinent observations concerning the year-round school proposal.[2] He notes that such proposals would still limit any one child to the normal 180 days of school per year and, at the same time, would drastically curtail, if not completely eliminate, the remedial and enrich-

[2] Robert P. Bullock, "Some Cultural Implications of Year-Round Schools," *Theory into Practice*, I (June, 1962), 154–61.

ment opportunities currently offered in summer school programs, as discussed above. In the summer time now available to pupils, many non-school agencies provide valuable civic, religious, physical fitness, and recreation programs that have important educational values for the children. Private and public agencies provide many children with student tours and summer work programs. All of these benefits would be unavailable to approximately three-fourths of the school-age group. It is doubtful if the advantages of the four-quarter school would overcome these disadvantages. Bullock goes on to list other objections that seem persuasive.

There is a history of individual schools that have attempted to operate on the four-quarter system in this country, but so far in almost every case these schools have changed back to the traditional two-semester pattern with summer vacation. Undoubtedly, other schools will try this system in the years to come. As with other proposals for flexible scheduling, we must await more detailed and conclusive reports of results and evaluations of total effectiveness compared with other patterns.

6. Many schools now are developing flexible schedules based on *time modules*. This is really another way of saying that the basic class period time has been changed, and that these modules become the building blocks from which a variety of class time lengths can be constructed, according to the best judgment of the teachers of each subject. In this system, it is necessary also to specify the *number of student modules* that will be involved. In other words, the module plan is based on the decision that specifies the smallest number of students and the shortest length of time that would be used for any instruction in the school. This is an arbitrary decision; and at this point in flexible scheduling experimentation, there are insufficient data to determine the best or optimum time module and number of students module. In the Bush-Allen proposal, the school day is organized into sixteen thirty-minute time modules. School begins at 8:00 A.M. and closes at 4:00 P.M. The number of students in the student module is fifteen. Time and student number modules thus can be organized in multiples of thirty minutes and fifteen pupils. An example of how this procedure works for physical education is presented later in this chapter.

Another facet of this module plan involves departing from another traditional restriction, namely, the *daily cycle* of instruction. Under this long-standing method of organizing instruction, classes are repeated daily in each subject. The new dimension is called the *weekly cycle*. Again, this is an arbitrary decision in the Bush-Allen plan. It could have been decided to have a four-week or six-week cycle; but in order to make a gradual transition from the traditional daily cycle, it was decided to begin with a weekly cycle. Thus, the weekly cycle permits the flexibility of planning the instructional time for each subject within an over-all framework of eighty periods over a five-day interval, rather than the restrictive five or six periods available daily.

There are many elaborations suggested in the Bush-Allen proposal that the teacher interested in the general problem of flexible scheduling for the entire school will desire to study. Space here only permits mention of one or two of these possibilities. Of the eighty periods available in a week cycle, it is suggested that fifteen periods be allotted to school-connected activities other than classroom instruction. Thus, the equivalent of two daily periods for the five days in a week's cycle are reserved for faculty meetings, departmental meetings, or team-teacher meetings. One thirty-minute period per day is designated for lunch, both for pupils and for teachers. Obviously, this permits the use of several periods for lunch assignment among the students and teachers and introduces more desirable flexibility. The equivalent of one period daily is used for group and individual guidance for all students. Starting with a total of eighty periods available per week and subtracting fifteen periods for non-instructional activities plus another five periods for guidance purposes, we note that *sixty periods* remain for instruction and study in the curriculum fields. The arrangement of these sixty periods then is determined by the school administration and is based upon the recommendations of the teaching staff as indicated in the discussion in the previous section of this chapter. One proposal for the flexible scheduling of physical education under the Bush-Allen plan is discussed in detail later in this chapter.

A useful summary of the flexibility provided by the Bush-Allen plan and the basic elements that make up the schedule is presented in Table 10–2.

It also might be useful to know that various school districts throughout the country have used the following modular units as a basis for planning their flexible schedules:

15 students for 30 minutes
15 students for 25 minutes
15 students for 20 minutes
30 students for 15 minutes
10 students for 10 minutes

While sufficient data have not yet been collected to establish one modular unit as being superior to the others, experience clearly indicates that the smaller the modular unit, the greater the flexibility possible and also the greater the complexity of the plan.

7. The Bush-Allen project suggests a rather unusual plan for attaining

TABLE 10-2

Specifications and Definitions for the Organization of the High School Program *

1. Six-year high school (grades 7–12); 300 students at each grade level		1,800 students
2. Smallest number of students to be scheduled for any group in any subject (defined as 1 student module)		15 students
3. Instructional periods to be scheduled (classes may be more than one period long)		30 minutes
4. Length of the school day (8 A.M. to 4 P.M.)		16 periods
5. Number of days before schedule repeats itself (defined as the schedule cycle)		5 days
6. Periods reserved for other than classroom instruction		15 periods
a. Faculty, departmental, grade level, and other staff meetings (2 periods daily × 5 days)	10 periods	
b. Lunch (1 period × 5 days)	5 periods	
	15 periods	
7. Guidance		5 periods
8. Periods remaining for instruction in subject areas		60 periods
9. Periods reserved for student independent study 20% (60 × 20%)		12 periods
10. Net time to be scheduled for classroom instruction for each student		48 periods

* From Robert N. Bush and Dwight W. Allen, "A New Design for High School Education: Assuming a Flexible Schedule" (unpublished material, Secondary Education Project, School of Education, Stanford University, July, 1961), p. 9.

flexibility in a given subject field relative to the interest and ability of the student.[3] One of the basic assumptions of the project is that every student in the six-year secondary school program should study each subject each year. The subjects to be required of all students are:

  a) Arts (visual, performing, practical)
  b) Languages (English and foreign)
  c) Mathematics
  d) Natural Sciences
  e) Physical Education and Health
  f) Social Sciences
  g) Guidance

Each student would study each subject every year, but the minimum requirement would be low. The plan suggests actual minimums for each subject in each grade level. For example, mathematics would be required for seven periods of the weekly cycle in the seventh and eighth grades, for five periods in the ninth and tenth grades, and for three

[3] Bush and Allen, *op. cit.*, pp. 22, 23.

periods in the eleventh grade, for all students in the school, for the weekly cycle. Similarly, minimum required periods are specified for each grade level in each subject area. In addition to these required minimums, provision is made for specialization and concentration by pupils in different subjects depending upon individual needs, interests, and abilities in each subject. In addition to the required minimums, three additional concentrations are suggested:

a. A *single concentration* consists of an additional *twelve periods* spread over the six-year span of high school, or an additional two periods per week each year. The Bush-Allen project has its own groupings of pupils; it suggests that the students falling in the comprehensive high-interest group in mathematics and the subject-talented students who do not hold a great interest in the subject would appropriately take the single concentration in addition to the basic minimum time requirement.

b. A *double concentration* in any subject consists of *twenty-four periods* of instruction added to the required minimum for that subject, spread over a six-year period, or an additional four periods per week each year. This extra time allotment probably is appropriate for students classified as subject-talented, with high interest in the particular subject.

c. Finally, there is a *gifted concentration* involving *forty-eight periods*, or eight periods per week each year, beyond the basic required minimum, which may be taken by the pupils who have superior ability and extreme interest in the subject. It is assumed that an individual student would take only one gifted concentration in the subject of his greatest competence and interest. It is possible for students to schedule single or double concentrations in two or three courses. The minimum requirements apply in general to students who are in the Bush-Allen comprehensive, low-interest group in the subject, which means those who are only capable of minimal satisfactory performance in that subject.

Thus, flexibility in the amount of work that can be scheduled in one or more subjects in which the pupil is interested and competent is a new dimension seldom found in most scheduling frameworks. Most schedules now permit the so-called "gifted" pupils to take courses at advanced levels of difficulty, such as in advanced placement programs; and some high schools even have arrangements with nearby colleges and universities whereby highly selected seniors may enroll in college courses. However, these plans do not usually allow for additional time to be spent in the area of the student's greatest interest and competence; they merely increase the level of difficulty of the course work within the same time allotment as for other subjects. Examples of how these additional time concentrations apply to physical education are to be found later in this chapter.

PHYSICAL EDUCATION FLEXIBLE SCHEDULING IN ELEMENTARY SCHOOLS

In actuality, elementary schools long have had the opportunity to schedule physical education, or for that matter any other class, on a flexible basis. Although in general most elementary schools operate on the basis of a time schedule guide, it is by no means rigid. The physical education class can be extended for a period longer than that indicated on the time schedule guide, or it can be made more brief. Such decisions depend upon the nature of the purposes to be achieved that day or the objectives and activities in a given block of instruction and participation.

Also, in the so-called "self-contained" classroom schools, the teacher may easily integrate physical education with on-going work in other subjects. She may discuss and illustrate native dances and costumes concerning a foreign country that is the topic of a social studies lesson; from that discussion, she may initiate a physical education unit that involves actually learning the music and the dance. The class may make costumes representing the country and can use them in giving a folk dance demonstration. In such a situation, it would be difficult to determine exactly when the social studies class ended and the physical education class began.

Opportunity for flexibility of scheduling is one of several distinguishing features of elementary schools when compared with traditional high schools. It would be surprising if it were not true that almost every reader of this book, upon reflection of his own elementary school experience, can recall many examples of this flexibility. Thus, it would not seem necessary to cite actual examples here.

PHYSICAL EDUCATION FLEXIBLE SCHEDULING IN SECONDARY SCHOOLS

Several examples of flexible scheduling innovations for physical education in high schools throughout the country are described in this section. Although pupil grouping and staff utilization are other essential elements in the total picture, this chapter only discusses the time dimension of flexible scheduling. Staff use and pupil grouping are subjects of other chapters.

One high school moved from the traditional daily period for each subject to scheduling each subject three times per week for one period and one time per week for two consecutive periods. Table 10–3 indicates how physical education is scheduled for one student under this time schedule.

TABLE 10-3
Individual Pupil Schedule

	Pupil: John Smith				
Periods	Monday	Tuesday	Wednesday	Thursday	Friday
1	English	English	English	English	Free
2	English	Social Studies	Social Studies	Social Studies	Social Studies
3	Science	Social Studies	Science	Science	Science
4	French	French	Science	French	French
5	Physical Education	Physical Education	Physical Education	French	Physical Education
6	Free	Free	Free	Free	Physical Education

It will be noted that the student has a double period every day in a different subject. After a trial of one semester, the boys and girls in this high school both gave generally favorable evaluations of the double period in physical education, which in this case totaled one hundred minutes. This requires all boys who are members of school athletic teams to take a class in physical education in their daily schedule. Many parents of these athletes questioned the desirability of requiring a boy to take a two-period block of physical education on a given day to be followed by athletic practice or an interscholastic contest later that afternoon. The authors subscribe to the principle that boys and girls engaged in voluntary school sports and athletics after school should be required to take the regular physical education requirement for all students. However, in this particular case, it would appear that the parents have a legitimate complaint regarding excessive vigorous participation by the athlete on the day the double period of physical education is scheduled. Perhaps, some further modification or flexibility could be introduced into such a program so that the athlete did not take the double period of physical education. The crux of the issue as to whether or not the athletic team member should also be required to take the regular physical education program hinges on the scope and type of program being offered to him in physical education. If physical education is used to introduce him to a wide variety of activities and skills that can be useful to him in later life and does not merely supplement the varsity football practice with a touch football game during the physical education class, then some type of reasonable requirement for the athletes seems to be highly desirable.

In an attempt to introduce greater flexibility, another high school operates on the basis of eight periods of forty minutes each. Various subject fields have combined two of these forty-minute periods one or two times during the week to obtain longer class meeting times. To date, the physical education department has not requested the double period time allotment, but prefers to remain on the daily schedule of forty minutes. Evaluations by both teachers and pupils clearly indicate that a forty-minute period is not of sufficient length to carry out many of the desirable activities of a well-balanced physical education program. When dressing, showering, and administrative time are subtracted from the forty-minute total, insufficient time remains for many of the activities that are highly desirable.

It is interesting to compare figures as to how the above five periods of forty minutes each could be rearranged in a weekly cycle to insure a longer period of activity and instruction for each pupil in the physical education program. In the traditional daily period of forty minutes, we can assume the following utilization of time each day:

15 minutes to dress, shower, dress
5 minutes for roll call, moving to areas
5 minutes for instructions and organization
25 minutes total used for non-active purposes

40 minutes per period per day
× 5 periods per week
200 minutes available per week for physical education
−125 minutes non-active time (from above calculations)
75 minutes available for activity and active instruction per week

Thus, we can see that on the daily forty-minute schedule, a student may average approximately seventy-five minutes of active participation and instruction per week. These five forty-minute periods in a weekly cycle might be rearranged as follows:

Monday: two forty-minute periods combined, or a total of	80 minutes
Wednesday: two forty-minute periods combined, or a total of	80 minutes
Friday: one forty-minute period, or a total of	40 minutes
Total minutes per week for physical education	200 minutes

15 minutes to dress, shower, dress
5 minutes for roll call, moving to areas, etc.
5 minutes for instructions and organization
25 minutes total used each day for non-active purposes
× 3 number of days the pupil has physical education per week
75 minutes total used for non-active purposes per week

Hence, 125 minutes per week are available for activity and instruction. In comparison, then, we find that the five daily periods of 40 minutes each provide a total of 75 minutes and the weekly schedule of one 40-minute and two 80-minute periods provides a total of 125 minutes of time available for activity and active instruction, using the exact same amount of total school time.

In view of the fact that an additional 50 minutes of activity time can be achieved by using the more flexible schedule, the authors cannot help but feel concerned about the apparently prevailing attitude in many parts of the country that a daily requirement in physical education is something "sacred." Further comments about this issue and its implications will be made at the end of this chapter.

Another example of flexible scheduling in physical education and athletics at Alexander Ramsey High School, Roseville, Minnesota, seems to be quite unique.[4] All sports activities, including practice of teams competing in interscholastic conferences, are held from 11:00 A.M. to 1:00 P.M. Lunch for these pupils is scheduled at 1:00 P.M., lasting until 1:35 P.M. Thus, the student enrolls for activities in the same manner as he registers for his regular classes. This registration is accomplished before school opens in the autumn. An example of a twelfth-grade boy's program is as follows:

Period	Class
1	English
2	Chemistry
3	Choir
4	Football
5	Football
1:00–1:30	Lunch
6	Senior Social Studies
7	Trig–Solid Geometry

On the surface, this type of schedule might appear to indicate an overemphasis upon football in comparison to other school offerings. Also, if school teams are scheduled during the regular school day, such teams undoubtedly will require the use of a major portion of the physical education facilities, which in turn will reduce the effectiveness of physical education classes that might be scheduled at the same hours. On the positive side, this type of scheduling is consistent with the Bush-Allen principle indicated earlier in this chapter, which provides for single and double concentrations of time for the talented and gifted students in a particular field. In this instance, the gifted students in physical education are scheduled in a single additional concentration of time. Another advantage, both to staff and students in the football program, is that school ends at 3:30 at the conclusion of the last scheduled period of the day, and team members and coaches do not have to remain for practice until 5:30 or 6:00 P.M.

It is doubtful if the trend of scheduling will move in this direction, at

[4] Bernice Bammann and John French, "A Variety of Improvements in Staff Utilization Are Tried in a Small High School at Beecher, Illinois," *The Bulletin of the National Association of Secondary School Principals*, XLII (January, 1958) 115–25.

least for physical education. In fact, the trend is moving strongly in the opposite direction in many schools. More than in any other subject, the added concentration of time for the gifted in physical education (members of school athletic teams) is being provided after school, rather than as part of the regularly scheduled school periods. One common practice is to schedule athletes into a physical education class during the last period of the day and to begin team practice at that time. This schedule has the advantage of releasing boys a period early for team practice and also makes it easier for team members to be excused from school early for trips on days of contests away from home. The major disadvantage is that these team members will not receive the benefit of a varied physical education instructional program while they are members of athletic teams. Some schools attempt to meet this problem at least half-way by requiring all boys, who do not become candidates for the succeeding sports at the close of their own team's season, to be in a regular physical education class during that last period of the day, from the date of termination of their sport to the end of the present semester. Usually, one of the coaches of the team that has just disbanded takes this class and plans a physical education program best suited to the needs of these athletes.

More and more high schools are reporting plans to undertake more flexible schedules. One school will use fifteen periods of twenty-seven minutes each and will schedule physical education, as well as other classes, in multiples of this time module. Other schools will have fifteen or sixteen periods of twenty minutes, while still others will use time modules of thirty minutes. Undoubtedly, the coming years will see a great variety of flexible scheduling through the use of more time modules of lesser length. At the same time schools cited above plan to group pupils into smaller size modules, they will use more team teaching and will emphasize more individual study and independent practice and participation as individual students demonstrate the responsible attitude and conduct required.

Flexible scheduling at the high school level unquestionably will see a great variety of innovations in the coming years. Physical educators should be in the vanguard of the planning and organization of such schedules and in the evaluation of their effectiveness.

PHYSICAL EDUCATION FLEXIBLE SCHEDULING IN THE FUTURE

It is difficult to forecast any major trends that may occur in the coming years concerning flexible scheduling for physical education. It would seem logical to expect that, as an increasing number of schools adopt a more flexible schedule, physical education departments will be involved to the same extent as are other subjects in the curriculum. However, it is disconcerting to investigate the current literature carefully for examples of flexible scheduling in physical education and to observe that very few reports are available compared with those from other fields of study. There seem to be many examples of schools reporting flexible scheduling innovations and describing how they work for a variety of subjects, but in most cases there is little or no reference to physical education. There would appear to be at least three explanations of this scarcity of examples in physical education. It may be that physical education examples exist to a much larger extent than are reported in the literature. Why such practices would not be reported in professional publications to the same extent as those in other fields is difficult to explain. A second reason may be that physical educators are not as anxious to participate in flexible scheduling experimentation as are teachers from other fields. It is the experience of the authors in surveying the literature and in discussing this problem with secondary school physical educators across the country that perhaps the latter explanation is the more tenable of the two. If this is a valid assumption, again it offers cause for deep concern. A third possible explanation is that school administrators have decided to begin flexible scheduling projects on a limited basis for a trial period, and that they have explicitly selected certain so-called "academic" subjects for such experimentation.

To analyze the situation in physical education still further, perhaps it is not logical to expect schools in different sections of the country to be moving ahead in any degree of uniformity as they participate, or fail to be included, in flexible scheduling programs. One reason that compounds this problem when attempting to discuss it in national terms is the wide discrepancy that exists between states concerning laws and boards of education rulings relevant to time allotment required of high school students in the field of physical education. California requires all students in grades one through twelve to take physical education daily, except students excused for medical reasons. Several states require a specified number of minutes per week for health and physical education. Still other states have lesser requirements; and, finally, some states do not have any time requirements for physical education.

A dilemma exists for the profession where such diverse requirements are present. A state favored with a daily requirement in physical education for all pupils finds its professional leaders reluctant to accept any form of flexible scheduling that deviates from this daily pattern, because it appears to be a backward step, and one that might result in the loss of a favorable time requirement in the total curriculum in the face of the previously mentioned "curriculum squeeze." Even when it can be demonstrated that a more flexible time allotment scheduled for three or four days per week provides more actual activity time for pupils in physical education than the equivalent total school time allotment spread over five days, there is great fear and trembling in the ranks of physical educators that we are not standing by our basic belief, namely, that every child should have *physical education daily.*

On the question of the need for a daily program of physical education on the assumption that all children need a certain (but usually unknown) amount of vigorous physical activity each day, one of the authors has made an extensive study of available basic research in physiology, physiology of exercise, and in physical education. He was able to locate many research reports that concluded that *regular* vigorous activity was desirable for most children, barring medical restrictions. But it was most surprising to find that not a single study was able to conclude, on the basis of data presented, either (1) that vigorous activity should be required *daily* for the subjects in the study or (2) that any specified *number of minutes* of vigorous activity should be prescribed on any other designated regular basis for the subjects of the research. It well may be that such conclusions do exist in the research literature; but, if so, one wonders why they are not cited as references in the physical education literature to support the many claims made by individuals and professional organizations of the need for the daily required physical education program for all children.

A review of the physical education literature reveals many such statements concerning the need for a daily program for all students in all grades. The authors of this book have made this same recommendation in other publications. But the significant point under discussion is that these citations in the physical education literature are not supported by research data. Therefore, the most disturbing implication of the refusal of physical educators, who now conduct a daily program, to engage in experimentation in a more flexible type of schedule is that they appear to be interested only in maintaining the "status quo" instead of making comparative studies of learning and fitness outcomes in physical education under varying time allotments. If the latter were accomplished, the profession would be advanced, and an optimum time allotment, which would enable us most effectively to meet the needs of the pupils in the schools, might be found.

There is nothing sacred about a daily requirement per se. If sufficient research evidence could be accumulated to indicate that a three-day-per-week program, utilizing the same amount of total school time as a daily program, would do an effective job of meeting school objectives in physical education, would we not be willing to accept such a time allotment as satisfactory? Would we still hold out for the five-day program?

At this point, the authors would like to make it perfectly clear that at the present time they, too, believe that a daily program of physical education for all pupils is the best time allotment standard according to available evidence and the preponderance of experienced, professional judgment. However, we also believe that we are in need of additional knowledge and experiences in physical education programs that are scheduled and conducted in a manner different from the predominantly traditional programs we find in schools today. Such knowledge and experience may enable us to develop new insights and understandings, as well as additional data, that may well serve as a basis for the reassessment of our present practices and beliefs. Administrators and other interested persons are now frequently asking the questions: Can physical education be conducted on some type of flexible scheduling basis rather than on a daily basis? Can the program be administered so as to achieve equal or greater effectiveness in meeting the program objectives when compared with more traditional ways of scheduling? The authors strongly encourage schools to give careful thought to the development and testing of new proposals in the actual school situation to see if they will lead to more effective physical education programs. In concluding this plea for the "experimental attitude" and the acceptance of responsibility to attempt to move the physical education profession forward through such action research as has been suggested in flexible scheduling and other areas of administrative problems mentioned in other chapters, it is worth pointing out that one of the possible outcomes of additional research on flexible scheduling is that the daily requirement may emerge as the most desirable requirement. If this be the case, then at long last we will be able to support our fervent recommendations with more basic data than we can at present. If some other time allotment proves to be superior for our purposes, then, again, the children and the teachers both will have been the benefactors.

At the other end of the scale of various time allotments presently existing in secondary schools throughout the country, it is now apparent that a large percentage of high school boys and girls receive little or no physical education on a regular basis throughout the school year. In order to upgrade these programs, several professional organizations have developed strong statements of desirable time allotment standards. A typical standard is that one period daily be assigned for the teaching of health education and physical education. Because it is deemed necessary to adopt a strategy of stating desirable, yet practically feasible, standards, rather than "idealistic" ones, such a standard from a national professional organization in physical education appears to undercut the laws and regulations of states that presently have time allotments that exceed those recommended in the standard. Thus, national standards stated by professional organizations now are appearing in such a form as to indicate both an optimum or maximum time allotment, and an intermediate standard to be achieved as a step toward the meeting of the optimum standard in the long run. The optimum standard is that physical education should be required daily of all students and that, in addition, a one-semester course in health and safety education should be required at both the junior and senior high school levels.

It is encouraging to note reports that the President's Physical Fitness Council is urging the governors of the various states to review the time allotment laws and regulations in their respective states pertaining to health and physical education, and to initiate legislation in instances where prevailing state practices do not meet recommended minimum standards.

In the Stanford Secondary Education Project, referred to in Chapter 9, it will be noted that the proposed school day is organized into sixteen periods of thirty minutes each. There is no additional time for moving from class to locker and from class to class. Neither are there any school bells. Teachers and pupils are responsible for leaving one class in time to arrive at the next class at its starting time. Each subject in the curriculum specifies how it desires to schedule the basic number of time modules (thirty minutes per module) assigned to it for each grouping of pupils based on interest and ability. Also, each subject may schedule the single, double, and gifted concentrations of additional time modules, as the departmental staff recommends.

Two examples of time allotment for different pupil groups in physical education are shown in Tables 10–4 and 10–5 to illustrate the degree of flexibility that is possible with this type of time schedule.

Table 10–4 for Group II-B, Comprehensive, High Interest Boys, indicates in column four the Total Periods (or number of thirty-minute time modules) allotted to this group of pupils in each grade. In this particular chart, the same number of time modules per week is allotted at each of the six grade levels. In other cases, varying numbers of time modules will be assigned in different grade levels, such as in Group V-G, shown in Table 10–5.

An example of how these time modules may be scheduled for any one grade is shown by reading across the seventh grade line. Column 1 indicates the grade level, seventh in this case. Columns 2 and 3 show ninety students, made up of six student modules (one student module has fifteen students). This means that ninety seventh-grade boys, of the 150 total number of boys in the seventh grade, have been classified as Comprehensive, High Interest for physical education. These ninety pupils have been allotted seven time modules (or thirty minutes each) for physical education during one week's cycle. The physical education staff may

TABLE 10-4

Boys' Physical Education
Group II-B: Comprehensive, High Interest

Grade	Number of Student Modules	Number of Students	Total Periods	Periods Each Line	Type of Instruction	Staff	Other Groups Included		Student Modules from Other Groups	Total Student Modules	Student Modules per Section	Sections To Be Scheduled	Periods per Meeting	Meetings per Week
1	2	3	4	5	6	7	8		9	10	11	12	13	14
7	90		7	1	SG	6T	7II(G)	(g)	5	11	2	6	1	1
		6		6	Lab	3T-TA		(b)	–	6	2	3	2	3
8	90		7	1	LG	T-4TA-R	8II(G)	(a)	5	11	11	1	1	1
		6		6	Lab	4T-2TA	9II B	(b)	5	11	3	4	2	3
9	75		7	1	LG		9II(G)	(a)	4	9	9	1	1	1
		5		6	Lab		8II(B)	(b)	6	–	–	Dup	2	3
10	75		7	1	LG	T3TA-R	10II(G)	(a)	4	9	9	1	1	1
		5		6	Lab	3T-2TA	11II(B)	(b)	3	8	3	3	2	3
11	45		7	1	LG	T-2TA-R	11II(G)	(a)	4	7	7	1	1	1
		3		6	Lab	3T-2TA	10II(B)	(b)	5	–	–	Dup	2	3
12	30		7	1	SG	T-I	(c) (d) (g)		–	2	1	2	1	1
		2		6	Lab	T	(b) (c) (d)		–	2	2	1	2	3

NOTE: The meanings of symbols (a), (b), (c), (d), (e), (f), and (g) are explained on pages 264–65.

arrange these seven half-hour periods any way they think is best in their professional judgment. Columns 5 and 6 indicate that the seven time modules will be divided so that one thirty-minute period per week will be devoted to Small Group (SG) instruction, and that six thirty-minute modules will be assigned to Laboratory (Lab) instruction. Column 7 shows that the Small Group Instruction will require the services of six teachers (T). Column 8 indicates that seventh-grade girls, who have been classified as Group II-G, Comprehensive, High Interest, may be combined with this group of boys for this Small Group Instruction. The symbol (g) refers to a footnote that states that small groups are desirable for seventh-graders to assist them in making an adjustment to a new school and a new type of program, in most cases. Column 9 tells us that five student modules comprise the Girls Comprehensive, High Interest group in the seventh grade, and these five modules will join the six modules of the boys. Column 10 then summarizes the six student modules for boys, and the five student modules for the girls, which means that a total of eleven modules will be scheduled for Small Group Instruction. Small groups, by definition, will consist only of one or two student modules (fifteen or thirty students). Column 11 lists two student modules per section or class. We started with eleven modules, so in reality, there will be five classes composed of two student modules (or thirty students), and one class of one student module (or fifteen students), for a total of six "sections (or classes) to be scheduled." Referring back to column 7, we can now see that six teachers (T) are required to teach these six Small Group classes. Columns 13 and 14 combine to indicate that each Small Group class meets for one period (thirty minutes) one meeting or time per week.

Moving to the twelfth grade, we see that now there are only two student modules, or a total of thirty boys assigned to the Comprehensive, High Interest Group. It is presumed that sixty of the ninety boys, who began in this group in the seventh grade, will have learned to participate at a higher level of skill and they will maintain their interest in physical education so that they can be moved into a higher classification by the time they are seniors. In fact, this progression from lower to higher classifications is evident from a perusal of columns 2 and 3 from seventh to twelfth grades. Again, in the twelfth grade, there still are seven periods of thirty minutes allotted; and these will be divided into one thirty-minute period for Small Group discussion, and six laboratory periods. One teacher and one intern are assigned to the Small Group class so that intensive discussion and study groups can be set up for fifteen students per group, which is one of the features of the program for seniors, emphasizing the highest degree of self-responsibility, a considerable degree of election of activities and allied study, and study and discussion in depth on pertinent physical education topics. No student modules from other groups are combined with this group. The Small Group will consist of the two student modules (thirty students) classified in this group in the twelfth grade. Each section (or class) will be composed of one student module (fifteen pupils), so there will be two sections (or classes) to be scheduled. These classes will meet for one time module (thirty minutes) one time per week.

Similarly, the thirty boys in the twelfth grade will have six periods of laboratory instruction to be taught by one teacher. No other students from other classifications will join them. Thus, a total of two student modules need to be scheduled, and there will be two student modules (thirty pupils) per section or class. There will be only one section or class, and it will meet for two time modules (sixty minutes) three times per week.

It should be apparent from Table 10–4 that a great degree of flexibility is possible in the variable factors of number of students classified in each group, number of student modules in each group, total periods assigned to each group at each grade level, the types of instruction that can be offered, the types of staff personnel required to instruct each class, the arrangement of total time modules allotted to each type of instruction, the combination of student modules from other groups, and the size and number of sections and meeting times per week.

Each figure on a chart, such as the one above, is the result of the best professional judgment a group of highly experienced and trained physical education teachers can render. There is an explicit rationale for each individual decision. Innumerable alternatives might have been decided upon. These particular recommendations, and others that might be suggested by other teacher groups, should be given a trial and the results carefully evaluated. Eventually, the more successful and efficient practices can be preserved and improved upon, and the less desirable ones can be eliminated or modified. Hence, progress should be achieved.

Chart Group V-G, Gifted, Girls (Table 10–5), indicates even greater flexibility than did the previous chart. For example, note that only one student module (fifteen girls) is assumed for the seventh grade. Nine periods of thirty minutes per week are allotted, and these nine periods will be scheduled in four different ways. There is one Small Group period requiring the services of a teacher. Seventh-grade gifted boys are combined with the girls in this Small Group class. Reference to the chart for Group V-B (see Appendix) will indicate that there is one module (fifteen pupils) for this group. This information is not repeated on the present chart, V-G, so that staff load computations will not be spuriously elevated. The addition of the boys' module will give us a total of thirty

TABLE 10-5

Girls' Physical Education
Group V-G: Gifted

Grade	Number of Student Modules / Number of Students	Total Periods	Periods Each Line	Type of Instruction	Staff	Other Groups Included		Student Modules from Other Groups	Total Student Modules	Student Modules per Section	Sections To Be Scheduled	Periods per Meeting	Meetings per Week
1	2/3	4	5	6	7	8		9	10	11	12	13	14
7	15 / 1	9	1	SG	T	7V(B)	(a) (g)	–	–	–	Dup	1	1
			4	Lab	T-I	7IV(G)	(b)	–	–	–	Dup	2	2
			3	Lab	T-I	7IV(G)	(b)	–	–	–	Dup	3	1
			1	Lab	T		(b)	–	1	1	1	1	1
8	15 / 1	9	1	LG	T-2TA-R	8IV(B&G), 9IV(B&G)		–	–	12	Dup	1	1
						8V(B), 9V(B&G)							
						8VI(B&G)							
						9VI(B&G)	(a)						
			4	Lab	T	9V(G)	(b)	1	2	2	1	2	2
			3	Lab	T	9V(G)	(b)	1	2	2	1	3	1
			1	Lab	T		(b)	–	1	1	1	1	1
9	15 / 1	8	1	LG	T-2TA-R	8IV(B&G), 9IV(B&G)		–	–	12	Dup	1	1
						8V(B&G), 8VI(B&G)							
						9V(B&G), 9VI(B&G), (a)							
			4	Lab	T	8V(G)		–	–	–	Dup	2	2
			3	Lab	T	8V(G)		–	–	–	Dup	3	1
10	15 / 1	8	1	LG	T-TA-R	10V(B), 11V(B&G)	(a)	–	–	5	Dup	1	1
			6	Lab	T	11V(G)	(b)	1	2	2	1	2	3
			1	Lab	T		(b)						
11	15 / 1	7	1	LG	T-TA-R	10V(B&G), 11V(B)	(a)	–	–	5	Dup	1	1
			6	Lab	T	10V(G)	(b)	–	–	–	Dup	2	3
12	15 / 1	7	1	SG	T		(b) (c) (g)	–	1	1	1	1	1
			6	Lab	T	12IV(G)	(b) (c) (d)	–	–	–	Dup	2	3

Note: The meanings of symbols (a), (b), (c), (d), (e), (f), and (g) are explained on pages 264–65.

pupils in the small group. There will only be one class or section, and it will meet one period (thirty minutes) per week.

Then, four of the total nine periods will be devoted to laboratory instruction, using a teacher and an intern, being combined with seventh-grade girls from Group IV (Talented, High Interest), there being one student module (fifteen pupils) from this group. There will be one class of thirty students meeting twice a week for two time modules (sixty minutes).

Additionally, this same group of girls will have three time modules (ninety minutes) devoted to laboratory instruction; and this class will require a teacher and an intern because it will be combined with fifteen girls from the seventh-grade Group IV, as in the other laboratory period. These thirty girls will meet as a class one time per week for three time modules (ninety minutes). Because all thirty girls are either talented or gifted, it is assumed that they will benefit from the longer, intensive period of ninety minutes, once per week. This is an example of an added *concentration* in a field of high talent or giftedness mentioned earlier as one of the unique features of the Stanford Secondary Education Project.

Completing the analysis of the seventh-grade girls in Group V-G, we find that one more period (time module of thirty minutes) remains to be scheduled and is designated as a laboratory period, which means that the girls will be dressed in appropriate physical education costume, even though only thirty minutes are available. In this laboratory period, these fifteen girls will not be combined with girls from any other group, so they may have the benefit of a small class and intensive participation and instruction. The class will meet one time per week for thirty minutes.

A further perusal of this chart shows other examples of flexibility of the various components.

The remaining charts developed by the Stanford Secondary Education Project on flexible scheduling in physical education and an explanation of the footnote references within the charts are shown in the Appendix.

The opportunities for flexible scheduling are innumerable, as the examples in the Appendix will indicate. It behooves the physical educator to "stretch his mind," to suggest reasonable alternatives for more effective use of time, to cooperate with on-going innovative programs in his school or district, and to take the lead in conducting and evaluating newer practices that seem to hold promise for the more effective achievement by pupils of school physical education objectives.

11

Facilities and Instructional Technology

As schools seek more effective ways of teaching and organizing educational experiences, one more set of conditions must be considered, namely, facilities. Again, we must free our thinking of restricted concepts and traditional ways of planning and building the school plant and grounds in order to make it possible for staff utilization plans, flexible scheduling, and grouping of students to occur and operate under the most desirable conditions. We need new "breakthroughs" in school facilities.

DEFINITION

The term "educational facilities" today has a very broad connotation. The definition is no longer restricted only to the narrow meaning of school buildings. It now encompasses all permanent structures that the school erects and also includes all devices and machines that might be classified under the heading of modern technological equipment. Obvious examples are radios, motion picture projectors, television studios and receivers, overhead projectors, teaching machines, and many other types of machines and electronic equipment. The term "facilities" is derived from the verb "to facilitate," and that is the function not only of the buildings and permanent structures, but also of the technological aids, namely, "to facilitate" instruction and learning.

For purposes of discussion, this chapter has been arbitrarily structured so that school buildings and grounds are described first, followed by a section on instructional technology and the many recent developments that are fast descending upon the educational scene.

BUILDINGS, STRUCTURES, AND AREAS FOR PHYSICAL EDUCATION

The rapid increase in the school-age population in the United States has well-known crucial implications for school construction. School districts face staggering financial problems as they attempt to procure adequate school sites and erect desirable school buildings to keep up with the increasing school population. Physical education, athletic and recreational areas and facilities require a large percentage of the school site land area and the largest expenditure of funds for buildings and structures of any single subject-matter area in the curriculum, particularly at the secondary level.

Although it is not within the scope of this book to discuss school finance in detail, it is essential to stress the pressures currently facing physical educators with respect to competition for school facilities funds. Certainly, these pressures will continue to increase as more school districts reach their maximum bonded indebtedness and their maximum tax rate levels. If physical education, athletics, and recreation are to be continued as fundamental areas in the total school curriculum, physical educators must have a thorough knowledge of school finance problems and of school planning procedures.

In order to interpret the needs for physical education, athletic, and recreation programs, not only in terms of educational objectives, but also translated into financial terms for action by the decision-makers who determine curriculum policy and school facility budgets, physical educators should take the lead in developing techniques for the careful analysis of cost factors involved in their programs. Indicative of the required types of analyses and the new techniques for making more adequate studies of school costs are two recent studies that are mentioned briefly.

A recent study conducted by Gordon Peak at Stanford University involved the analysis of the complete cost of site acquisition and development, school building construction, and landscaping required to build a new high school to the point of readiness for occupancy. Peak then prorated the cost of physical education, athletic, and recreation areas and facilities to determine their relative percentage cost in relation to the cost of the entire high school. He found that 22.6 per cent of the capital outlay cost of the school was devoted to physical education, athletics, and recreation. He also found that 54.75 per cent of the area of the total school site was allocated for use in physical education, athletics, and recreation.

In order to justify such a high proportion of total expenditures and school site use to the public and the school board, physical educators must also know more precisely how much physical education costs per pupil "exposure" in relation to the per pupil participation cost of the other subjects in the curriculum. Being unable to locate cost data based on pupil time participation bases that would be comparable to similar data from other subjects, Hallberg devised an apparently new technique in school finance studies to determine this information, not only for physical education, but for all other subjects in the curriculum as well. Although Hallberg's major research contribution was the development of the new technique for estimating the cost of instruction per pupil per unit of participation and to determine what this cost was for physical education in the schools used in his study, he also found some preliminary data by which he could compare physical education pupil cost to pupil cost of instruction in other subjects in two of those schools.[1] The cost per student hour of participation in these two schools is shown in Table 11-1.

TABLE 11-1

Comparative per Pupil Participation Costs

Subject	Costs per Student Hour	
	School A	School B
Mathematics	$.48	$ .64
Science	.54	.75
English	.55	.60
Industrial arts	.98	1.10
Safety education	.45	.74
Art	.81	.67
Business education	.50	.52
Home economics	.70	.67
Physical education	.53	.53
Language	.49	.58
Social studies	.43	.43
Mean =	.59	.66
S.D. =	.13	.14

It is evident from the data in Table 11-1 that cost per student hour of physical education was below the mean cost of all classes combined in both schools, and that in School A physical education costs less than five other subjects and in School B it costs less than eight other subjects.

[1] Edmond C. Hallberg, "A Cost Analysis of Physical Education Programs in Terms of Utilization of Facilities" (unpublished Ed.D. dissertation, School of Education, Stanford University, 1960), p. 82.

The challenge to physical education becomes more apparent when we combine the findings of Peak and Hallberg with our interpretations and descriptions of the areas and facilities required to conduct an effective program. If we are confronted with the Peak data only, we will be very hard pressed to obtained favorable financial decisions. Advocates of other subject areas may feel that their subjects are not receiving a sufficient share of the total expenditures and that physical education "obviously" (look at the figures!) is receiving too much of the total funds expended. However, we must then call attention to the Hallberg data that give indications that physical education costs per pupil participation unit are not excessive in relation to other subjects; in fact, that cost is exceeded by several other subjects.

More data of the above types are urgently needed. Newer and better techniques for making careful financial analyses are required. Physical education seems to be slow in producing such new information and improved techniques in school finance.

EDUCATIONAL SPECIFICATIONS

If we are to provide schools in the future that will "facilitate" new designs in curriculum, better use of curriculum materials, improved staff utilization, instructional technology, pupil grouping, and flexible scheduling, physical education teachers, supervisors, teacher education consultants, and research experts must be strongly involved in school plant planning from its very inception. It has been observed many times in the past that school planning frequently proceeds with little or, in some unfortunate instances, no involvement of physical education teachers in the school or district concerned. There are hopeful signs that school boards, school administrators, architects, and engineers are realizing now that teachers also should be members of the school planning team.

School planning should be based on the concept of "educational specifications." MacConnell describes in detail the role of educational specifications in school planning and gives examples of this method in physical education.[2] Essentially, the steps are:

1. An explicit statement of educational philosophy by the school district and a more definitive statement of the educational philosophy of the particular school to be constructed should be formulated. Ramifications of the socioeconomic status of the pupils; the vocational and educational goals of the students; the value systems of the ethnic groups in the community; the industrial, business and cultural components in the area; and similar factors are taken into consideration.

[2] James D. MacConnell, *Planning for School Buildings* (Englewood Cliffs, N.J.: Prentice-Hall, Inc., 1957), pp. 145–67.

2. Within the context of the general educational philosophy of the new school, the physical education program's objectives and specific behavioral goals for the students should be written out and officially adopted by the school board of the district.

3. Next, the physical education chairman or consultant spells out the program of activities and other learning experiences that will best accomplish the objectives and goals.

4. It should then be determined with the school administration what the prevailing policies will be concerning physical education class size, length of class periods, number of classes per period, and maximum number of pupils the school will serve.

5. Climatic conditions should be studied in order to know the average amount of inclement weather to be expected and the implications for indoor facility usage.

6. Every activity in the program, including interscholastic athletic activities, recreational activities, and spectator considerations, should be analyzed; the physical conditions necessary for the proper conduct of those activities should be described in detail. For example, the floor or field area required for an activity according to prevailing rules and the estimated number of pupils to be instructed on the area at any one time should be indicated. Safety factors, types of surfaces, ventilation, entrances, exits and traffic patterns, utilities, and all other considerations that affect the proper use of the facility for each activity must be spelled out so that the architect and the contractor can understand them. Relationships of areas should be indicated in schematic form by the physical educators.

The above information, when developed in detail by the physical educator, is designated as "educational specifications." It is the function of the professional education staff members to produce these specifications based on foreseeable educational requirements. It is the responsibility of the architect and contractor to plan and build a facility that will house and "facilitate" the conduct of the learning experiences and auxiliary services according to the specifications detailed by the professional staff.

Examples of detailed educational specifications for physical education facilities are to be found in the reports by Arce,[3] Elliott,[4] Cornacchia and Nixon,[5] and Neilson and Nixon.[6] The use of educational specifications in

[3] William B. Arce, "Planning Boys' Gymnasium Facilities for Secondary Schools" (unpublished Ed.D. dissertation, School of Education, Stanford University, 1956).

[4] Allan R. Elliott, "Space and Facilities for Physical Education and Community Use in Public Schools" (unpublished Ed.D. dissertation, School of Education, Stanford University, 1956).

[5] Harold J. Cornacchia and John E. Nixon, *Playground Facilities for Rural and Small Elementary Schools* (Stanford, Calif.: Stanford University Press, 1955).

[6] Donald W. Neilson and John E. Nixon, *Swimming Pools for Schools* (Stanford, Calif.: Stanford University Press, 1954).

physical education as a planning procedure and suggestions for developing facilities for the future are ably presented by Scott.[7,8]

7. The physical education staff should then relate data concerning class size, number of classes, time schedule, weather, and similar controlling factors to the information concerning desirable areas and facilities. The entire facility needs, with all educational specifications attached for reference, should then be produced in schematic form. This total plan is presented to the school administration personnel responsible for the over-all planning of the school.

8. Continual interaction should be arranged by the administration from this point on so that the physical educators are given full opportunity to explain their educational specifications to school planners and the architect in charge. As financial decisions are made and as the architect brings in preliminary drawings, the physical educators should have full opportunity to study, react, and make recommendations at each stage of progress. With this process of full partnership and with each specialist operating in his own area of competence, excellent facilities should result.

In summary, the program should determine the facilities and the facilities should "facilitate" the program, not vice versa.

PHYSICAL EDUCATION FACILITIES FOR THE FUTURE

It is freely predicted that in the future pupils will make extensive use of community facilities as locales for learning experiences involving business offices, industrial plants, libraries, museums, government offices, and many other types of facilities. There will be times when groups of students will travel considerable distances away from school for a specific learning purpose. It might be noted in passing that the interscholastic athletic program, as a phase of physical education, for many years has provided such experiences away from home, probably to a greater extent than any other subject in the curriculum. Also, school outdoor education programs are examples of this procedure for extending educational opportunities beyond the narrow confines of the school grounds.

Many European countries have long made extensive use of community facilities for school physical education classes. Students walk or go on streetcars for several blocks, or even several miles on occasion, to use swimming pools, athletic fields, ice skating rinks, and other athletic areas, as part of the regular school physical education program. In Austria, it is the national policy in physical education for entire classes of pupils in

[7] Harry A. Scott, "Facilities for the Future," *Journal of Health, Physical Education and Recreation*, XXXIII, No. 4 (April, 1962), 34–36.
[8] Harry A. Scott and Richard B. Westkaemper, *From Programs to Facilities in Physical Education* (New York: Harper & Row, 1958).

large city schools to spend one or two weeks at government supported sport-dormitories, located high in the Austrian Alps, where the majority of the time is devoted to ski instruction, recreation, and outdoor education.

New school buildings will be designed for maximum flexibility and multipurpose use so as to accommodate individual, small and large group instruction, team teaching, and independent study, and to facilitate technological instruction. Physical education facilities will follow the same criteria. With the advent of greater freedom of pupil movement, with more responsibility placed upon pupils for their own practice and individual study, and with the subsequent use by students of school facilities and equipment with less teacher supervision than is traditional today, new views of student control and new methods of administration will have to be developed. Also, a whole new concept of school law in the area of legal liability will have to emerge, if these new educational trends are to receive the necessary support to elicit their full potential for improved learning.

INSTRUCTIONAL TECHNOLOGY

This term is applied to the entire array of mechanical and electrical machines and appliances that are being utilized as aids to instruction in many phases of the school program. A look into the future school shows that we can expect to find each school having a central studio, or control center, from which various media of communication will be transmitted to many areas within the school. Motion picture films, television programs (live and taped), tape recordings, and radio will provide the source of much instructional material. Many rooms will be constructed and furnished with screens, television outlets and receivers, recording devices, listening aids, control panels, and other forms of mechanical aids. Schoolwide intercom systems will reduce or eliminate the need for individual motion picture projectors and films in each room.

Many other types of instructional aids will be available to students and teachers such as microcards, microfilms, slides, filmstrips, mockups, models, books, tape recordings, overhead projector slides, and others. The future of instructional technology is unlimited, and probably many of the instruments and machines to be found in the school of the future are unknown to us at this time.

Trump makes three interesting observations about education and technology:

> Although technological advances are made by educated people, education makes relatively little use of the advances.

Where technology is used in schools, it usually is used to embellish established programs rather than as planned parts of those programs.

In using technological facilities, education has most often modified or adapted those designed for other occupations rather than created designs specifically for educational purposes.[9]

There are three major trends in instructional technology: mass instruction, individual instruction, and instructional systems development.

Mass instruction is not new to education. For years educators have used the standard audio-visual aids, such as movies, filmstrips, and recordings to present special material to fairly large groups of pupils. Mass instruction now is being further facilitated by newer instruments and machines.

Individualized instruction is a newer trend and actually is in the opposite direction from mass instruction. It involves the use of the highly publicized teaching machine, language laboratory listening equipment, and other forms of mechanical and electrical equipment.

The term "instructional systems" has been used to describe a combination of individual instruction and mass instruction technology. For example, there are systems of television kinescope films that are combined with teaching machine programed instruction or with programed textbooks.

Trump indicates how large group, small group, and individual study instruction can be facilitated by proper use of audio and visual aids.

Large-Group Instruction

1. Closed- and open-circuit television to provide enrichment, magnification, simultaneous instruction in several rooms, etc.
2. Projectors with overhead, rear projection for writing, printing, and other presentations in black and white and color, with overlays, for use in light or semi-darkened rooms.
3. Micro-, opaque, and other projectors for specific tasks.
4. Electronic tape and other recordings to reduce repetition, provide uniformity, and permit re-use.
5. Films, filmstrips, and slides of various sizes for photographed materials.
6. FM radio to distribute information simultaneously to several rooms.
7. Charts, pictures, flannelboards, models, mock-ups, museum materials, etc.
8. Duplicated materials to provide uniformity, involvement, and concrete illustrations.

Individual Study

1. All of the above that are portable should be available in project areas and material centers.
2. Science and language laboratory, workshop, and library supplies and equipment of best design.
3. Self-teaching and appraisal machines-information, instructions, and ques-

---

[9] J. Lloyd Trump and Dorsey Baynham, *Focus on Change: Guide to Better Schools* (Chicago: Rand McNally & Co., 1961), pp. 11, 12.

FACILITIES AND INSTRUCTIONAL TECHNOLOGY

tions placed on machine in advance by teachers so students can use with minimum of teacher assistance.

4. Self-appraisal tests to permit self-examination and scoring.

Small-Group Discussion

1. All *of above* that are portable should be available for students to bring to discussion group meetings as aids in explaining and presenting convincing evidence.[10]

Several types of machines and instruments in the armament of instructional technology are described in the following pages. It is the belief of the authors that physical education teachers can make very effective use of these instruments and that we all need to be imaginative and bold in new attempts to innovate and experiment with their use in order to further advance our instructional procedures. Physical education classes frequently are larger than any other class in school, and it is the more imperative that every advantage be gained from the potential values of instructional technology to do a more effective instructional job.

Digital Computer

A digital computer, as described by Silberman,[11] is an extension of the old, well-known hand calculator. It requires a "program," written by human beings, that outlines the task of the instrument. Program information and other data may be fed into the machine, where it can be stored. A control unit can then follow directions fed into the machine to produce a variety of arithmetical and logical operations. An output device assembles the desired information in forms, such as a punch card, a printed message, or a picture on a TV screen.

Computers can perform three operations: calculation, stimulation, and simulation. These are illustrated in the following paragraphs.

Computers can calculate attendance records and bus schedules, process test scores and report cards, and can handle fiscal accounting and many other clerical tasks. One important new use is that of flexible scheduling of the school program.

In the area of stimulation, the computer can present material to pupils, lead students to make responses, evaluate these responses, and provide additional information relevant to the performance of the child on that lesson. Several types of computer-controlled teaching machines are now on the market. Some of these systems can provide individual instruction to a number of pupils simultaneously.

The computer also can simulate, as for example, a cluster of neurons or a biological organ. It can simulate a school, an organization, or a busi-

---

[10] J. Lloyd Trump, *Images of the Future* (Washington, D.C.: National Education Association, 1959), p. 29.

[11] Harry F. Silberman, "The Digital Computer in Education," *Phi Delta Kappan*, May, 1962, pp. 345–47.

ness. As an educational aid, simulation can enable us to learn more about the system under study. In addition, it can serve as a teaching tool. It provides for detailed analysis of problem situations, it indicates probable results of alternate courses of action, and it provides a very close control of the teaching situation. Also, potentially dangerous or hazardous innovations can be tried out in a safe manner until the results are indicated. Furthermore, simulation is a technique used to assist in long-range educational planning.

Silberman indicates at least seven possible effects of computers on education in the years ahead: [12] (1) School organization will be more of a man-machine system than the man system that it is today. There will be more division of labor between the machine and persons in the school organization. (2) Administrators will be given needed relief from "information overload" and clerical detail, which in turn will free them for dealing with more significant problems and for more continuous, long-range planning. (3) Computers will speed up the rate at which knowledge will become obsolete so that more rapid curriculum changes will be required than previously. The basic theory and structure of knowledge in the sciences is changing rapidly also, because of the aid of computers in research work. As the structure and content of knowledge changes in subject fields, school curricula must change. (4) Preparation of instructional material will be quite different. Much more emphasis will be placed on adequate preparation of materials, with the help of the computer in assembly, preparation, and quality control. Also, there will be a much more empirical or scientific approach to curriculum material development. (5) Computers will tend to make education more democratic, because education will be more responsive to individual differences and needs. (6) At the same time, it will become more responsive to social needs. (7) Greater individualization of instruction will become possible.

The future possibilities of the computer are made most dramatic by Bushnell and Cogswell:

> Visualize a computer-based library connected to a national library system where students seated in front of consoles can call up information on the current state of knowledge in any area of the sciences or arts. Consider a student study area where students in their individual study cubicles are instructing themselves with the aid of a machine tutor which is linked via the school-system computer to a national information-retrieval system that is processing written data into courses of study, developing diagnostic questions, and searching for answers to questions students ask.[13]

---

[12] *Ibid.*, p. 347.
[13] Don D. Bushnell and John F. Cogswell, "A Computer-based Laboratory for Automation in School Systems," *Audio-Visual Communication Review*, IX (July–August, 1961), 173–85.

Constructing the School Schedule with Computer Assistance

Constructing the master time schedule for the school is one of the most difficult and important tasks of the administration. It is also one of the most frustrating assignments for administrators and counselors. Yet, if the suggestions made in this book for more effective educational outcomes for each student are to be fully applied in practice, it is essential that the school schedule be made more flexible so that it may best serve the needs of individual students, improve staff utilization, and provide for maximum efficiency in the utilization of educational areas and facilities. A potentially promising procedure for solving this complex problem is being investigated as part of the Secondary Education Project at Stanford University, namely, the use of electronic data-processing machines in formulating the high school schedule. Oakford, the chief investigator in this study, makes several observations that should be of interest to physical educators and to school administrators who deal with physical education and athletic scheduling problems.[14]

In traditional scheduling procedures, physical education classes frequently are the last to be filled in on the individual student's study card. This practice results in an imbalance in numbers of pupils assigned to specific classes. Also, it frequently results in a widely heterogeneous group of pupils being assigned to one class, which, in turn, greatly complicates the instructor's problem in providing an instructional program that will meet these great individual differences. It is obvious that, if the above conditions exist to a considerable extent in many schools, the successful solution to the problem of machine scheduling the high school program will greatly benefit the physical education and athletic programs as well as other subject fields. Physical education then will be assigned automatically desirable time allotments and schedule patterns equal to those made available to the other subjects.

Oakford [15] says that this experimental work in flexible scheduling with machine assistance is important, because the full-scale use of principles underlying flexible scheduling is impossible until such time as a breakthrough is made in the management and coordination of the variable factors involved in scheduling, which to date have not been brought under proper control by present scheduling methods. Also, a machine program could relieve the time and energies presently devoted to scheduling by highly trained and talented professional teachers, counselors,

[14] Robert V. Oakford, "Machine Assistance for Constructing the High-School Schedule," in Robert N. Bush and Dwight W. Allen, "A New Design for High School Education: Assuming a Flexible Schedule" (unpublished material, Secondary Education Project, School of Education, Stanford University, July, 1961), Appendix B, pp. 1–6.
[15] *Ibid.*, pp. 1–4.

and administrators; these persons then could apply more time to other professional tasks.

Inasmuch as the logic of scheduling is the basis for the development of computer assistance, a clear-cut distinction is essential concerning administrative decisions that require sound educational judgment by qualified administrators and routine decisions that can be delegated to people in lesser positions of authority, or that can even be delegated to the machine. Oakford explains at more length the implications of the problem in this statement. He holds out hope for being able to develop the computer method of constructing the school schedule, indicating that computers presently are being used to solve problems of comparable scope and difficulty.

For the practical-minded reader, Oakford indicates that the computer's assistance will be needed for the following specifications of the master schedule:

1. The set of courses to be offered, with a specification of the structuring of each of the courses and special room requirements.
2. The set of student programs. In some cases students may be grouped by program as in elementary school, or alternatively there may be an individual program for each student.
3. The set of teachers with qualifications of each.
4. The set of rooms available with seating capacity and type classification.[16]

Bush and Allen add their optimistic view:

The time may be near when basic scheduling information can be listed on cards; the program of studies that each pupil selects—under the guidance of proper persons in the school, available teachers, available rooms and other special data. An electric computer may then be used to formulate the master schedule, class lists, teacher assignments, and any other data relevant to the master schedule.[17]

In point of fact, pilot runs have now been accomplished in actual high school situations, and computer master scheduling has been successfully achieved for more than 95 per cent of the students in the school. This scientific "breakthrough" seems assured in the near future.

Communications Media

A brief list of various machines currently available for communicating audio and visual instructional material to pupils and teachers is listed below. There are many others not included in this list, and almost every

---

[16] *Ibid.*, p. 5.
[17] Robert N. Bush and Dwight W. Allen, "A New Design for High School Education: Assuming a Flexible Schedule" (unpublished material, Secondary Education Project, School of Education, Stanford University, July, 1961), p. 6.

day sees a new addition to the range of possibilities of instructional technology.

1. *Home Video Tape Recorder and Television Receiver.* A regular television receiver with a built-in video tape recorder. It will be available in a few years. Available now is a portable video tape recorder that weighs 90 pounds and is the size of a small suitcase.

2. *Automated Data Retrieval Center.* The University of Michigan has a partially automated library that utilizes a digital computer system, which will rapidly find and transmit information on a variety of subjects.

3. *Videofile.* The Videofile is being developed by the Ampex Corporation to assist in automatic data retrieval. A student dials a code number related to the topic on which he desires information. The material appears on a TV screen in front of him. It is also possible to make copies of this information by pressing a button on the machine. There is a possibility that a satellite system could be developed that would connect major libraries throughout the world, so that the enormous store of human knowledge available could be obtained in an instant.

4. *The Voice Typewriter.* This machine will transcribe spoken words. By setting a dial, it can transcribe in any of several languages.

5. *Portable Video Tape Camera.*

6. *Motion Picture Camera and Film.* This film can be developed in seventy seconds.

7. *Textorient.* J. D. J. Holbil has reduced whole books to a single symbolic diagram that he calls a textorient and that summarizes the book and gives the reader the basic issues or topics without the necessity of reading the book.

8. *Eight mm. Sound Film.* Much more widespread usage may be made of 8 mm. sound film as an instructional medium than in the past. It may become more commonplace than 16 mm. film, which schools have relied on so heavily heretofore. Some audio-visual authorities predict that the use of 8 mm. film may eventually foreshadow television instruction in the years to come.

First, the cost of 8 mm. film is considerably less. Second, with the current "breakthrough" in projector construction, the 8 mm. projector has become so simple to load and use that virtually any pupil or teacher can now serve as his own operator.

One of the current objections to television instruction is the "accessibility problem" of obtaining and showing a closed-circuit film at the preplanned time in the course when it is most appropriate to the topic of study. This handicap could be overcome by using 8 mm. film.

9. *EDEX Teaching System.* The EDEX Teaching System is a machine that presents combined audio and visual stimuli to groups of students, that involves each student in responses to the stimuli, and that records individual and group responses. It asks multiple-choice questions at key points in the lesson, directing them to each student. Each student must respond, his answers are recorded, and he is informed of the correct response without delay. By use of two projectors, the teacher can employ alternately films and film strips as the basis for the instructional program. Each student has a small box on his desk with buttons that he pushes to indicate his answers. Every student is actively engaged in a "dialogue" with his teacher.

10. *Mach-tronics MVR-10.* This machine is a portable television tape recorder.

It is incumbent upon physical educators to become acquainted with the capabilities of these instructional media and to learn to utilize and adapt them for optimum effect. Also, we must keep up-to-date with each new development in instructional technology and determine appropriate uses of them in the teaching of physical education and the coaching of athletics.

Instructional Television

Television is well known today on the educational scene. It is possible to classify educational television into four types: (1) educational stations, (2) commercial stations granting time for educational broadcasts, (3) closed-circuit televising with the aid of "live" instructors, and (4) closed-circuit broadcasting using filmed programs.

Millions of children now receive these types of television instruction. Many educational television stations are in operation and many more are on the planning boards. We can even foresee now the possibilities for international programing through the use of an educational communications satellite! Some educational authorities have predicted that in another ten years a majority of children in America's schools will be receiving television instruction.

In 1952 the FCC approved 259 television channels for educational agencies. In 1962 it was estimated that more than 2,000 hours per week of television instruction were being offered to approximately 26,000,000 children and adults.[18] Many states have passed enabling legislation and have appropriated funds to support educational television, and other states are planning to do likewise.

---

[18] Chalmer G. Hixson, "The Status and Potential of Instructional Television for Physical Education," *Journal of Health, Physical Education and Recreation,* XXXIII (May–June, 1962), 25.

The claimed advantages of educational television listed by Hixson [19] are:

1. More widespread use of the best teachers to serve more pupils in many schools.

2. Television teachers are afforded more time and resources for the proper planning of their lessons.

3. Unusual or expensive learning materials and resources can be brought to any classroom through television.

4. Television instruction is more efficient, because large numbers of students can be served by one broadcast, as contrasted to the necessity for repeated lessons given by the same classroom teacher to several classes. Also, lessons are available for reuse and for future classes.

5. Television instruction frees the regular classroom teacher from some of the time he used to spend in lesson preparation; with the use of television, he can devote more time to individual and small group counseling and instruction.

6. Television can provide closeup views of important learning materials that in most cases are superior to the view a pupil might obtain in a regular classroom lesson.

7. The good studio teacher gives the impression of communicating directly on a one-to-one basis with each pupil in the room and thus motivates him to keep his attention on the lesson.

8. Television lessons can be received in a room with light, thus enabling pupils to carry on supplementary learning activities such as note taking, instructional material examination, and similar activities that reinforce and further elucidate the instruction coming over the television.

Television instruction can be classified into four major types:

1. *Complete Course Teaching.* In this case, a television program is the complete instructional method. A pupil learns on his own responsibility from the program, which usually is taught by very prominent experts in the subject. Sometimes the sponsoring agency or institution provides a self-test that can be taken at the end of the course and submitted for evaluation. The famous "Continental Classroom" series is an example of this type of television instruction.

2. *Major Resource Teaching.* In this category, television lessons may be utilized two to four or five times per week and are amplified by a classroom teacher who supplements these lessons, oversees applications in the classroom of ideas presented on television, tests the pupils, and supervises laboratory work.

3. *Enrichment Instruction.* This type of instruction involves noted or expert resource personnel with a high degree of special competence in

[19] *Ibid.,* p. 26.

the subject of instruction, usually offered only once, or perhaps for a short series of television appearances. Such enrichment programs are used to supplement the instruction of the classroom teacher.

4. *Supplementary Instruction.* Television programs are developed that serve mainly to supplement the work of the classroom teacher and usually involve experts who deal with instructional materials not normally available to the teacher or the school.

It has been estimated that a majority of television instruction in the United States is of the enrichment and supplementary types.

An interesting study by the Research Division of the NEA revealed that "a majority of the teachers, 81.6 per cent, and a majority of the principals in districts having 50 or more teachers believe that, with teaching by television, classes cannot be increased in size without detrimental effects on quality of education." [20]

One of the major conclusions of the study by the Educational Media Panel, an advisory group to the Commissioner and the United States Office of Education that was established in 1960, states that:

Experience indicates that the most effective uses (of TV instruction) have been where television has been combined carefully with other activities in a total learning situation; and where students were strongly motivated to learn from it. This challenges educators to make a broad review and restructuring of what happens in the classroom.[21]

One study reviewed 141 reports that compared the effectiveness of television instruction with traditional instructional methods and found the following results. Forty studies showed television instruction to be superior, whereas twelve studies favored the traditional instructional method. Eighty-nine studies showed no significant difference in favor of either type of instruction. Hixson summarizes these findings by stating that: "In summation, students can learn as well when television is used by the teacher as in the conventional classroom situation; frequently, they learn better." [22]

A review of more than four hundred research studies related to television instruction reveals the following tentative conclusions: [23]

1. Much information can be learned as well by TV as it can by traditional instructional methods.
2. TV instruction can be effective for pupils of varying learning abilities.

[20] "Teaching by Television," *NEA Research Bulletin,* XL (February, 1962), 7, 8.
[21] Institute for Communications Research, *Educational Television: The Next Ten Years* (Stanford, Calif.: Stanford University Press, 1962), p. 19.
[22] Hixson, *op. cit.,* p. 26.
[23] Mendel Sherman, "MPATI's Promise, A Summing Up," *Phi Delta Kappan,* XLIII (May, 1962), 326–28.

3. There is a great variation in attitudes toward TV both by pupils and teachers. So far, learning has not seemed to be affected by the student's attitude toward TV.
4. Class size does not appear to be a crucial factor in learning from TV instruction.
5. No individual subject nor particular grade level seems to be any more appropriate for TV instruction than others.
6. Filmed and recorded instruction seems to be as effective as "live" teaching on TV.
7. Students indicate a preference for an experienced teacher on TV as compared with an inexperienced one in the regular classroom.

Television Instruction in Elementary School Physical Education

Several examples follow of the varied use of television to provide physical education instruction to pupils and in-service training to teachers at the elementary level.

The Tucson, Arizona, Public Schools, District #1 conducted a pilot study in the use of educational television in six elementary schools. Physical education was one of the subjects under study.[24]

Physical education lessons numbered ten in a thirty-lesson series that was shown each Tuesday over Station KUAT-TV. Each lesson was fifteen minutes long and was viewed by each teacher and her class. A total of twenty classes viewed each physical education program. Teachers were provided with television lesson guide sheets before each lesson to enable the classroom teacher to utilize more effectively the material presented in the television lesson.

One of the main topics in the series for the sixth grade was the AAHPER Fitness Test battery, for the purpose of making these tests more meaningful to parents, pupils, and teachers, and to promote their widespread use in the district. Second-graders had seven lessons in movement education, with both the children and the classroom teacher being active the entire time working with the television instructor. The lessons in movement education were carefully correlated with instructional units in other subjects, such as reading, social studies, and science.

The Philadelphia Public Schools produced a television series entitled "Fit As a Fiddle" for grades four through six.[25] The purpose was to help pupils and teachers become acquainted with the objectives of health and physical education and to motivate improved pupil performance. The program was fifteen minutes long, shown once per week for thirty-six weeks, and was produced by Station WHYY-TV. A comprehensive

---

[24] Virginia Robinson, "An Experiment in Instructional Television," *Journal of Health, Physical Education and Recreation*, XXXIII (May–June, 1962), 30.

[25] Martha A. Gable, "Fit As a Fiddle . . . via TV Teaching," *Journal of Health, Physical Education and Recreation*, XXXIII (May–June, 1962), 27,28.

program of advanced publicity was carried out to insure a large and interested audience of teachers and pupils in many schools throughout the district.

Among the topics presented on the program were diagnostic tests performed by two or three pupils; demonstrations of individual and dual stunts; techniques for games involving balls and other apparatus, and featuring well-known sports performers to demonstrate correct fundamentals; methods for organizing and using pupil leadership in physical education; a dance demonstration; remedial physical education activities for the feet and posture; and several health education topics. These television programs were shown in regular classrooms or in larger rooms that could accommodate as many as four or five normal-size classes. Mimeographed materials, including definitions of key terms, questions for discussion, reference reading lists, and suggested homework projects, were sent to classroom teachers in advance of the program.

Teachers, together with physical education supervisors, evaluated the results of this series of programs. It was reported that the programs were very productive for both teachers and pupils.

The Columbus Public Schools, Columbus, Ohio, have had several years of experience with instructional television in physical education. One report indicated that television lessons were being provided in physical education for three separate groups of children: first and second grades, third and fourth grades, and fifth and sixth grades.[26] These lessons were taped at the studio and consisted mainly of demonstrations of physical education skills and activities taught by an elementary school physical education instructor who used selected elementary students for demonstration purposes. Detailed television lesson outlines were provided for each viewing group. At the time of this report, it was indicated that this television instruction was useful and effective and that the district planned to continue to utilize this medium as a means of assisting elementary classroom teachers throughout the system.

The Detroit Public Schools report that television has been used for the in-service education of elementary school teachers in physical education.[27] Programs included demonstrations and lecture-panel discussions and were concerned with sports skills, dance, games, and corrective physical education. Student demonstration was utilized to a limited degree.

The Board of Education of Worcester County, Maryland, reports a

---

[26] Letter from Edna Lambert, Department of Physical and Health Education, Columbus Public Schools, Columbus, Ohio, to John E. Nixon, December 11, 1962.

[27] Letter from Robert R. Luby, Divisional Director, Detroit Public Schools, Detroit, Michigan, to John E. Nixon, November 8, 1962.

one-year television program in physical education for elementary pupils.[28] Each child received one lesson every three weeks. A qualified teacher, using eight pupils, taught in the studio, using suitable games and relays. He also demonstrated fundamental skills and stunt-type activities. After the program, classroom teachers organized the children into groups and helped them to practice and refine their skills. Classroom teachers evaluated the television programs as being "valuable." The administration reports that elementary school physical education was appropriate for television.

Atlanta and Fulton County Schools in Georgia combined to present an elementary school physical education program based on requests from more than 2,000 teachers who had experienced an eight-week TV workshop after school hours.[29] Atlanta TV station 30 carried the program and provided a TV technical team to work with a team of five highly selected teachers. Together this group selected the program's goals, such as to help teachers gain more competence and self-confidence in teaching elementary school physical education; to learn and develop new skills; to introduce new activities; to improve fitness; and to learn the concepts of good sportsmanship, fair play, and self-discipline. The program included games, stunts, self-testing activities, and one folk dance on each program. Manuals were written to accompany each program, with additional explanatory material for teacher and pupil reference.

Typically, two teachers taught each program, sharing the total thirty minutes available. From three to twelve children from various schools in the districts concerned were used on the program. Programs were video-taped on Thursday and were shown twice on Friday, once in the morning and again in the afternoon. There was one program per month for each grade level. Sixty schools provided approximately 600 children for the programs during the entire series.

In evaluating the results, it was agreed that many schools showed a marked improvement in their physical education programs at the end of the series. Also, elementary school classroom teachers indicated that physical education was the second most desired subject for additional TV programs the following year. In addition, it appears that one-time workshop programs would be very valuable, that TV is an excellent way to demonstrate new equipment, and that TV has great potential for the orientation of new teachers.

Undoubtedly, many other elementary schools are making constructive use of educational television in physical education. Only a few of these

[28] Letter from Paul S. Hyde, Superintendent, Board of Education of Worcester County, Snow Hill, Maryland, to John E. Nixon, November 6, 1962.
[29] Isabel L. Brooksher et al., "Fitness and Fun on Educational Television," *Journal of Health, Physical Education and Recreation*, XXXIV (February, 1963), 24–26.

programs, unfortunately, are reported in the professional literature. In fact, an interested investigator, who searches the literature for such reports, is doomed to a feeling of considerable frustration as well as disappointment at the paucity of reports in the field of physical education. More reports seem to be available concerning elementary school television than about secondary school programs.

The following examples of television programs in physical education at the secondary level, and for elementary and secondary schools combined, are again indicative of the wide potential of this medium of communication for effective instruction, both of pupils and teachers.

Television Instruction in Secondary School Physical Education

The Baltimore Public Schools have been using television instruction in physical education since 1952.[30] Sixteen programs in one school year have been the maximum number attempted. These programs are twenty-five minutes long. The major purposes are to provide in-service training for teachers and to serve as a public relations endeavor to inform parents and the public as to the objectives of the total physical education curriculum, its place in the educational program, and physical education course content.

Some programs, including swimming, golf, tennis, soccer, and several phases of the aquatics program, have been recorded on 16 mm. film. Two programs have been scheduled on Saturday mornings for the viewing public. Also, television is used extensively to show interscholastic athletic contests. It is reported that these programs have been of value both to the performers and the viewers.

The Oklahoma City Public Schools report a physical education television program series for high school athletes, both boys and girls, during the off-season of their sport.[31] The major emphasis of the class was physical fitness. It was presented on Monday, Wednesday, and Thursday of each week for twenty-five minutes and lasted for one semester.

Fifteen to twenty minutes of each program were devoted to a discussion of body structure, physiological operation of body components, and bodily changes that result from physical activity. Exercises were demonstrated and described during the remaining time each day, and some time was devoted to minimum fitness test description and demonstration.

[30] Letter from Julian L. Dyke, Supervisor, Secondary Boys' Physical Education, Baltimore Public Schools, Baltimore, Maryland, to John E. Nixon, November 30, 1962; letter from Mary E. McCoy, Supervisor, Secondary Girls' Physical Education, Baltimore Public Schools, Baltimore, Maryland, to John E. Nixon, November 28, 1962.
[31] Letter from Gene Bipboye, Studio Teacher, Oklahoma City Public Schools, Broadcasting Center, Oklahoma City, Oklahoma, to John E. Nixon, November 20, 1962.

An expert television teacher of physical education conducted the program. This person occasionally brought in authorities to aid in the discussions, and he utilized teachers and students from local high schools for demonstrations. Extensive use was made of audio-visual aids, such as films, manikins, skeletons, charts, diagrams, cards, pictures, posters, and printed materials. A lesson study guide was distributed to each pupil to use in conjunction with the television series. The television teacher of the course suggested that next time the course is offered it should be made available to a wider group of students, which might include high school juniors and seniors interested in careers in physical education, coaching, community recreation, nursing, medicine, and similar vocations, and students who were unable to enroll in regular physical education classes.

Television Instruction in Elementary and Secondary School Physical Education

The Fresno County Schools Office, Fresno, California, has presented instructional television broadcasts over local commercial stations for the past several years.[32] The major purposes of these broadcasts were (1) to interpret the curriculum and services of the schools to the public and (2) to provide in-service education for school personnel. Programs usually are shown at 7:30 A.M. on Wednesdays so that teachers can see them at school and have an opportunity for guided group discussion immediately after the showing of the film.

Program topics are selected by countywide surveys through committees of school personnel, aided by television coordinators from each school in the district. One program, developed because of teacher requests, was a kinescope demonstrating the national physical fitness program of the President's Youth Fitness Council. This program was made by various physical education instructors from selected schools, from Fresno State College, and by the county physical education consultant.

Weekly guide sheets are distributed to schools, indicating program objectives, an outline of the program content, suggestions for using material from the broadcast in actual classes, and a reference list of pertinent materials. Also, evaluation forms are distributed with the weekly guides.

Evaluation of the county television instructional services indicated that:

1. Television instruction should involve coordinated teamwork among school personnel and lay leaders.

[32] Kathryn D. Kendig, "ETV-Fresno," *California Journal of Elementary Education,* XXXI (November, 1962), 95–101.

2. Instructional television is most effective when combined with other educational media and patterns of social interaction.
3. Television instruction is best suited to stimulate thinking and to present materials, information, and ideas that will lead to further discussion, experimentation, research, and creative expression.
4. In order best to contribute to the in-service function, television should be planned as an integral part of a total program, rather than being an isolated experience.

The Bay Section of the California Association for Health, Physical Education, and Recreation, through the cooperation of commercial television station KGO-TV, San Francisco, produced and showed sixty-five educational programs to inform teachers and parents of new ideas and techniques in physical education for school and the home. Each program was ten minutes in length and was programed at 6:50–7:00 A.M. Monday through Friday for thirteen consecutive weeks. Since its first showing, the entire program has been rerun on KGO-TV in response to heavy public demand. Programs were taped in advance in local schools selected to show the instructional progression in physical education from intermediate grades through the college level. The moderator for the series was Mr. Stanley Friese, Director of Physical Education, Berkeley City Schools, Berkeley, California, who gave continuity to the program. In addition to the film clips of on-going school programs in the Bay Area, each program also included a recommended exercise for the day for the home audience.

In order to make the most effective use of television instruction in physical education in the future, studies must be conducted to provide guiding evidence on such problems as: What activities, at what grade levels, and in what size groups, can best be taught by television? Can television be used to teach the informational and intellectual content of physical education, such as the physiological and health aspects of the program, the rules, strategy, history, and other facets? To what extent should television be interwoven with regular instruction in the gymnasium and on the athletic field? What roles should teachers perform before, during, and after television broadcasts? Many similar problems could be added to this list. Physical education in the public schools has been slow, in relation to other subjects in the curriculum, to utilize this medium of communication and instruction.

There are many untapped possibilities for the effective use of educational television as an instructional medium for physical education, not only in the schools, but in the home as well. It seems safe to predict that television will be used in the future in physical education instruction to about the same extent it will be employed in other subject fields.

Teaching Machines

Henry describes a teaching machine as a device that (1) presents a unit of verbal or symbolic information visually, usually in question form; (2) provides the student with some means of responding to each unit; and (3) informs the student of the correctness of each response.[33] Actually, mechanical devices, in one form or another, have been used in American schools for more than fifty years.

In recent years, we have seen a tremendous growth of interest and use in teaching machines and much speculation and research concerning their potential values. In schools using them today, perhaps not more than one-fifth of the student's time per day is occupied by this type of instruction. Some authorities predict that in the school of the future teaching machines will use about one-third of the pupil's total school time, which indicates that the school must furnish one teaching machine for every three students, plus the proper facilities for their use.

Most machines in use today are designed for one student working individually. Machines are now being developed that are able to provide automated instruction to twenty pupils at a time; and, as manufacturers gain experience, many more pupils will be able to work from one "system." Machines of the future will provide automatic storage and analysis and print out administrative and counseling information desired by school administrators, counselors, and teachers. Much controversy rages today about the relative merits of teaching machines. The research evidence to date is far from conclusive. Advantages and disadvantages claimed by supporters and critics may be summarized as follows.

Positive values of teaching machines are listed by Broudy.[34] He indicates that some evidence shows that machine programs, which produce efficient learning, tend to negate individual differences in I.Q. Also, teachers using machines seem to find more time for non-instructional duties than they did formerly under traditional teaching methods. Further, teaching machines seem to provide a better opportunity for differentiated instruction for each pupil. And last, teaching machines make possible a differentiation of personnel and their duties.

Hilgard indicates that programed learning is supported by the following psychological principles of learning.[35] (1) Programed learning recognizes individual differences by beginning where the learner is and letting him proceed at his own speed. (2) The learner must be active; the

---

[33] William G. Henry, Jr., "What Makes the Teaching Machine Teach?" *Audiovisual Instruction*, VI (April, 1961), 126–29, 145.

[34] Harry S. Broudy, "Teaching Machines: Threats and Promise," *Educational Theory*, XII (July, 1962), 151–56.

[35] Ernest R. Hilgard, "What Support from the Psychology of Learning," *NEA Journal* (November, 1961), 20–21.

learner learns by doing. (3) Immediate knowledge of results is provided by reward, reinforcement, or cognitive feedback. (4) Programed learning emphasizes the organized nature of knowledge. (5) It provides spaced review. (6) By reducing the threat to the pupil, his anxiety is reduced.

A list of disadvantages seems to include a greater number of items than does the above list of values. Perhaps the critics are more vocal and more impelled to state their reservations in the literature than are the advocates. At any rate, a partial list of disadvantages of teaching machines would include these remarks.

The single answer format assumes that knowledge is fixed and that all facts and conclusions are orderly. It has no place for the intellectual abilities of inference, intuition, insight, and inquiry. It disregards exploring, conceptualizing, experimenting, and valuing. It is rigid; it does not permit taking an over-all view. It provides one "correct" answer, thus leaving much possibility for ambiguity, although not permitting any appeal to alternative answers that might be "reasonable" under certain specified conditions. Many educators and psychologists believe that the theoretical basis underlying teaching machine instruction is tenuous and unconvincing. They do not agree with underlying philosophical assumptions, and they differ with the viewpoint of educational process implied in this teaching method. It ignores the use of questions and questioning in the learning process and does not provide for verbal expression as a mode of learning.

Some teachers view teaching machines as a threat, although this fear would seem to be unwarranted. They believe that machines may replace teachers; they fear that administrators will use machines as a basis for increasing pupil-teacher ratios in classrooms. Many teachers genuinely believe that the quality of instruction will suffer. Also, they think there may be a loss of direct teacher control over the materials of educational instruction.

In attempting to evaluate the positive and negative claims about the efficacy of teaching machines, available research studies seem to provide incomplete and inconclusive data up to this time. There is some evidence that "automated programed instruction teaches facts and verbally mediated responses as effectively as conventional procedures do." [36] A further observation by Cronbach is that "the evidence now available gives little support for the original view that instruction calling for one active response after another will teach better than a straightforward lecture or text." [37] Cronbach's conclusions hardly would seem to constitute a ring-

[36] Lee J. Cronbach, "Programed Instruction," *NEA Journal* (December, 1962), 45–47.
[37] *Ibid.*, p. 46.

ing endorsement for programed instruction as an improvement over more traditional instructional forms.

In attempting to summarize the current state of professional judgment about the merits of teaching machines and programed instruction, it seems sound to observe that the profession should require more thorough and critical research evidence before teaching machines are adopted for widespread use. To date, there has been insufficient evaluation of so-called "experimental" programs using teaching machines in many parts of the country.

Gates shows his skepticism by stating that: "The pity is not that considerable money and expert time are being poured into developing mechanical devices; the pity is that equally great efforts are not being devoted to the possibilities of other media and other approaches, including older ones."[38] Gates also believes that ". . . vigorous efforts should be made to explore the possibilities of developing new forms of printed materials that will teach effectively without elaborate and expensive machinery."[39]

Teaching Machines and Physical Education

No published reports of the use of teaching machines for physical education instruction were available to the authors at the time of writing of this book. It does seem to be a professional responsibility for physical education teachers, administrators, and teacher education personnel to keep abreast of teaching machine developments and evaluations and to experiment with this device. There are many topics in physical education that could be "programed," taught as individual study, and assigned as homework in connection with the physical education class. Health facts and principles; physiological and anatomical knowledge relevant to physical education; and the history, rules, strategy, facilities, and equipment involved in many of the activities of the physical education curriculum should be studied. Knowledge of proper techniques for performing various skills should be learned. The above and similar types of instructional materials are amenable to "programing" and instruction on teaching machines.

PHYSICAL EDUCATION AND INSTRUCTIONAL TECHNOLOGY

In addition to the many machines and devices listed previously, there are many more machines and "gadgets" that can assist the physical education teacher. Space forbids a complete listing and description. Profes-

---

[38] Arthur L. Gates, "Teaching Machines in Perspective," *The Elementary School Journal*, LXII (October, 1961), 11.
[39] *Ibid.*, p. 12.

sional journals keep the teacher informed through articles and advertisements of the development and availability of these mechanical aids to teaching. It is the prediction of the authors that physical education in the future will make far greater use of such aids than it has in the past, as it attempts to deal with larger numbers of pupils in smaller areas and facilities. Automatic tennis-throwing machines, pitching machines, golf-driving machines that plot a drive electronically on a three-dimension screen and require only limited space, and many similar devices will enable physical educators to schedule the use of facilities on a continuous basis throughout the school day. It will enable more flexible scheduling of individual and small group instruction and individual study and practice by small numbers of pupils as an assignment to be carried out on individual pupil responsibility.

Many physical educators have demonstrated a flair for inventing and building new equipment and teaching aids. This imaginative ability will be in even greater demand in the future. The age of automation and of instructional technology is here for physical education. It can be a most helpful ally, if we respond to the challenges and opportunities thus presented.

Appendix

TABLES OF
FLEXIBLE SCHEDULING
POSSIBILITIES

TABLE A

Boys' Physical Education
Group I-B: Comprehensive, Low Interest

Grade	Number of Student Modules / Number of Students	Total Periods	Periods Each Line	Type of Instruction	Staff	Other Groups Included	Student Modules from Other Groups	Total Student Modules	Student Modules per Section	Sections To Be Scheduled	Periods per Meeting	Meetings per Week
1	2/3	4	5	6	7	8	9	10	11	12	13	14
7	15 / 1	5	1	SG	T	(a) (g)	–	1	1	1	1	1
			4	Lab	T	(b)	–	1	1	1	2	2
8	15 / 1	5	1	LG	T-2TA-R	8I(G), 8III(G)	7	8	8	1	1	1
						9I(B&G), 9III(G) (a)						
			4	Lab	T-TA	9I(B) (b)	2	3	3	1	2	2
9	30 / 2	5	1	LG	T-2TA-R	8I(B&G), 9I(G) (a)	–	–	8	Dup	1	1
			4	Lab	T-TA	8I(B)	–	–	–	Dup	2	2
10	30 / 2	5	1	LG	T-4TA-R	10I(G), 10III(G)	9	11	11	1	1	1
						11I(B&G), 11III(B&G) (a)						
			4	Lab	2T-2I	11I(B), 11III(B) (b)	3	5	5	1	2	2
11	30 / 2	5	1	LG	T-4TA-R	10I(B&G), 10III(G)	–	–	11	Dup	1	1
						11I(G), 11III(B&G) (a)						
			4	Lab	2T-2I	10I(B), 11III(B) (b)	–	–	–	Dup	2	2
12	45 / 3	5	1	SG	T-2I	(c) (g)	–	3	1	3	1	1
			4	Lab	T-I-A	12III(B) (c)	1	4	4	1	2	2

Note: The meanings of symbols (a), (b), (c), (d), (e), (f), and (g) are explained on pages 264–65.

TABLE B

Girls' Physical Education
Group I-G: Comprehensive, Low Interest

Grade	Number of Student Modules / Number of Students	Total Periods	Periods Each Line	Type of Instruction	Staff	Other Groups Included		Student Modules from Other Groups	Total Student Modules	Student Modules per Section	Sections To Be Scheduled	Periods per Meeting	Meetings per Week
1	2/3	4	5	6	7	8		9	10	11	12	13	14
7	15 / 1	5	1	SG	T		(a) (g)	–	1	1	1	1	1
			4	Lab	T-I	7III(G)	(b)	1	2	2	1	2	2
8	15 / 1	5	1	LG	T-2TA-R	8I(B), 8III(G)		7	8	8	Dup	1	1
						9I(B&G), 9III(G)	(a)						
			4	Lab	2T 2TA	9I(G), 8&9III(G)	(b)	4	5	5	1	2	2
9	30 / 2	5	1	LG	T-2TA-R	8I(B&G), 9I(B)		6	–	8	Dup	1	1
						8III(G), 9III(G)	(a)						
			4	Lab	2T 2TA	8I(G), 8&9III(G)	(b)	3	2	–	Dup	2	2
10	30 / 2	5	1	LG	T-4TA-R	10I(B), 10III(G)		9	–	11	1	1	1
			1	1		11I(B&G), 11III(B&G)	(a)						
			4	Lab	2T-2I	11I(G), 10&11III(G)	(b)	4	6	6	1	2	2
11	30 / 2	5	1	LG	T-4TA-R	10I(B&G), 11I(B)		–	–	3	Dup	1	1
						10III(G), 11III(B&G)	(a)						
			4	Lab	2T-2I	10I(G), 10&11III(G)	(b)	–	–	–	Dup	2	2
12	45 / 3	5	1	SG	T-2I		(g)	–	3	1	3	1	1
			4	Lab	T-2I	12III(G)	(c)	1	4	4	1	2	2

NOTE: The meanings of symbols (a), (b), (c), (d), (e), (f), and (g) are explained on pages 264–65.

TABLE C

Girls' Physical Education
Group II-G: Comprehensive, High Interest

Grade	Number of Student Modules / Number of Students	Total Periods	Periods Each Line	Type of Instruction	Staff	Other Groups Included		Student Modules from Other Groups	Total Student Modules	Student Modules per Section	Sections To Be Scheduled	Periods per Meeting	Meetings per Week
1	2 / 3	4	5	6	7	8		9	10	11	12	13	14
7	75 / 5	7	1	SG	6T	7II(B)	(g)	6	–	11	Dup	1	1
			6	Lab	3T		(b)	–	5	2	3	2	3
8	75 / 5	7	1	LG	T-4TA-R	8II(B)	(a)	6	–	11	Dup	1	1
			6	Lab	2T-TA	9II(G)	(b)	4	9	3	3	2	3
9	60 / 4	7	1	LG	T-3TA-R	9II(B)	(a)	5	–	9	Dup	1	1
			6	Lab	2T-TA	8II(G)	(b)	5	–	–	Dup	2	3
10	60 / 4	7	1	LG	T-3TA-R	10II(B)	(a)	5	10	9	Dup	1	1
			6	Lab	3T-2TA	11II(G)	(b)	4	8	3	3	2	3
11	60 / 4	7	1	LG	T-2TA-R	11II(B)	(a)	3	–	7	Dup		
			6	Lab	3T-2TA	10II(G)	(b)	–	–	–	Dup	2	3
12	45 / 3	7	1	SG	T-2I		(c) (d) (g)	–	3	1	3	1	1
			6	Lab	T-TA		(b) (c) (d)	–	3	3	1	2	3

NOTE: The meanings of symbols (a), (b), (c), (d), (e), (f), and (g) are explained on pages 264–65.

TABLE D

Boys' Physical Education
Group III-B: Talented, Low Interest

Grade	Number of Student Modules	Number of Students	Total Periods	Periods Each Line	Type of Instruction	Staff	Other Groups Included	Student Modules from Other Groups	Total Student Modules	Student Modules per Section	Sections To Be Scheduled	Periods per Meeting	Meetings per Week
1	2	3	4	5	6	7	8	9	10	11	12	13	14
11		15		1	LG	T-4TA-R	10I(B&G), 11I(B&G)	10	–	11	Dup	1	1
			5				10III(G), 11III(G)						
		1		4	Lab	2T-2I	10I(B), 11I(B)	4	–	–	Dup	2	2
12		15		1	SG	T	(c) (d) (g)	–	1	1	1	1	1
			5										
		1		4	Lab	T-I-A	12I(B) (c)	3	–	–	Dup	2	2

In constructing this chart, it was assumed that boys who are talented in physical education also are sufficiently interested in it to be classified in Group IV-B, Talented, High Interest, in grades 7, 8, 9, and 10. The experience of many teachers has shown, however, that a small number of boys who have outstanding ability (Talented) in physical education lose interest in the 11th and 12th grades. Hence, one student module for such boys is assumed in this chart and is labeled Group III-B: Talented, Low Interest.

NOTE: The meanings of symbols (a), (b), (c), (d), (e), (f), and (g) are explained on pages 264–65.

TABLE E

Girls' Physical Education
Group III-G: Talented, Low Interest

Grade	Number of Students / Number of Student Modules	Total Periods	Periods Each Line	Type of Instruction	Staff	Other Groups Included	Student Modules from Other Groups	Total Student Modules	Student Modules per Section	Sections To Be Scheduled	Periods per Meeting	Meetings per Week
1	2/3	4	5	6	7	8	9	10	11	12	13	14
7	15 / 1	5	1	SG	T	(g)	–	1	1	1	1	1
			4	Lab	T-I	7I(G) (b)	–	–	–	Dup	2	2
8	15 / 1	5	1	LG	T-2TA-R	8I(B&G), 9I(B&G)	–	–	8	Dup	1	1
					2T	9III(G) (a)						
			4	Lab	2TA	8I(G), 9I(G)	–	–	–	Dup	2	2
						9III(G) (b)						
9	15 / 1	5	1	LG	T-2TA-R	8I(B&G), 9I(B&G)	–	–	–	Dup	1	1
					2T	8III(G) (a)						
			4	Lab	2TA	8I(G), 9I(G)	–	–	–	Dup	2	2
						8III(G) (b)						
10	15 / 1	5	1	LG	T-4TA-R	10I(B&G), 11I(B&G)	10	–	11	Dup	1	1
						11III(B&G) (a)						
			4	Lab	2T-2I	10I(G), 11I(G)	5	–	–	Dup	2	2
						11III(G) (b)						
11	15 / 1	5	1	LG	T-4TA-R	10I(B&G), 11I(B&G)	10	–	11	Dup	1	1
						10III(G), 11III(G) (a)						
			4	Lab	2T-2I	10I(G), 11I(G)	–	–	–	Dup	2	2
						10III(G) (b)						
12	15 / 1	5	1	SG	T	(c) (d) (g)	–	1	1	1	1	1
			4	Lab	T-2I	12I(G) (c)	–	–	–	Dup	2	2

NOTE: The meanings of symbols (a), (b), (c), (d), (e), (f), and (g) are explained on pages 264–65.

TABLE F

Boys' Physical Education
Group IV-B: Talented, High Interest

Grade	Number of Student Modules / Number of Students	Total Periods	Periods Each Line	Type of Instruction	Staff	Other Groups Included	Student Modules from Other Groups	Total Student Modules	Student Modules per Section	Sections To Be Scheduled	Periods per Meeting	Meetings per Week
1	2/3	4	5	6	7	8	9	10	11	12	13	14
7	15 / 1	9	1	SG	T	7IV(G) (a) (g)	1	2	2	1	1	1
			4	Lab	T-I	7V(B) (b)	1	2	2	1	2	2
			3	Lab	T-I	7V(B) (b)	1	2	2	1	3	1
			1	Lab	T	(b)	-	1	1	1	1	1
8	15 / 1	9	1	LG	T-2TA-R	8IV(G), 9IV(B&G)	11	12	12	1	1	1
						8V(B&G), 9V(B&G)						
						8VI(B&G), 9VI(B&G) (a)						
			6	Lab	T-TA	9IV(B) (b)	1	2	2	1	2	3
			2	Lab	I	(b)	-	1	1	1	2	1
9	15 / 1	8	1	LG	T-2TA-R	8IV(B&G), 9IV(G)	-	-	12	Dup	1	1
						8V(B&G), 9V(B&G)						
						8VI(B&G), 9VI(B&G) (a)						
			6	Lab	T-TA	8IV(B)	-	-	-	Dup	2	3
			1	Lab	I	(b)	-	1	1	1	1	1
10	15 / 1	8	1	LG	T-TA-R	10IV(G), 11IV(B&G) (a)	4	5	5	1	1	1
			6	Lab	T	11IV(B) (b)	2	3	3	1	2	3
			1	Lab	I	(b)	-	1	1	1	1	1
11	30 / 2	7	1	LG	T-TA-R	10IV(B&G), 11IV(G) (a)	3	-	5	Dup	1	1
			6	Lab	I	10IV(B) (b)	1	-	-	Dup	2	3
12	30 / 2	7	1	SG	T	(c) (g)	-	2	2	1	1	1
			6	Lab	T-TA	12V(B) (b) (c) (d) (g)	1	3	3	1	2	3

NOTE: The meanings of symbols (a), (b), (c), (d), (e), (f), and (g) are explained on pages 264–65.

TABLE G

Boys' Physical Education
Group V-B: Gifted

Grade	Number of Student Modules / Number of Students	Total Periods	Periods Each Line	Type of Instruction	Staff	Other Groups Included	Student Modules from Other Groups	Total Student Modules	Student Modules per Section	Sections To Be Scheduled	Periods per Meeting	Meetings per Week
1	2/3	4	5	6	7	8	9	10	11	12	13	14
7	15 / 1	9	1	SG	T	7V(G) (a) (g)	1	2	2	1	1	1
			4	Lab	T-I	7IV(B) (b)	–	–	–	Dup	2	2
			3	Lab	T-I	7IV(B) (b)	–	–	–	Dup	3	1
			1	Lab	T	(b)	1	1	1	1	1	1
8	15 / 1	9	1	LG	T-2TA-R	8IV(B&G), 9IV(B&G)	–	–	12	Dup	1	1
						8V(G), 9V(B&G)						
						8VI(B&G), 9III(B&G) (a)						
			4	Lab	T	9V(B) (b)	1	2	2	1	2	2
			3	Lab	T	9V(B) (b)	1	2	2	1	3	1
			1	Lab	T	(b)	1	1	1	1	1	1
9	15 / 1	8	1	LG	T-2TA-R	8IV(B&G), 9IV(B&G)	–	–	12	Dup	1	1
						8V(B&G), 8VI(B&G)						
						9V(B), 9VI(B&G) (a)						
			4	Lab	T	8V(B) (b)	–	–	–	Dup	2	2
			3	Lab	T	8V(B) (b)	–	–	–	Dup	3	1
10	15 / 1	8	1	LG	T-TA-R	10V(G), 11V(B&G) (a)	3	4	5	1	1	1
			6	Lab	T	11V(B) (b)	1	2	2	1	2	3
			1	Lab	T	(b)	–	1	1	1	1	1
11	15 / 1	7	1	LG	T-TA-R	10V(B&G), 11V(G) (a)	–	–	5	Dup	1	1
			6	Lab	T	10V(B) (b)	–	–	–	Dup	2	3
12	15 / 1	7	1	SG	T	(b) (c) (g)	–	1	1	1	1	1
			6	Lab	T	12IV(B) (b) (c) (d) (g)	2	–	–	Dup	2	3

NOTE: The meanings of symbols (a), (b), (c), (d), (e), (f), and (g) are explained on pages 264–65.

TABLE H

Boys' and Girls' Physical Education
Group VI-B & G: Adapted

Grade	Number of Student Modules / Number of Students	Total Periods	Periods Each Line	Type of Instruction	Staff	Other Groups Included	Student Modules from Other Groups	Total Student Modules	Student Modules per Section	Sections To Be Scheduled	Periods per Meeting	Meetings per Week
1	2 / 3	4	5	6	7	8	9	10	11	12	13	14
7	30 / 2	6	1	SG	T	(a) (g)	–	2	2	1	1	1
			2	Lab	2T	(e) (f)	–	2	2	1	2	1
			3	Lab	2T	(e) (f)	–	2	2	1	1	3
8	30 / 2	6	1	LG	T-2TA-R	8IV(B&G), 9IV(B&G)	–	–	12	Dup	1	1
			2	Lab	3T-TA	8V(B&G), 9V(B&G) (a) 9VI(B&G) (f)	2	4	4	1	2	1
			3	Lab	2T	(e) (f)	–	2	2	1	1	3
9	30 / 2	6	1	LG	T-2TA-R	8IV(B&G), 9IV(B&G)	–	–	12	Dup	1	1
			2	Lab	3T-TA	8V(B&G), 8VI(B&G) 9V(B&G) (a) 8VI(B&G) (f)	–	–	–	Dup	2	1
			3	Lab	2T	(e) (f)	–	2	2	1	1	3
10	30 / 2	6	1	LG	T-TA-R	11VI(B&G) (a)	2	4	4	1	1	1
			4	Lab	4T	11VI(B&G) (f)	2	4	2	2	2	2
			1	Lab	2T	(e) (f)	–	2	1	2	1	1
11	30 / 2	6	1	LG	T-TA-R	10VI(B&G) (a)	–	–	4	Dup	1	1
			4	Lab	4T	10VI(B&G) (f)	–	–	–	Dup	2	2
			1	Lab	2T	(e) (f)	–	2	1	2	1	1
12	30 / 2	6	1	SG	2T	(e) (g)	–	2	1	2	1	1
			4	Lab	2T	(f)	–	2	2	1	2	2
			1	Lab	2T	(e) (f)	–	2	1	2	1	1

NOTE: The meanings of symbols (a), (b), (c), (d), (e), (f), and (g) are explained on pages 264–65.

APPENDIX

EXPLANATORY NOTES FOR THE PHYSICAL EDUCATION STRUCTURE

Selected Basic Assumptions

1. The instructional staff should be assigned on the basis of a ratio of one staff member (senior teacher, teacher, intern, or teacher aide) for each twenty-five to thirty students, a desirable standard in physical education to ensure adequate *instruction*, which is the key element in a superior program.

2. The seventh grade usually is a crucial transitional period for the students as they move along the educational ladder. The physical education program usually is significantly different (dressing, showering, costume, specialized instruction, more and larger facilities, longer instructional periods, more testing, etc.) from the typical elementary school program. Therefore, it would seem that seventh-graders should *not* be grouped with students of higher grades. Also, it seems crucial to assign experienced teachers to seventh-grade groups.

3. Eighth and ninth grades, and tenth and eleventh grades, in similar ability-interest groups, probably can be combined into one class satisfactorily. This combination of grades would require a *cycle program for two years duration*, one program for the eighth- and ninth-grade group, another for the tenth- and eleventh-grade group.

4. Seniors (twelfth grade) are permitted more elective choices and more time and concentration in fewer activities in order better to prepare them for independent responsibility that soon will face them in adult life.

5. Co-educational combinations for instructional, practice, and competitive purposes can be worked out between groups shown on the Schedule, at the discretion of the teachers.

6. This proposal puts more emphasis on instruction aimed at "intellectualizing" the physical education program to a greater extent than typically is the case in traditional programs, hence, the provision for large group instruction periodically for one thirty-minute period. It would seem that boys and girls can be grouped together for this purpose for most topics that will be presented in such a period. Occasional thirty-minute periods could be scheduled for boys and girls separately if a particular subject (i.e., menstrual problems) is best presented in this manner.

7. As the interested students (comprehensive-interested; subject talented-interested; and gifted) advance in grade, the number of periods required for instructional physical education classes increases. Group II, Comprehensive, High Interest students, receives a single concentration of twelve additional periods added to the basic thirty minimum required periods. Group IV, Talented, High Interest students, receives a concentration of eighteen additional periods, which is only three-fourths of a double concentration. Group V, Gifted students, also receives a concentration of eighteen additional periods, which is only three-eighths of a gifted concentration. The reason for not assigning the maximum concentrations to these physical education groups is that presum-

ably most of the interested and able students will take advantage of voluntary opportunities available for participation in a wide variety of well-conducted intramural and interscholastic sports, dance, exercise, and recreational programs that the school will administer to supplement the instructional program. Thus, interested and able physical education pupils will achieve the recommended concentrations of time in the above manner. See page 212 for an explanation of three types of "concentrations" used in this project.

8. The time allotment for the Adapted group remains the same for each grade because these students, as they progress from grade to grade, will continue to need all of the specialized attention and instruction the school can provide at each grade level.

9. Whenever possible, handicapped students should be grouped with other pupils in large group sessions to help integrate them into the total program and reduce their isolation from the regular students in the physical education program.

Group Designations

1. *Large Groups.* Instructions will be predominantly by classroom lecture and other formal teaching techniques of the classroom. By definition, large groups will contain three or more student modules (forty-five or more students).

2. *Small Groups.* Small groups will emphasize discussion and other formal individual and small group learning techniques. Small groups, by definition, will consist only of one or two student modules (fifteen or thirty students).

3. *Laboratory (Lab) Groups.* Students in these groups will normally be dressed in appropriate physical education costume and will be in the activities phase of the instructional program taking place in the various activity areas and facilities (gymnasiums, sports fields, swimming pool, dance studio, corrective room, and similar classrooms). Laboratory groups may consist of one or more student modules.

Key to Notes Accompanying the Charts

(a) This thirty-minute period one time per week could offer, for example, instruction in the classroom concerning the "why" of physical education in the school program, and in adult life; basic kinesiology, physiology of exercise, and body mechanics; the values of exercise, dance, sports, and gymnastics; the role of sports in American and world cultures; physical training values and techniques; mental and emotional health aspects; preventative, therapeutic, and maintenance values and techniques of physical activity; individual assessment of physical interests and capabilities and a coordinated guidance program to develop physical education habits, attitudes, knowledges, and skills for a lifetime; tests and evaluations; theory and practice of relaxation; rules, strategy, equipment, and facilities; spectator appreciation; and similar valuable "academic" content.

These topics could be presented and studied by a variety of techniques including extensive use of audio-visual aids; use of noted, highly qualified resource personnel from the community, state, and nation; homework assignments; and use of texts, written examinations, etc.

Different teachers might conduct the large group sessions to best utilize the special interests and talents of each staff member. When desirable, boys and girls can be scheduled to meet separately.

(b) Groups of boys and girls in similar ability-interest groups can be combined into co-educational classes once per week or at other intervals deemed desirable.

(c) Seniors can have more opportunity to elect activities in their programs and can practice and compete in a few selected activities at a more advanced level of skill. Laboratory sessions for small groups may be used for intensive-, repetitive-type practice of skills or teamwork required at advanced skill levels, under expert instruction; students may investigate and try out new activities.

(d) The senior teacher may be replaced at specified times by (1) a teacher of less experience, (2) an intern, or (3) a community resource person, when any of these persons has a specialized skill and teaching competence at an advanced level appropriate to the activity assigned at the time.

(e) Large group instruction could be held once each two weeks, rather than weekly as shown, for handicapped students.

(f) Physicians and adapted physical education specialists recommend that adapted physical education classes for handicapped pupils not exceed a ratio of one specially trained corrective physical education teacher per twenty students. The state of California provides excess cost aid to districts on this basis to encourage and support physical education for the handicapped with special teachers.

(g) The small group will be utilized for seventh and twelfth grades because it is believed that seventh-graders will be enabled to make better adjustment to a new program, and because twelfth-graders can better achieve terminal interests connected with their impending departure from high school. Seniors should be ready for discussion and study in depth of specific topics.

(h) Certain less-active phases of the program could be carried on in this thirty-minute period, such as testing, demonstration-instruction, social dance, etc.

SCHEDULE FOR PHYSICAL EDUCATION STUDENT

The chart on page 266 is an illustrative schedule for a tenth-grade student. He is enrolled in foreign languages, science, mathematics, English, arts, social studies, and physical education. He is also scheduled for five thirty-minute periods for guidance and eleven periods for independent study. His physical education schedule includes three sixty-minute laboratory periods and two thirty-minute periods of large group instruction, in addition to one thirty-minute period of health education.

TABLE I

Schedule for Student Beta: Grade Ten

Per.	M.	T.	W.	Th.	F.
1	FM	FM	FM	FM	FM
2	G	G(IS)	G	G(IS)	G
3	FL Lab IV-2	IS	FL Lab IV-2	PE(H) LG IV	FL Lab IV-2
4	FL SG IV-2	IS	SS LG IV	IS	SS LG IV
5	Sci LG III	Sci Lab III	Sci LG III	Sci SG III	Sci SG III
6	PE Lab IV	Sci Lab III	PE Lab IV	Sci SG III	PE Lab IV
7	PE Lab IV	PE LG IV	PE Lab IV	PE SG IV	PE Lab IV
8	IS	IS	IS	IS	IS
9	Lunch	Lunch	Lunch	Lunch	Lunch
10	Math LG I	Math Lab I	Math LG I	Math Lab I	Math LG I
11	Eng Lab III	FL Lab IV-1	Eng SG III	FL Lab IV-1	FL SG IV-1
12	Eng Lab III	Eng LG III	IS	Eng Lab III	FL SG IV-1
13	Arts LG III	SS SG IV	SS Lab IV	Eng Lab III	IS
14	Arts LG III	SS SG IV	SS Lab IV	SS SG IV	Arts LG III
15	Arts LG III	SS SG IV	SS Lab IV	SS SG IV	Arts LG III
16	SS LG IV	IS	SS Lab IV	SS SG IV	Arts LG III

NOTES

FM—Faculty Meeting
G—Guidance Period
IS—Independent Study

Three sixty-minute periods of PE Lab
Two thirty-minute periods of Large Group PE
One thirty-minute period of Health Education

SCHEDULE FOR PHYSICAL EDUCATION TEACHER

The chart on page 268 is an illustrative schedule for a physical education teacher. This teacher is provided with a large block of time each day for preparation, conferences, and other non-instructional activities. This teacher's responsibility is with the eighth and ninth grades (a cycle) and primarily with average-ability students in physical education. His program includes two large group lecture classes (co-educational).

The majority of his classes are two periods long (1 hour), and he also teaches one three-period lab and two one-period labs. He spends the first hour of the school day in faculty meetings and guidance duties (both group and individual). His department has scheduled five periods per week for meetings. He has the last period free each day to organize for the next day or to prepare for his after-school activities. He teaches physical education thirty-nine periods per week (19.5 hours), two of these in the classroom and the other thirty-seven in the gymnasium and on outdoor fields and courts.

SUGGESTED CURRICULUM FOR GROUP V, GIRLS, GIFTED

An example of a curriculum for one of these groups of students follows. It is assumed that the school year has thirty-six weeks. It will be noted that varying numbers of periods are assigned for the total school year to each of the grades for this group of girls. The following outline indicates activity units that might be appropriate at each grade level.

SEVENTH GRADE   325 Total Periods

Unit Division
1. Five units—thirty-two periods per unit
2. Five units—twenty-four periods per unit
3. One orientation unit—nine periods
4. One period per week of small group instruction

Guide to Activity Selection
1. At least two team sports
2. One unit of tumbling
3. One unit of swimming
4. One unit of rhythmic activity
5. One unit of track and field
6. One unit of physical fitness
7. One unit of a dual sport

At this level, the program is designed to orient the student to high school physical education. For the majority of the students, this will be the first year of an organized physical education program.

EIGHTH GRADE   325 Total Periods

Unit Division
1. Five units—thirty-two periods per unit
2. Five units—twenty-four periods per unit

TABLE J

Schedule for Physical Education Teacher

Per.	M.	T.	W.	Th.	F.
1	FM	FM	FM	FM	FM
2	G	G(IS)	G	G(IS)	G

3	⌈Lab 8II(B)
	  9II(B)
		⌈Lab 8I(B)
		  9I(B)
			⌈Lab 8II(B)
			  9II(B)
				⌈Lab 8I(B)
				  9I(B)
					⌈Lab 8II(B)
					  9II(B)

4	⌊Lab 8II(B)
	  9II(B)
		⌊Lab 8I(B)
		  9I(B)
			⌊Lab 8II(B)
			  9II(B)
				⌊Lab 8I(B)
				  9I(B)
					⌊Lab 8II(B)
					  9II(B)

5	⌈Lab 8II(B)
	  9II(B)
		⌈Lab 8V(B)
		  9V(B)
			⌈Lab 8II(B)
			  9II(B)
				⌈Lab 8V(B)
				  9V(B)
					⌈Lab 8II(B)
					  9II(B)

6	⌊Lab 8II(B)
	  9II(B)
		⌊Lab 8V(B)
		  9V(B)
			⌊Lab 8II(B)
			  9II(B)
				⌊Lab 8V(B)
				  9V(B)
					⌊Lab 8II(B)
					  9II(B)

7	⌈Lab 8II(B)
	  9II(B)
		⌈Lab 8II(B)
		  9II(B)
			⌈Lab 8II(B)
			  9II(B)
				⌈Lab 8II(B)
				  9II(B)
					⌈Lab 8II(B)
					  9II(B)

8	⌊Lab 8II(B)
	  9II(B)
		⌊Lab 8II(B)
		  9II(B)
			⌊Lab 8II(B)
			  9II(B)
				⌊Lab 8II(B)
				  9II(B)
					⌊Lab 8II(B)
					  9II(B)

9					
10					
11					⌈Lab 8IV(B)
12					⌊Lab 8IV(B)
13	LG 8I, 8III, 9I, 9III (B&G)		LG 8II(B&G)		⌈Lab 8V(B) 9V(B)
14	DM		DM	Lab 8V(B)	Lab 8V(B) 9V(B)
15	DM	Lab 9IV(B)	DM	DM	⌈Lab 8V(B) ⌊ 9V(B)
16					

3. One unit for opening and closing school—nine periods
4. One period per week of large group instruction

Guide to Activity Selection
1. One unit of soccer
2. One unit of basketball, softball, or volleyball
3. One unit of paddle handball or recreational games
4. One unit of tumbling
5. One unit of swimming
6. One unit of folk or square dance
7. One unit of marching
8. One unit of track and field
9. One unit of physical fitness

NINTH GRADE   284 Total Periods

Unit Division
1. Five units—twenty-seven periods per unit
2. Five units—twenty-one periods per unit
3. One unit for opening and closing school—eight periods
4. One period per week of large group instruction

Guide to Activity Selection
1. One unit of speedball
2. One unit of basketball, softball, or volleyball
3. One unit of badminton
4. One unit of tumbling or gymnastics
5. One unit of swimming
6. One unit of social dance
7. One unit of grooming and posture
8. One unit of track and field
9. One unit of physical fitness

TENTH GRADE   252 Total Periods

Unit Division
1. Five units—twenty-seven periods per unit
2. Five units—twenty-one periods per unit
3. One unit for opening and closing school—eight periods
4. One period per week of large group instruction

Guide to Activity Selection
1. One unit of a team sport
2. One unit of badminton or tennis
3. One unit of bowling
4. One unit of gymnastics or body mechanics
5. One unit of social dance
6. One unit of modern dance
7. One unit of track and field
8. One unit of physical fitness
9. One unit of grooming and posture

ELEVENTH GRADE   253 Total Periods

Unit Division
1. Five units—twenty-four periods per unit

2. Five units—eighteen periods per unit
3. One unit for opening and closing school—seven periods
4. One period per week of large group instruction

Guide to Activity Selection
1. One unit of field hockey
2. One unit of a dual sport
3. One unit of bowling
4. One unit of gymnastics
5. One unit of body mechanics
6. One unit of synchronized swimming
7. One unit of modern dance
8. One unit of physical fitness
9. Two elective units or extended units.

At this level, unit organization should not be so rigid. In other words, a student may wish to continue on in one activity through two units rather than just one.

TWELFTH GRADE   253 Total Periods

Unit Division
1. Five units—twenty-four periods per unit
2. Five units—eighteen periods per unit
3. One unit for opening and closing school—seven periods
4. One period per week of individual study and small group instruction

Guide to Activity Selection
1. One unit of field hockey
2. One unit of archery
3. One unit of golf
4. One unit of modern dance and/or body mechanics
5. One unit of physical fitness
6. Electives

As much as possible, this program should be elective in scope. The student should be given the opportunity to develop and perfect skills in activities in which she has particular interest.

SUGGESTIONS FOR SMALL AND LARGE GROUP ACTIVITIES

1. Rules, strategy
2. Movement analysis
3. Co-ed activities
4. Guest lectures
5. Individual and group research
6. Testing
7. Measurement and evaluation

Selected References

To the reader who wishes to pursue his study further, the authors recommend the following references to supplement the discussions in each chapter.

CHAPTER 1

ASSOCIATION FOR SUPERVISION AND CURRICULUM DEVELOPMENT. *New Insights and the Curriculum.* Washington, D.C.: National Education Association, 1963.

A yearbook offering contributions from leading social scientists and educators. New knowledge classified in the categories of potentiality, knowledge, self-management, relationships, across cultures, citizenship, and creativity is analyzed and summarized. Curriculum implications are reported for each.

ASSOCIATION FOR SUPERVISION AND CURRICULUM DEVELOPMENT. *Perceiving, Behaving, Becoming.* Washington, D.C.: National Education Association, 1962.

A yearbook that examines current theory about the nature of human capacity and adjustment and discusses implications of personality theory for educational thought and practice. It summarizes important knowledge concerning the supremely healthy, self-actualizing, fully functioning personality and provides guidelines for applying this knowledge in school practice.

BLOOM, BENJAMIN S., et al. *Taxonomy of Educational Objectives.* London: Longmans, Green & Co., 1956.

An excellent classification of educational objectives. Behavioristic descriptions of objectives are also included.

BRAMELD, THEODORE. *Cultural Foundations of Education.* New York: Harper & Row, 1957.

The author brings to educational theory substantial ideas and facts from anthropology, philosophy, psychology, sociology, and other fields. A threefold conceptual scheme for categorizing human experience is used: order, process, and goals. Each is considered in terms of cultural components and education is viewed through the lens of each of these categories.

BUTTS, R. FREEMAN, and LAWRENCE A. CREMIN. *A History of Education in American Culture.* New York: Holt, Rinehart & Winston, Inc., 1953.

Recommended to provide a sound historical foundation upon which to base judgments about American education. The authors stress the cultural and problems approach to the study of education, combining this with a factual and chronological approach to the study of history. For each of four chronological periods in American history, they discuss political, economic, sociologial, and religious institutions influencing American education; intellectual, philosophical, psychological, religious, and scientific outlooks influencing education; educational viewpoints; and actual practices in education.

GARDNER, JOHN W. *Excellence: Can We Be Equal and Excellent Too?* New York: Harper & Row, 1961.

A provocative discussion of the "pursuit of excellence," with important implications for curriculum development.

GESELL, ARNOLD, and FRANCES L. ILG. *The Child from Five to Ten.* New York: Harper & Row, 1946.

A classic text on child deevlopment. It delineates the progressive growth stages with systematic reference to ten major fields of behavior: motor characteristics, personal hygiene, emotional expression, fears and dreams, self and sex, interpersonal relations, play and pastimes, school life, ethical sense, and philosophic outlook.

GESELL, ARNOLD, FRANCES L. ILG, and LOUISE BATES AMES. *Youth: The Years from Ten to Sixteen.* New York: Harper & Row, 1956.

A series of descriptions based on extensive clinical study. For each age level, the authors have summarized their findings as "maturity traits" (behavior patterns and guidance problems), "maturity trends" (growth gradients and sequences), and "maturity profiles" (delineations characterizing each age zone). The third in a series, the first two of which are: *Infant and Child in the Culture of Today* (1943) and *The Child from Five to Ten* (1946).

HAVIGHURST, ROBERT J. *Human Development and Education.* London: Longmans, Green & Co., 1953.

A basic reference on the developmental task concept for education. Provides an overview of the developmental tasks of infancy, childhood, adolescence, adulthood, and old age. Parts II and III treat the developmental tasks as objectives of education. Part V describes an empirical test of some of the hypotheses about developmental tasks and contains a set of rating scales for estimating achievement.

HAVIGHURST, ROBERT J., and BERNICE L. NEUGARTEN. *Society and Education.* Rockleigh, N.J.: Allyn & Bacon, Inc., 1962.

An analysis of major educational topics and problems from a sociological point of view. The authors examine the place of the educational system in the society it serves. Content is organized in terms of the social environment of the child and the adolescent; the school as a social institution; and the teacher's crucial role in interaction between child, school, and society.

JERSILD, ARTHUR T. *Child Psychology.* 5th ed. Englewood Cliffs, N.J.: Prentice-Hall, Inc., 1960.

The author considers motor, social, emotional, and language development; the growth of understanding and intelligence; children's imaginative and play activities; ideals and morals; and personality problems.

JERSILD, ARTHUR T. *The Psychology of Adolescence.* New York: The Macmillan Co., 1963.

An overview of adolescent psychology with emphasis on normal development. The author discusses physical, mental, emotional, social, vocational, and personality development. A companion volume to *Child Psychology.*

LERNER, MAX. *America as a Civilization.* New York: Simon & Schuster, Inc., 1957.

An analysis of contemporary American civilization that studies technological, economic, political, and philosophical characteristics; describes present-day structure of our society; and analyzes typical life patterns.

MURPHY, GARDNER. *Human Potentialities.* New York: Basic Books, Inc., 1958.

About the changing qualities of human individuals and their societies; the author discusses approaches to realizing our potentialities as human beings, stressing individual creativeness and the freeing of intelligence.

TORRANCE, E. PAUL. *Guiding Creative Talent.* Englewood Cliffs, N.J.: Prentice-Hall, Inc., 1962.

Concerned with the discovery and development of creative talent, this book stresses the necessity for developing creativity as a function of education, offers suggestions for assessing creative talent, and discusses problems resulting from the expression and repression of creative abilities.

CHAPTER 2

CRONBACH, LEE J. *Educational Psychology.* New York: Harcourt, Brace & World, Inc., 1963.

Concerned with giving the teacher an understanding of the way pupils learn, psychological principles are clearly stated and amply illustrated. Major topical areas include readiness; acquiring ideas, attitudes, and skills; planning, motivation, and evaluation; and emotional learning.

GWYNN, J. MINOR. *Curriculum Principles and Social Trends.* New York: The Macmillan Co., 1960.

Curriculum development is viewed in terms of needed changes in elementary and secondary schools. Topics include historical overview of curriculum development in schools, conflicting educational theories, problems concerned with child growth and development, social and economic factors, teacher education, curriculum aides, influence of the textbook, development of the unit technique, the community approach to the curriculum, national and international movements, propaganda and the curriculum, and the curriculum crisis at midcentury. Annotated references include special bibliographies for elementary school and secondary school curriculum workers.

HAND, HAROLD C. *Principles of Public Secondary Education.* New York: Harcourt, Brace & World, Inc., 1958.

Nine basic principles of American public secondary education are defined and illustrated. These are applied to the solution of major curriculum problems: improving the school's "holding power," school-community relations, discipline, extraclass activities, guidance, and appraisal. The teacher's role in curriculum improvement is discussed in Chapter 11.

HILGARD, ERNST R. *Theories of Learning.* New York: Appleton-Century-Crofts, Inc., 1956.

An exposition of the major learning theories from Thorndike's connectionism to current developments in studies of reinforcement, motivational aspects of learning, and the problems of learned discrimination.

KRUG, EDWARD A. *Curriculum Planning.* New York: Harper & Row, 1957.

Deals with curriculum planning practices and the problems involved in making curriculum planning an effective process. Chapter 11 includes an excellent statement of guiding principles for future curriculum planning.

LEONARD, J. PAUL. *Developing the Secondary School Curriculum.* New York: Holt, Rinehart & Winston, Inc., 1960.

Curriculum development theory is combined with extensive discussion of current practices. Stress is placed on recent changes and proposals in secondary education, reports of national committees and commissions, and practical ways to initiate curriculum change.

MCNALLY, HAROLD J., A. HARRY PASSOW, *et al. Improving the Quality of Public School Programs.* New York: Bureau of Publications, Teachers College, Columbia University, 1960.

Describes and appraises organized efforts at curriculum improvement. The first four chapters discuss the social changes and forces that demand curriculum change. The concluding chapter summarizes guidelines and principles for curriculum improvement.

SMITH, B. OTHANEL, WILLIAM O. STANLEY, and J. HARLAN SHORES. *Fundamentals of Curriculum Development.* New York: Harcourt, Brace & World, Inc., 1957.

An analysis of curriculum development with emphasis on the social-reconstruction approach and a diagnosis of theoretical curriculum issues. Part II is particularly useful in this context.

STRATEMEYER, FLORENCE B., HAMDEN L. FORKNER, MARGARET McKIM, and A. HARRY PASSOW. *Developing a Curriculum for Modern Living.* New York: Bureau of Publications, Teachers College, Columbia University, 1957.

Reviews the foundations of curriculum development and provides detailed proposals for curriculum designs based on the persistent life situations concept.

TABA, HILDA. *Curriculum Development: Theory and Practice.* New York: Harcourt, Brace & World, Inc., 1962.

Examines the theory of curriculum development, strengthens the basis for curriculum improvement by reaching into fields other than education, and focuses upon current ideas and problems. Discussions in depth concerning foundations, the process of curriculum planning, curriculum design, and strategy for curriculum change are given.

CHAPTER 3

ASSOCIATION FOR SUPERVISION AND CURRICULUM DEVELOPMENT. *Balance in the Curriculum.* Washington, D.C.: National Education Association, 1961.

This yearbook contains a description of modern curriculum development and stresses the need for balance in the selection and placement of subjects in the curriculum.

BRUNER, JEROME S. *The Process of Education.* Cambridge: Harvard University Press, 1960.

A discussion of curriculum development emphasizing the role of structure in learning, readiness for learning, the nature and importance of intuition, and motives for learning.

CASSIDY, ROSALIND. *Curriculum Development in Physical Education.* New York: Harper & Row, 1954.

Chapter 1 defines the need for curriculum redirection and describes patterns of curriculum change.

FAUNCE, ROLAND C., and NELSON L. BOSSING. *Developing the Core Curriculum.* Englewood Cliffs, N.J.: Prentice-Hall, Inc., 1958.

This book contains an analysis of the core curriculum, including its definition, the strengths and weaknesses, philosophy and purposes, the relationship of theories of learning, the role of guidance, the role of the teacher, use of resource units, and evaluation.

MILLER, ARTHUR G., and M. DOROTHY MASSEY. *A Dynamic Concept of Physical Education for Secondary Schools.* Englewood Cliffs, N.J.: Prentice-Hall, Inc., 1963.

Presents the nature, scope, and potential of physical education in today's secondary school curriculum. Chapter 10 advocates as much interaction as possible between different academic disciplines in any school and describes several examples of subject-matter correlation involving physical education and other subjects.

SELECTED REFERENCES

MILLER, ARTHUR G., and VIRGINIA WHITCOMB. *Physical Education in the Elementary School Curriculum.* 2d ed. Englewood Cliffs, N.J.: Prentice-Hall, Inc., 1963.

Part III discusses how physical education can be integrated with the social studies, language arts, and arithmetic in the elementary school.

OBERTEUFFER, DELBERT, and CELESTE ULRICH. *Physical Education.* 3d ed. New York: Harper & Row, 1962.

Chapter 9 stresses associated or concomitant learnings, the integrated curriculum, and the value of the core curriculum.

SMITH, B. OTHANEL, WILLIAM O. STANLEY, and J. H. SHORES. *Fundamentals of Curriculum Development.* Rev. ed. New York: Harcourt, Brace & World, Inc., 1957.

Chapters 10 through 15 contain detailed description of the subject curriculum, the activity curriculum, and the core curriculum.

SOWARDS, G. WESLEY, and MARY-MARGARET SCOBEY. *The Changing Curriculum and the Elementary Teacher.* Belmont, Calif.: Wadsworth Publishing Co., Inc., 1961.

Chapter 7 presents an analysis and critique of major curriculum patterns that evolved in elementary education in the United States. The authors conclude with their reasons for believing that many elements of the core curriculum have great promise as bases for further improvement in the curriculum of elementary schools.

STALEY, SEWARD C. "Graduate Study in Physical Education and Scholarship." In *College Physical Education Association Annual Proceedings.* Washington, D.C.: American Association for Health, Physical Education, and Recreation, 1961.

An eloquent plea for a higher quality of scholarly endeavor by physical educators. Advocates the encouragement of a core of "scholars" of physical education.

TABA, HILDA. *Curriculum Development, Theory and Practice.* New York: Harcourt, Brace & World, Inc., 1962.

Chapter 21 reviews the major curriculum patterns and analyzes the strengths and weaknesses of each. Chapter 22 discusses the elements of the curriculum and their relationships and emphasizes the necessity for an underlying conceptual framework for any curriculum pattern.

CHAPTER 4

AMERICAN ASSOCIATION OF SCHOOL ADMINISTRATORS. *New Insights and the Curriculum.* Washington, D.C., 1963.

A yearbook that gives recent curriculum trends and influences.

EDUCATION POLICIES COMMISSION. *School Athletics-Problems and Policies.* Washington, D.C.: National Education Association, 1954.

Recommends that all boys and girls in public schools be afforded the educational benefits of participation in school athletic programs properly conducted.

EDUCATIONAL POLICIES COMMISSION. *The Central Purpose of American Education.* Washington, D.C.: National Education Association, 1961.

Emphasizes the necessity for a strong physical basis to underlie the development of the "rational powers" of pupils in schools.

GWYNN, J. MINOR. *Curriculum Principles and Social Trends.* 3d ed. New York: The Macmillan Co., 1960.

Chapter 8 describes the "powerful influence" of the textbook on curriculum development. Chapter 17 describes how teacher training and curriculum improvement are very closely "interwoven."

KENNEDY, JOHN F. "The Soft American," *Sports Illustrated*, XV (December, 1960), 15–17.

Written while President-elect. Indicates his deep personal concern for the physical welfare of every citizen of this country and cites his determination to exercise leadership in this area from the office of the President. Obviously, a strong influence upon the school physical education curriculum.

LEESE, JOSEPH, KENNETH FRASURE, and MAURITZ JOHNSON. *The Teacher in Curriculum Making*. New York: Harper & Row, 1961.

Emphasizes the involvement of the individual teacher in curriculum evaluation and change. Indicates the influences that affect teacher attitudes toward curriculum improvement.

MICHAEL, LLOYD S. "New Directions for the High School Curriculum," *California Journal of Secondary Education*. xxxiii (October, 1958), 356–361.

Indicates the potentialities for improving education programs by the use of flexible scheduling, team teaching, instructional technology, and similar innovations. Implications for curriculum change are listed.

National Conference on Interpretation of Physical Education. Chicago: The Athletic Institute, Inc., 1962.

A clear statement on the interpretation of physical education. It is supplemented by the Institute's interpretation film, "Readiness, the Fourth R."

PRESIDENT'S COUNCIL ON YOUTH FITNESS. *Youth Physical Fitness: Suggested Elements of a School-Centered Program*. Washington, D.C., 1961. Parts One and Two.

An excellent example of a strong influence toward curriculum change.

CHAPTER 5

ASSOCIATION FOR SUPERVISION AND CURRICULUM DEVELOPMENT. *Research for Curriculum Improvement*. Washington, D.C.: National Education Association, 1957.

A yearbook on curriculum research providing a theoretical and historical background, an analysis of the research process and of specific problems, and a discussion of personnel who participate in curriculum research. An annotated bibliography is included as Appendix A.

BROWN, CAMILLE, AND ROSALIND CASSIDY. *Theory in Physical Education: A Guide to Program Change*. Philadelphia: Lee & Febiger, 1963.

A study of physical education theory. The authors have formulated a theoretical framework for guiding program change in physical education. A concept of the field as "the art and science of human movement" is emphasized.

CASSIDY, ROSALIND. *Curriculum Development in Physical Education*. New York: Harper & Row, 1954.

A resource on the development of the physical education curriculum, with many examples of practice. Problems encountered in program planning, and the processes and principles applicable in building the curriculum at each level, are stressed. A bibliography is included.

COWELL, CHARLES C., and HELEN W. HAZELTON. *Curriculum Designs in Physical Education*. Englewood Cliffs, N.J.: Prentice-Hall, Inc., 1955.

A plan for designing physical education curricula. Reviews the foundations for curriculum development, outlines the steps in curriculum building, and provides a series of tables relating suggested physical education activities to developmental goals for each grade level.

SELECTED REFERENCES

KRUG, EDWARD A., CHESTER D. BABCOCK, JOHN GUY FOWLKES, and H. T. JAMES. *Administering Curriculum Planning.* New York: Harper & Row, 1956.

Deals with curriculum planning with emphasis on a concept of participation in curriculum development by all concerned and upon the actual administration of curriculum-improvement programs. The teacher's role is stressed.

LEONARD, J. PAUL. *Developing the Secondary School Curriculum.* New York: Holt, Rinehart & Winston, Inc., 1960.

Stresses the need and possible procedures for curriculum change. Chapter 12 is of special interest in studying procedures for curriculum improvement.

MCNALLY, HAROLD J., A. HARRY PASSOW, et al. *Improving the Quality of Public School Programs.* New York: Bureau of Publications, Teachers College, Columbia University, 1960.

Presents descriptions and appraisals of organized efforts at curriculum improvement. Guidelines and principles for curriculum improvement are summarized in the last chapter.

NATIONAL SOCIETY FOR THE STUDY OF EDUCATION. *Social Forces Influencing American Education.* Chicago: University of Chicago Press, 1961. Sixtieth Yearbook. Part II.

Designed to identify the dominant forces influencing American education and to aid in providing understanding of current social changes affecting the schools. The contemporary situation is analyzed from the viewpoints of eight different social-science disciplines. Political science, economics, demography, social class, values, the student social system, teachers' organizations, and mass media are examined as forces influencing education.

SHEPARD, NATALIE M. *Foundations and Principles of Physical Education.* New York: The Ronald Presss Co., 1960.

Derives principles from facts, philosophic beliefs, basic assumptions, and experience. Specific principles are presented in the areas of curriculm, instruction, administration, and evaluation. The relationship of principles to program is emphasized.

SMITH, B. OTHANEL, WILLIAM O. STANLEY, and J. HARLAN SHORES. *Fundamentals of Curriculum Development.* New York: Harcourt, Brace & World, Inc., 1957.

Part Four discusses curriculum change as action research, analyzing the roles of various personnel, techniques for diagnosing the local school-community situation, and ways of initiating and controlling curriculum change.

STRATEMEYER, FLORENCE B., HAMDEN L. FORKNER, MARGARET G. MCKIM, and A. HARRY PASSOW. *Developing a Curriculum for Modern Living.* New York: Bureau of Publications, Teachers College, Columbia University, 1957.

Part V analyzes the process of curriculum improvement, suggests techniques for stimulating and guiding curriculum change, and discusses the place of research in curriculum development.

TABA, HILDA. *Curriculum Developement: Theory and Practice.* New York: Harcourt, Brace & World, Inc., 1962.

Most portions of this text, especially Part Four, are relevant to the topics discussed in this chapter.

CHAPTER 6

ANDREWS, GLADYS, JEANNETTE SAURBORN, and ELSA SCHNEIDER. *Physical Education for Today's Boys and Girls.* Rockleigh, N.J.: Allyn & Bacon, Inc., 1960.

Treats the nature of movement as the basis of physical education, current persistent problems facing movement education, and the evaluation process. Stresses creativity in teaching and provides descriptions of the various forms of movement that make up the physical education program: exploration of movement, games and sports, stunts and related activities, and rhythms and dance.

ASSOCIATION FOR SUPERVISION AND CURRICULUM DEVELOPMENT. *A Look at Continuity in the School Program.* Washington, D.C.: National Education Association, 1958.

An exploration of current conditions with respect to articulation and learning continuity in elementary and secondary schools. Discusses the foundations for continuity and explores current efforts at solving articulation problems. A classified bibliography is provided.

BROER, MARION R. *Efficiency of Human Movement.* Philadelphia: W. B. Saunders Co., 1960.

Pertinent to a consideration of the nature of fundamentals in physical education. Discusses basic mechanical principles underlying efficient movement, the application of these principles to fundamental physical skills and to sports and dance, and considers the use of a foundation course in efficient movement in the physical education program.

BROWNELL, CLIFFORD LEE, and E. PATRICIA HAGMAN. *Physical Education: Foundations and Principles.* New York: McGraw-Hill Book Co., Inc., 1951.

Chapter 9 presents criteria for selecting program activities and also deals with scope of physical education programs, principles of curriculum development, and their application to physical education.

COWELL, CHARLES C., and HELEN W. HAZELTON. *Curriculum Designs in Physical Education.* Englewood Cliffs, N.J.: Prentice-Hall, Inc., 1955.

A curriculum text based on current professional education concepts and curriculum development theory. Aids the physical educator in establishing local standards and organizing a given school curriculum. Part III includes detailed curriculum design tables and sample seasonal programs and daily schedules.

FORSYTHE, CHARLES E. *Administration of High School Athletics.* Englewood Cliffs, N.J.: Prentice-Hall, Inc., 1962.

A resource on the administration of athletic programs. Deals with all aspects of the boys' interscholastic program as well as treating intramural athletics, athletics for girls, and junior high school athletics.

HALSEY, ELIZABETH, and LORENA PORTER. *Physical Education for Children.* New York: Dryden Press, Inc., 1958.

This volume on elementary school physical education is written from the developmental point of view and gives particular emphasis to the use of movement exploration and problem-solving activities. Descriptions, analyses, and references for games, movement exploration, dance, and self-testing activities are given.

LAPORTE, WILLIAM RALPH. *The Physical Education Curriculum.* 6th ed. Los Angeles, 1955.

A basic resource on curriculum organization in physical education.

LA SALLE, DOROTHY. *Guidance of Children Through Physical Education.* 2d. ed. New York: The Ronald Press Co., 1957.

A source book of teaching methods, presenting materials of instruction, classified according to age and grade levels. Stresses the promotion of democratic values through physical education.

LEAVITT, NORMA M., and HARTLEY D. PRICE. *Intramural and Recreational Sports— For High School and College.* 2d ed. New York: The Ronald Press Co., 1958.

SELECTED REFERENCES

Presents suitable activities, desirable practices, and recommended policies and procedures for planning and conducting a program of intramurals in high schools and colleges.

MEANS, LOUIS E. *Intramurals: Their Organization and Administration.* Englewood Cliffs, N.J.: Prentice-Hall, Inc., 1963.

A resource for materials on the intramural facet of the physical education curriculum. Suggestions for planning and administering intramural programs are given. Topics included are organization of units for competition, planning time for intramurals, the program of activities, awards and recognition, co-recreational activities, and community relationships.

METHENY, ELEANOR, and LOIS ELLFELDT. "Dynamics of Human Performance," *International Seminar in Health and Fitness in the Modern World.* Rome: University of Rome, 1960.

A statement of a theory of movement education developed by the authors. It "identifies structured movement experiences as a source of mental-emotional concepts that are not only significant but essentially unique forms of human knowledge and understanding."

MILLER, ARTHUR G., and M. DOROTHY MASSEY. *A Dynamic Concept of Physical Education for Secondary Schools.* Englewood Cliffs, N.J.: Prentice-Hall, Inc., 1963.

Analyzes a variety of physical education activities and includes sample unit plans, suggested teaching techniques, and a bibliography.

OBERTEUFFER, DELBERT, and CELESTE ULRICH. *Physical Education: A Textbook of Principles for Professional Students.* New York: Harper & Row, 1962.

Chapter 8 presents foundational principles or standards for curriculum development and includes sample programs and a discussion of controversial areas related to competitive athletics.

SALT, E. BENTON, GRACE I. FOX, and B. K. STEVENS. *Teaching Physical Education in the Elementary School.* 2d ed. New York: The Ronald Press Co., 1960.

A source book of activities in a number of classifications: small group play, large group play, rhythms and dances, team games, directed play, stunts and pyramids, and classroom games. Suggested teaching methods and techniques are also included.

SOUDER, MARJORIE A., and PHYLLIS J. HILL. *Basic Movement—Foundations of Physical Education.* New York: The Ronald Press Co., 1963.

A reference for the movement education approach to physical education. Provides a developmental sequence of activities basic to the more complex and coordinated activities of sports, games, and dance.

VANNIER, MARYHELEN, and HOLLIS F. FAIT. *Teaching Physical Education in Secondary Schools.* Philadelphia: W. B. Saunders Co, 1957.

Part III discusses course content, class organization, teaching procedures, and evaluation in a variety of activities classified in eight categories: body building and physical fitness, individual sports, track and field sports, aquatics, team sports, dance, tumbling and gymnastics, and adapted activities. Part IV is devoted to the extraclass program: intramural activities, interscholastic athletics, recreational activities, drill teams and pep squads, and public demonstrations.

CHAPTER 7

ALPENFELS, ETHEL. "The Role of Values in a Changing American Scene," In *NAPECW Biennial Record, 1957–59.* Washington, D.C.: American Association for Health, Physical Education, and Recreation, 1959. Pp. 36–44.

Discusses the role of values in American society from an anthropologist's viewpoint. Comments on the conflict between individualism and conformity, earlier maturation, clock watching, roles of men and women, and our honoring of youth.

AMBROSE, EDNA, and ALICE MIEL. *Children's Social Learning.* Washington, D.C.: National Education Association, 1958.

Report of a study of children's social learnings and how they are acquired. Examines social learnings, their interrelationships with the components of healthy personality development, and the school's role in furthering social learnings. Analyzes the school environment as a means of developing social learnings for democratic living and offers proposals for further research, experimentation, and study.

AMERICAN ASSOCIATION FOR HEALTH, PHYSICAL EDUCATION, AND RECREATION. *Spectator Sportsmanship.* Washington, D.C.: National Education Association, 1961.

Analyzes the problems of spectator sportsmanship. Suggestions for improvement are offered from the standpoint of the school administrator, the athletic director, the coach, the player, the official, the student council, the cheerleader, and the sports editor. Sample sportsmanship codes, ratings, and tests are included.

AMERICAN ASSOCIATION FOR HEALTH, PHYSICAL EDUCATION, AND RECREATION. *Values in Sports and Athletics.* Washington, D.C.: National Education Association, 1963.

Report of a national conference sponsored jointly by the Division of Girls and Women's Sports and the Division of Men's Athletics. Papers presented by consultants representing several fields of specialization are printed in entirety as well as several recorded panel presentations and question-answer session proceedings.

CASSIDY, ROSALIND. *Counseling in the Physical Education Program.* New York: Appleton-Century-Crofts, Inc., 1959.

A guide for physical educators in fulfilling the teacher's role in guidance. Emphasis is placed on the guidance role of the teacher in contrast to that of the guidance specialist.

COLEMAN, JAMES S. "Athletics in High School," *The Annals of the American Academy of Political and Social Science,* CCCXXXVIII (November, 1961), 33–43.

Reports the conclusions of a research study of the role of athletics in ten middle western high schools in 1957–1958.

COZENS, FREDERICK W., and FLORENCE S. STUMPF. *Sports in American Life.* Chicago: University of Chicago Press, 1953.

A study of the basic sociological significance of games, sports, and recreational activities in American culture.

DUBOIS, CORA. "The Dominant Value Profile of American Culture," *The American Anthropologist,* LVII, Part I (December, 1955), 1232–39.

A synthesis and systematizing of the relevant insights on American values. Three focal values are discussed: effort-optimism, material well-being, and conformity.

EDUCATIONAL POLICIES COMMISSION. *Moral and Spiritual Values in the Public Schools.* Washington, D.C.: National Education Association, 1951.

A basic statement of the role of the public schools in the development of moral and spiritual values.

FOSHAY, ARTHUR W., KENNETH D. WANN, et al. *Children's Social Value.* New York: Bureau of Publications, Teachers College, Columbia University, 1954.

Report of a cooperative research study in the Springfield, Missouri, public schools. An action research approach was used in the study of follow-through and

SELECTED REFERENCES

group acceptance, independence and initiative, considerateness and aggression, ownership and sharing, and democratic behavior and security.

GINZBERG, ELI. *Values and Ideals of American Youth.* New York: Columbia University Press, 1961.

A series of essays presenting varied viewpoints concerning the values of American youth. Favorable and unfavorable conditions for the realization of individual potentialities are discussed. Problems treated include juvenile delinquency, pornography, youth and the automobile, and minority intergroup relations.

GORDON, IRA J. *Human Development: From Birth Through Adolescence.* New York: Harper & Row, 1962.

A self-psychology oriented text that attempts to combine an external approach and an internal approach to the study of the growth of human beings. Stresses development as a process of organization; the individual as a unique, functioning whole; and individual development of the self-system.

HARTFORD, ELLIS FORD. *Moral Values in Public Education.* New York: Harper & Row, 1958.

Affirms the point of view that the teaching of moral values is appropriate and timely for the public schools. Provides practical accounts and suggestions drawn from the experience of Kentucky schools in a program of emphasis upon the teaching of moral and spiritual values.

MASLOW, ABRAHAM H. *Toward a Psychology of Being.* Princeton: D. Van Nostrand Co., 1962.

An exposition of a positive, dynamic view of psychology. Parts IV and V are relevant to the topics discussed in this chapter.

PECK, ROBERT F., ROBERT J. HAVIGHURST, *et al. The Psychology of Character Development.* New York: John Wiley & Sons, Inc., 1960.

Analysis of case studies with emphasis on the concept of an underlying orientation in the individual's behavior. Provides a useful construct of five "developmental levels of character," and conclusions regarding personality development based on extensive study and analysis. Research techniques and instruments are described in detail.

ROCKEFELLER BROTHERS FUND, INC. *The Pursuit of Excellence: Education and the Future of America.* New York: Doubleday & Co., Inc., 1958.

A report of the Special Studies Project on the critical national problem of utilizing effectively the individual talents of our citizens. Topics include dignity of the individual, nature of the challenge, educational system, use and misuse of human abilities, and motivation and values.

CHAPTER 8

ASSOCIATION FOR SUPERVISION AND CURRICULUM DEVELOPMENT. *Perceiving, Behaving, Becoming.* Washington: D.C.: National Education Association, 1962.

A yearbook that examines current theory about the nature of human capacity and adjustment and discusses implications of personality theory for educational thought and practice. Summarizes important knowledge concerning the healthy, self-actualizing, fully functioning personality and provides guidelines for applying this knowledge in school practices.

BUSH, ROBERT N., and DWIGHT W. ALLEN. "A New Design for High School Education: Assuming a Flexible Schedule." Unpublished material, Secondary Education Project, School of Education, Stanford University, July, 1961. This material, revised and expanded, has been published by McGraw-Hill Book Co. under the title, *A New Design for High School Education: Assuming a Flexible Schedule*, by Robert N. Bush and Dwight W. Allen, 1964.

A report of a research project on flexible scheduling, staff utilization, pupil grouping, and computer scheduling of the master schedule of the high school, concerning grades seven through twelve. Contains a chapter on physical education, by John E. Nixon, with unique proposals for scheduling, grouping, and staff utilization.

GUILFORD, JOY P. *Personality.* New York: McGraw-Hill Book Co., Inc., 1959.

An approach to the study of personality, stressing individual differences. The factorial approach is used to systematize descriptions of individual personality. Offers detailed study of individual differences among human beings.

MCNALLY, HAROLD J., A. HARRY PASSOW, et al. *Improving the Quality of Public School Programs.* New York: Bureau of Publications, Teachers College, Columbia University, 1960.

Descriptions and appraisals of organized efforts at curriculum improvement. Summary of guidelines for curriculum improvement.

MORSE, ARTHUR D. *Schools of Tomorrow—Today!* New York: Doubleday & Co., Inc., 1960.

A report on ten educational experiments, selected as a cross-section of current experimentation. The projects described include studies in team teaching, ungraded primary schools, teacher aides, television, the gifted child, the new technology, improvement of rural schools, and teacher recruitment.

NATIONAL SOCIETY FOR THE STUDY OF EDUCATION. *Individualizing Instruction.* Chicago: University of Chicago Press, 1962. Sixty-first Yearbook. Part I.

A compendium of current knowledge in the area of individualizing instruction. Discussed are theoretical issues, the extent of individual differences, current school practices for individualizing instruction, and implications for teacher preparation and school-community relationships.

TORRANCE, E. PAUL. *Guiding Creative Talent.* Englewood Cliffs, N.J.: Prentice-Hall, Inc., 1962.

Concerned with the discovery and development of creative talent, this book stresses the necessity for developing creativity as a function of education, offers suggestions for assessing creative talent, and discusses problems resulting from the expression and repression of creative abilities.

TRUMP, J. LLOYD. *Images of the Future.* Washington, D.C.: National Education Association, 1959.

Report of the Commission on the Experimental Study of the Utilization of the Staff in Secondary Schools. Describes new patterns for flexible-size pupil groups and differentiated roles for school personnel.

TRUMP, J. LLOYD. *New Directions to Quality Education.* Washington, D.C.: National Education Association, 1960.

A further report of the Commission on the Experimental Study of the Utilization of the Staff in Secondary Schools. Provides more detailed suggestions for flexible scheduling, staff utilization, pupil grouping, and instructional technology.

TRUMP, J. LLOYD, and DORSEY BAYNHAM. *Focus on Change: Guide to Better Schools.* Chicago: Rand McNally & Co., 1961.

Another report of the Commission on the Experimental Study of the Utilization of the Staff in Secondary Schools. Stresses innovations in high schools throughout the country and actual examples of newer practices.

WAETJEN, WALTER B. *Human Variability and Learning.* Washington, D.C.: National Education Association, 1961.

Papers and reports from the Fifth Curriculum Research Institute of the Association for Supervision and Curriculum Development concerning educational implications of human individual differences.

CHAPTER 9

BAMMANN, BERNICE, and JOHN FRENCH. "A Variety of Improvements in Staff Utilization Are Tried in a Small High School at Beecher, Illinois," *National Association of Secondary School Principals Bulletin,* XLII (January, 1958), 115–25.

An actual example of how a small high school has experimented with various staffing patterns in different school subjects.

BUIKEMA, KENT A., and JAMES E. SMITH. "Effective Staff Utilization," *Journal of Health, Physical Education, and Recreation,* XXXIV (March, 1963), 19–21.

A description of a variety of practices that have been adopted in an Illinois high school involving not only more effective staff utilization, but also including flexible scheduling, pupil grouping, and individual practice and study in physical education. Shows how imagination, leadership, and hard work can improve the physical education program.

COLEBANK, AL. "Team Teaching Improves Elementary School Physical Education," *CAHPER Journal,* January–February, 1962, p. 10.

Describes a plan of classroom teacher utilization to improve instruction in physical education in elementary schools.

EMPEY, DONALD W. "Student Self-Direction, Flexible Scheduling, and Team Teaching," *National Association of Secondary School Principals Bulletin,* XLVII (February, 1963), 118–24.

Describes actual practices in staff utilization, flexible scheduling, and individual study, and evaluates the outcomes of these practices.

HELLER, M. P., and ELIZABETH BELFORD. "Team Teaching and Staff Utilization in Ridgewood High School, *National Association of Secondary School Principals Bulletin,* XLVI (January, 1962), 105–22.

Describes staff utilization innovations employed and evaluates their effectiveness.

LONSDALE, BERNARD J. "Television and Team Teaching in California Elementary Schools," *California Journal of Elementary Education,* XXXI (November, 1962), 75–94.

A summary report of instruction by television, and the use of team teaching, in elementary schools in California, with an evaluation of the strengths and weaknesses of these practices.

MALLORY, A. "Team Approach to Safety and Physical Fitness," *Safety Education,* XLI (May, 1962), 10–12.

An example of staff utilization for more effective instruction in safety education as well as in physical fitness aspects of the physical education program.

MILLER, ARTHUR G., and VIRGINIA WHITCOMB. *Physical Education in the Elementary School Curriculum.* 2d ed. Englewood Cliffs, N.J.: Prentice-Hall, Inc., 1963.

Chapter 2 describes team teaching in elementary school physical education.

TRUMP, J. LLOYD. "An Image of a Future Secondary School Health, Physical Education, and Recreation Program," *Journal of Health, Physical Education, and Recreation,* XXXII (January, 1961) 16–18.

A series of suggestions as to how physical education can be improved through more effective staff utilization, flexible scheduling, pupil grouping, and use of technological aids.

CHAPTER 10

Bush, Robert N., and Dwight W. Allen. "A New Design for High School Education: Assuming a Flexible Schedule." Unpublished material, Secondary Education Project, School of Education, Stanford University, July, 1961. This material, revised and expanded, has been published by McGraw-Hill Book Co. under the title, *A New Design for High School Education: Assuming a Flexible Schedule*, by Robert N. Bush and Dwight W. Allen, 1964.

    A report of a research project on flexible scheduling, staff utilization, pupil grouping, and computer scheduling of the master schedule of the high school, concerning grades seven through twelve. Contains a chapter on Physical Education, by John E. Nixon, with unique proposals for scheduling, grouping, and staff utilization.

Clein, Marvin I. "A New Approach to the Physical Education Schedule," *Journal of Health, Physical Education, and Recreation*, XXXIII (November, 1962), 34–36, 65, 66.

    Report of innovations at Evergreen Park High School, Evergreen Park, Illinois, concerning physical education program structure and class organization, which provide greater flexibility, more staff unity and cohesion, greater provision for the individual differences of students, and similar benefits.

Trump, J. Lloyd. "New Directions in Scheduling and Use of Staff in the High School," *California Journal of Secondary Education*, XXXIII (October, 1958), 362–82.

    Indicates the possibilities for improving the quality of secondary education through flexible scheduling and more effective staff utilization.

Trump, J. Lloyd. *New Horizons for Secondary School Teachers*. Washington, D.C.: National Education Association, 1958.

    One of the earliest reports of the Commission on the Experimental Study of the Utilization of the Staff in Secondary Schools suggesting improvements in secondary education through innovations in flexible scheduling, staff utilization, pupil grouping, and instructional technology.

Trump, J. Lloyd. *Images of the Future*. Washington, D.C.: National Education Association, 1959.

    An early report of the Commission on the Experimental Study of the Utilization of the Staff in Secondary Schools explaining the work of the Commission and the potentialities for the improvement of secondary education through newer practices of flexible scheduling, staff utilization, and pupil grouping.

Trump, J. Lloyd. *New Directions to Quality Education*. Washington, D.C.: National Education Association, 1960.

    An elaboration of an earlier report of the Commission on the Experimental Study of the Utilization of the Staff in Secondary Schools on the potentialities of flexible scheduling, staff utilization, pupil grouping, and instructional technology for the improvement of the quality of secondary education.

Trump, J. Lloyd, and Dorsey Baynham. *Focus on Change: Guide to Better Schools*. Chicago: Rand McNally & Co., 1961.

    A report of the work of the Commission on the Experimental Study of the Utilization of the Staff in Secondary Schools and the citation of actual examples of innovations in high schools throughout the country in the areas of flexible scheduling, staff utilization, pupil grouping, instructional technology, and new facilities.

SELECTED REFERENCES

CHAPTER 11

AMERICAN ASSOCIATION FOR HEALTH, PHYSICAL EDUCATION, AND RECREATION. *Audio-Visual Materials in Physical Education.* Washington, D.C., 1956.

    A listing of many types of audio-visual materials available to the teacher of physical education and the athletic coach.

ARCE, WILLIAM B. "Planning Boys' Gymnasium Facilities for Secondary Schools." Unpublished Ed.D. dissertation, School of Education, Stanford University, 1956.

    An example of how to plan a gymnasium by the procedure of developing "educational specifications." Includes practical suggestions for the planning and constructing of a high school gymnasium. Available on Micro-card from the University of Oregon.

BARTA, JUDY. "Automation Arrives on the Tennis Courts," *Journal of Health, Physical Education, and Recreation,* XXX (February, 1959), 29, 30, 82.

    Explains the values of the tennis teaching machine and illustrates how a teacher can use it most effectively. One example of how automation may be applied to sports instruction.

BROUDY, HARRY S. "Teaching Machines: Threats and Promise," *Educational Theory,* XII (July, 1962), 151–56.

    A discussion of the pros and cons of teaching machines and their effectiveness as an instructional medium.

FINN, JAMES D., and DONALD G. PERRIN. *Teaching Machines and Programed Learning: A Survey of the Industry.* Washington, D.C.: National Education Association, 1962.

    This book provides information about the current status of teaching machines and programed learning materials, their uses, strengths, and weaknesses, and an assessment of their probable use in the future.

FINN, JAMES D., and ELINOR RICHARDSON. "The New Technology," *The National Elementary Principal,* XL (January, 1961), 18–22.

    A description of the major elements to be found in present-day instructional technology, and some pertinent observations by authorities in this field of specialization.

FITZGERALD, H. T. "Teaching Machines: A Demurrer," *The School Review,* LXX (Autumn, 1962), 247–56.

    A criticism of teaching machines. Pleads for caution, careful evaluation, and balance in their use.

"Focus on Facilities: Planning Space for Physical Activity," *Journal of Health, Physical Education, and Recreation,* XXXIII (April, 1962), 33–48.

    Sixteen plans of physical education facilities that will "turn your idealized teaching station into reality."

FOSTER, B. "Role of the Portable Tape Recorder in Basketball Coaching," *Scholastic Coach,* XXXI (January, 1962), 38.

    A practical illustration of how one mechanical aid can be of great help to an athletic coach.

GATES, ARTHUR L. "Teaching Machines in Perspective," *The Elementary School Journal,* LXII (October, 1961), 1–13.

    A critical evaluation of the value of teaching machines by a specialist in learning theory.

HALLBERG, EDMOND C. "A Cost Analysis of Physical Education Programs in Terms of Utilization of Facilities." Unpublished Ed.D. dissertation, School of Education, Stanford University, 1960.

Reports a unique procedure for determining the per pupil per hour cost of physical education and athletic participation in a high school. The method can be applied to any school subject, thus affording a basis for comparison of costs. Available on Micro-card from the University of Oregon.

HIXSON, CHALMER G. "The Status and Potential of Instructional Television for Physical Education," *Journal of Health, Physical Education, and Recreation,* XXXIII (May–June, 1962), 25, 26, 46.

A summary of the use of television for instruction in physical education for pupils in school and for the in-service education of teachers. A prognosis of the future of educational television.

INSTITUTE FOR COMMUNICATIONS RESEARCH. *Educational Television, The Next Ten Years.* Stanford, Calif.: Stanford University, 1962.

Report of a detailed research study on educational television, its effects and progress to date, and implications for educational programs in the future.

KOVAL, MIKE. "Teaching Sports Skills on Television," *Journal of Health, Physical Education, and Recreation,* XXXIII (May–June, 1962), 30.

A practical example of the use of television as a medium of instruction in sports.

MACCONNELL, JAMES D. *Planning for School Buildings.* Englewood Cliffs, N.J.: Prentice-Hall, Inc., 1957.

A book on school planning philosophy and procedures that emphasizes the "educational specifications" approach. Stresses the need to build facilities that are adaptable for change and flexible use in the future. Excellent material on planning in physical education.

NATIONAL EDUCATION ASSOCIATION. *Automation and the Challenge to Education.* Washington, D.C., 1962.

An analysis of the impact of automation upon the education process as schools depend more and more on television, teaching machines, and other fruits of instructional technology.

"Physical Education Facilities for a Junior College," *Journal of Health, Physical Education, and Recreation,* XXXIV (February, 1963), 22–24.

A description with photographs of modern physical education and athletic facilities at a new community college. Contains many ideas and innovations for the consideration of planners of new physical education and athletic facilities at various educational levels.

SCOTT, HARRY A. "Facilities for the Future," *Journal of Health, Physical Education, and Recreation,* XXXIII (April, 1962), 34–36.

In this article, new developments in the planning of physical education and athletic facilites are stressed; planning for the future is the central theme.

SILBERMAN, HARRY F. "The Digital Computer in Education," *Phi Delta Kappan,* XLIII (May, 1962), 345–47.

An analysis of the uses and future implications of the digital computer in public education, which contends that the status of the individual student will be advanced and more clearly recognized by teachers as computers come into more widespread use.

TEXAS ENGINEERING EXPERIMENT STATION. *Shelter for Physical Education.* College Station, Texas: Texas A. & M. College, 1961.

A report of a research study of the factors that affect the design and construction of "limited" shelters for physical education. Information on providing sufficient covered areas to permit the conduct of physical education activities in inclement weather, at a cost much less than that of the traditional gymnasium, is presented.

Index

Ability grouping, 170-72
Action research, 31-32
Activities, extraclass, 23, 107-8, 133, 152, 172
American Association for Health, Physical Education, and Recreation, 55, 89
American Medical Association, 58-59
American public school, functions of, 3-21
American Red Cross, achievement standards, 171
Association for Supervision and Curriculum Development, 54-55, 135
Athletic Institute, 90, 165
Automated data retrieval center, 239

Broad-fields curriculum, 40-43
Bush-Allen plan, 171-72, 191-92, 200-201, 204, 209-12, 221-26, 238, 255-68

California Association for Health, Physical Education, and Recreation, 43
California Framework for Public Education, 61
Carnegie Unit, 183
Citizen's advisory committees, 68
Class activities, variations in, 164-65
Class size, 159, 169-70
Clerks, 191
Co-education, 131-32
College and university consultants, 68-70
College and university curriculum services, 73-75
Commission on the Experimental Study of the Utilization of the Staff in the Secondary School, 181, 188; see also Trump plan
Communications media, 238-40
Communications skills, 6, 7
Competences, teacher, 184-88
Competition, sports, 141-42, 151-52

Computer, digital, 235-38
Conference reports, professional, 89
Consultants, 64-65, 68-73, 190
Content selection, 105-35
Continuity of learning, 134-35
Core curriculum, 43-49
Council for Public Schools, 59
Council on Basic Education, 59-60
Counseling and guidance
 individualizing instruction through, 167-68
 teaching values through, 147-50
County school office and district consultants, 70-73
Course selection, 168-69
Critical incident reporting, 148-49
Cultural change, school's role in, 9-17
Cultural transmission, school's role in, 3-9
Curriculum
 activity, 49-50
 broad-fields, 40-43
  physical education in, 42-43
 content, 25-27, 82, 105-35
 continuity, 134-35
 core, 43-49, 50
  physical education in, 48-49
 correlated, 50-51
  physical education in, 51
 defined, 22
 formal, 22
 informal, 22-23
 integrated, 51-52
 objectives, 23-25, 81-82
 patterns, 34-52, 111-31
 separate-subjects, 34-40
  physical education in, 39, 52
 sequence, 27-29, 82
 standards, physical education, 105-8
Curriculum change
 and educational problems, 103-252
 challenges for, 101-2

287

Curriculum development
 defined, 23
 foundations for, 1–102
 influences on, 53–77
 participation in, 31–33
 physical education, challenges for, 101–2
 physical educator's role in, 78–102
 principles of, 22–33, 81–83
 teacher and, 93–101
Curriculum guides, 63, 89, 95

Dalton Plan, 162
Data, collecting, 86–91
Democracy
 citizenship education for, 16–17
 individual differences in, 10, 158–61
Differences, individual, 158
 instructional difficulties resulting from, 158–60
Digital computer, 235–36
Diversity, uniformity and, 160–61

Economic well-being, 12–14
EDEX Teaching System, 240
Educational Media Panel, 242
Educational Policies Commission, 54
Educational problems, curriculum change and, 103–252
Eight mm. sound film, 239
Elementary school physical education curriculum content, patterns for organizing, 111–14
 basic weekly schedule plan, 111–12
 informal yearly balance plan, 113–16
 seasonal units plan, 113
Evaluation, 30–31
 in core curriculum, 47
 in separate-subjects curriculum, 38
 phase of curriculum development, 92–93
Experimental Study of the Utilization of the Staff in the Secondary School, 181, 188
Extraclass activities, 23, 107–8, 133, 152, 172
Extramural program, 23

Facilities, 227–52
 buildings and grounds, 228–33
 cost of, 228–30
 defined, 227
 educational specifications for, 230–32
Family living, education for, 14–15
Fitness, 5, 12, 109–10, 129–31, 141; see also President's Council on Physical Fitness

General aides, 190
Group activities, small and large, 270
Group living, 8–9, 14–17
Group participation, 14–17
Grouping, pupil
 ability, 161, 170–72, 176
 individualizing instruction through, 168–72
 relationship to learning values, 151–52
Guidance, 167–68

Health
 as a public school objective, 5–6, 12
 mental, 6
Home video tape recorder and television receiver, 239

Illinois School Code, 39
In-service education, 73–77, 240–48
Individual development, 10–12
Individual differences, 10, 18, 158–61
 teacher, 172–73
Individual study, 165–67, 177, 234–36
Individualizing instruction, 18, 157–79, 234–36, 249–51
 significance of, 157–61
 through grouping, 168–72
 through methodology, 163–68
 through rate of progress, 161–62
Instruction, individualizing, 18, 157–79, 234–36, 249–51
 significance of, 157–61
Instruction assistants, 190
Instructional aids; see Technology, instructional
Instructional staff in a secondary school, 189
Instructional systems, 234
Intergroup relations, education for, 16–17
Interscholastics, 107–8, 133, 152
Intramurals, 23, 107–8, 133, 152

Lay public, role in curriculum development, 31–33, 83
Learning
 principles, 18–21, 29–31, 134–35
 values, 136–56
Leisure, worthy use of, 11

Mach-tronics MVR-10, 240
Massachusetts Council for Public Schools, 59
Materials, sequence of, 27–29
Methods, teaching, 29–31, 83
 in broad-fields curriculum, 41–42

INDEX

in core curriculum, 46–47
in separate-subjects curriculum, 38
individualizing instruction through, 163–68
Motion picture camera and film, 239
Movement education, 106–7, 108–11, 135

National Association for Mental Health, 6
National Education Association, 54
Project on Instruction, 55–56
Needs, basic and derived human, 23–24
New York State Commissioner of Education, 39

Objectives, curriculum, 23–25, 81–82, 135
Organization, 105–35

Patterns, curriculum, 34–52, 111–31
activity, 49–50
basic weekly schedule, 111–12
broad-fields, 42–43
concurrent unit, 119, 120
core, 43–49, 50
correlated, 50–51
elective, 119, 121–23
informal yearly balance, 113, 115–16
integrated, 51–52
prescribed single block, 116–19
seasonal units, 113, 114
separate-subjects, 34–40
Personnel, resource, 192
Physical education
and instructional technology, 251–52
basic core of, 108–11
buildings, structures, and areas for, 228–30
co-educational programs in, 131–32
facilities for the future, 232–33
flexible scheduling
in elementary schools, 213
in secondary schools, 213–17
in the future, 217–26
staff utilization in elementary school, 195–96
staff utilization in high school, 196–98
teaching machines and, 251
television instruction in, 243–49
Physical education curriculum, influences toward change in, 53–77
national, 53–60
Physical education programs, continuity in, 134–35
Portable video tape camera, 239

President's Council on Physical Fitness, 43, 57–58, 105–6, 221, 247
Principles
curriculum development, 22–33, 81–83
learning, 18–21, 29–31, 134–35, 249–50
Private business, services of, 89–90
Problem solutions
evaluating results, 92–93
selecting and testing, 91–92
Problem-solving, 13, 30, 46–47, 78–79, 164–65
curriculum change as, 78–93
Problems
defining, 79–86
identifying through curriculum development principles, 81–83
techniques for defining, 84–86
Professional educators, role of in curriculum development, 32–33
Programed learning, 249–51
Punishment, reward and, 152–55

Rate of progress, individualization through, 161–62
Recreation, 11, 133, 141
Related disciplines, study of, 86–87
Research, physical education, 87–88
Reward, in teaching values, 152–55
Role-playing, 146, 149–50

Schedule
back-to-back, 206
for physical education student, 265
for physical education teacher, 267
individual pupil, 214
Schedule modifications, 206–12
Scheduling
computer, 237–38
flexible, 200–201, 202–26, 255–70
basic assumptions concerning, 204–6
School, role of, 3–21
based on learning principles, 17–21
cultural change, 9–17
cultural transmission, 3–9
School Mathematics Study Group, 36
School plant planning, 228–33
School recreation programs, 133
School schedule, constructing with computer assistance, 237–38
Secondary school physical education content, patterns for organizing, 116–31
concurrent unit plan, 119
elective plan, 119–22
prescribed single block plan, 116–19

Secondary school physical education content (*Continued*)
    sample plans for boys' programs, 122–31
Self-sufficiency, occupational, 7–8
Separate-subjects curriculum, 34–40
Sequence, 27–29, 82
    in broad-fields curriculum, 41
    in core curriculum, 45–46
    in separate-subjects curriculum, 36–38
Social change
    curriculum change as, 79
    school's role in, 9–17, 27
Special services, guidance and, 167–68
Specifications, educational, 230–32
Staff
    professional, 191
    supporting, 191
Staff personnel, differentiation of, 188–92
Staff utilization, 180–201
    basic assumptions, 181
    in elementary school physical education, 195–96
    in high school physical education, 196–98
    in the future, 198–201
Standards, physical education curriculum, 105–8
Stanford Appraisal Guides, Teaching and Learning, 187
Stanford University Secondary Education Project, 191, 200, 221, 226, 237
State boards of education, 66–67
State departments of education, 60–65, 88
Study procedures, individual, 165–67
Subject content, studying values as, 143–47
Subject matter
    in broad-fields curriculum, 41, 42
    in core curriculum, 44–45
    in separate-subjects curriculum, 35–36
    physical education, 105–35
    selection of, 25–27, 82, 135
    values as, 143–47
Survival and self-protection, individual, 5–6

Teacher, and curriculum development, 93–101
Teacher-pupil planning, 30, 32, 38, 46
Teacher utilization, 182–84
    improving, 184
Teachers
    differences among, 172–73
    duties of, professional and non-professional, 184–88
    evolving roles of, 181–82
    professional, 190
Teaching machines, 249–51
Teaching values, 136–56
    significance of, 136–40
Team teaching, 192–201
Techniques, teaching, variety in, 163–64
Technology, instructional, 233–52
    communications media, 238–40
    defined, 233
    facilities and, 227–52
        definition, 227–28
    physical education and, 251–52
    teaching machines, 249–51
    television, 240–48
Television, instructional, 240–48
    complete course teaching, 241
    enrichment instruction, 241
    major resource teaching, 241
    supplementary instruction, 242
Textorient, 239
Time allotment
    among major content areas, 28–29
    for physical education, 39, 60, 105–6, 205–6, 213–26
    in separate-subjects curriculum, 35
Trump plan, 177–78, 181, 184–85, 188–92, 193–94, 198, 233–35

Uniformity, 160–61
United States Office of Education, 56–57, 88–89

Values
    development of, 137–39
    difficulties in teaching, 140
    learning by imitation, 142–43
    physical education's unique responsibility, 139–42
    school's role in teaching, 9, 14, 136–56
    studying as subject content, 143–47
    teaching, 136–56
    significance of, 136–40
    teaching through environmental modification, 150–52
    teaching through individual counseling, 147–50
Videofile, 239
Vocational education, 7–8, 13
Voice typewriter, 239

Well-being, economic, 12–14
Winnetka Plan, 162
Women, cultural role of, 15